The Economics and Planning of Transport

G. J. Bell, B.Sc., M.A., M.C.I.T.
Senior Lecturer in Transport Studies,
Central Manchester College

D. A. Blackledge, B.A., M.A.
Senior Planner (Transportation),
West Midlands Passenger Transport Executive

P. J. Bowen, B.Sc (Econ)
Senior Lecturer in Transport Studies,
Central Manchester College

Heinemann : London

William Heinemann Ltd
10 Upper Grosvenor Street, London W1X 9PA

LONDON   MELBOURNE   TORONTO
JOHANNESBURG   AUCKLAND

Photoset by Wilmaset, Birkenhead, Merseyside
Printed in Great Britain by
Redwood Burn Ltd., Trowbridge

Preface

Many people study transport-related subjects today. In most classes studying for the Qualifying Examination of the Chartered Institute of Transport you will find graduate management trainees, 'A' Level students, and those from overseas, all with little experience in the industry. On the other hand there will be those with few academic qualifications but a wealth of experience. In polytechnics and universities, there are students taking HNDs and degrees with a Transport Management bias and post-graduate civil engineers studying economics as part of their Master's degrees in Transportation Planning. Many of these students will be studying economics for the first time and yet, within one year, they will need to understand transport economics at a very high level.

This book introduces students to the elementary theory of economics and then applies it to the transport sector. Those who have studied economics before will, having refreshed their memory, be able to apply their existing knowledge to the problems of transport.

Chapter 1, *The Economic Function of Transport*, is particularly relevant to students from less developed countries to whom the problems presented are very real. It is also relevant to those from the developed world where the advantages of transport investment are often questioned.

Chapters 2 and 3 deal with demand and supply. Both begin with the basic theory but the student is quickly presented with the difficult conceptual problems faced in transport economics and shown the way the industry itself deals with them.

In Chapter 4, which deals with pricing policy, we explain the concept of marginal cost pricing by using actual figures in pounds and pence because classroom experience shows that this is much more meaningful to most students to whom the reading of graphs presents problems. Included in this chapter is the very important question of how, from the economist's viewpoint, we can best deal with the urban traffic congestion problem. We also discuss in some detail the way in which a particular industry, in this case road passenger transport, approaches the pricing of its services, and show clearly the more practical factors which transport operators have to consider.

Chapter 5 deals with the ever-topical subject of subsidy in transport and we include in this a discussion of the worsening rural transport problem. Chapter 6 is concerned with investment appraisal including an up-to-date assessment of the role of cost benefit analysis.

The next two chapters, *The Role of Government* and *Transport Planning* have been included because the former has a strong influence on the working of the transport sector and the latter is closely related to transport economics. We have taken the opportunity to provide the student with information that is difficult to find in most transport textbooks. Thus there is examination of the way that local government and nationalized industries are financed and controlled and the various planning documents that local authorities are required to produce. In addition, the structure of the Department of Transport is outlined as are the procedures in trunk road planning.

Chapter 9 develops the theme introduced earlier of the free market economy, departures from it, and their significance in the international context. Included in this chapter is a discussion on the progress towards the Common Transport Policy of the EEC.

Inaccuracies, inconsistencies and illogicalities are all our own but we would like to thank for their helpful advice Paul Fawcett, Peter Jackson and Peter Smith. We would also like to thank the Chartered Institute of Transport for allowing us to reproduce past examination questions and the editor of *Flight International* and the Greater Manchester Council for permission to use some of their material. In a textbook of this kind great reliance is placed on other, more learned, texts and we are most grateful to those publishers who have allowed us to use their material and whom we have acknowledged in the text.

Thanks are also due to typists Elain Mulroy, Malathi Raghava, Helen Swiercz, Sue Green and Linda Corbett. Finally, to our wives, Sarah, Steph (who also helped considerably with the typing) and Margaret, for their constructive criticisms and for waiting patiently for the DIY to be finished, our utmost gratitude.

Contents

1

Economic Function of Transport

1.1 Introduction

In this chapter we will attempt to determine how important the role of transport is in the economy of a country, particularly its role in economic development. Notice the word 'attempt'. Economics is an inexact science and is, therefore, one which lends itself to a variety of views on almost any subject within it. We only have to look at the arguments which rage over the causes of inflation or unemployment to appreciate the problems involved! The economics of transport does not escape such problems and in this first chapter we must present the opposing arguments and try to reach a conclusion. First of all we will present figures to show that transport accounts for a large part of the economic activity in the United Kingdom. Then we will outline the theory of the economic function of transport. This will show why transport plays an important role in the development of an economy, encouraging economic growth and increasing the general standard of living of the population. Having set out the theory we must look for evidence to support it. This means looking at economic history. At this point, problems arise because people interpret events differently and, consequently, form differing opinions, and this makes it difficult to outline policies for encouraging economic development today. However, at the end of the chapter we will make some suggestions and look at the type of transport·projects that have been undertaken in the developing world.

1.2 The importance of transport

Only transport enthusiasts travel for the pleasure travel itself gives. Most of us travel not for its own sake but because we want to get somewhere to carry out some further activity. The demand for transport is, therefore, a *derived* rather than a *direct* one. This does not mean, of course, that it is unimportant. After all, coal and oil, two of our most important products, experience a derived demand. In fact transport is a significant part of the economy and we can show its importance in a variety of ways. First of all transport is a large and labour-intensive industry. In 1980, Government Statistics[1] showed that those employed in this field (excluding vehicle manufacture) numbered 1.5 million, about 6.7% of the total labour force. A study undertaken a few years ago for the Chartered Institute of Transport[2] suggested that if those employed in physical distribution were included then the transport labour force comprised about 9% of the total working population. Table 1.1 shows the major employment areas.

Road transport, (including vehicle maintenance and repair and physical distribution) is by far the largest employer with 74% of the total. Rail transport employs 12% and sea ports, inland waterways and air transport together employ another 12%. Central and local government, education and consultancy account for the rest.

In terms of energy consumption, transport comprised nearly 25% of the 56,547 million therms consumed in 1980 and Government expenditure on transport was £3,545 million out of a total £90,660 million. Two further statistics deserve particular attention. The first is the contribution that the industry makes to the Gross Domestic Product, one measure of the wealth of a country. Of a total Gross Domestic Product of £193,488 million for the United Kingdom in 1980 transport contributed £10,084 million (5.2%). Secondly, some indication of the investment in the industry can be seen in figures for the Gross Domestic Fixed Capital Formation. Of the total

Table 1.1   Transport employment in the United Kingdom by function

	Function	Total employment	Percentage (%) of totals
1	Operations, safety and security	1,705,300	74
2	Engineering maintenance and technical development	395,200	17
3	Financial, economic and procurement services and general administration	149,800	7
4	Sales and marketing	28,100	1
5	Personnel, education and training, medical and welfare	12,700	1
6	Research and planning	5,700	—
7	Regulations, legal and licencing services	4,200	—
	Totals	2,301,000	100

amount of £38,563 million, transport—buses and coaches, other road vehicles, rail rolling stock, ships and aircraft, accounted for nearly 14%.

We can see, therefore, that the sums involved are immense and the relative size of the transport sector in terms of employment, energy consumption and Government expenditure makes it one of the most important parts of the economy and one well worth examination. However, the figures shown merely indicate the size of the sector at one point in time. They do not explain the economic function of transport. To this we now turn.

1.3 The economic function of transport

One of the first things we learn in economics is that mankind has unlimited wants but limited resources with which to satisfy those wants. In economics we are concerned with the way in which we allocate our scarce resources to use them most efficiently. These scarce resources are used to produce goods or services which if they satisfy a want are said to have *utility*. We can distinguish three types of utility which might be best described by considering a manufacturing process such as that making bricks. Step one involves extracting clay from the ground and moulding it into brick shapes. This provides *utility of form*. Step two requires bricks to be baked in an oven—*utility of state*. However, those bricks will be of little use or value if they remain in the brickyard; transport provides the third type, *utility of place*.

It does this by ensuring that goods are taken from the producer to the consumer. In transport jargon, we say it *bridges the producer—consumer gap*. This is true not only of freight but of passenger transport. For example, when you go to the hairdresser or dentist you, the consumer, are taken by one form of transport to the producer of a service and an employee is the producer transported to the employer who is the consumer of the employee's skills and knowledge.

1.4 Gains from specialization

Lord Lugard in 1922 stated 'the material development of Africa may be summed up in one word—transport'.[3] Why should this be so, and can such a claim be justified? One of the main arguments in favour of Lord Lugard's view is that transport enables trade to take place on a larger scale than was hitherto possible and this trade between groups of people increases the well-being of society. To show this we must turn to economic theory and look at the advantage of specialization. Consider the following example. Suppose both England and France are self-sufficient in mushrooms and courgettes and one unit of resources produces the following:

	Mushrooms	Courgettes
England	12	4
France	6	10

England is therefore better at producing mushrooms and France, courgettes. Would it not be better for each country to specialize? If one unit of resources in England was transferred to mushroom production and in France to courgette production we can show that more of both vegetables would be produced.

	Mushrooms	Courgettes
England	+12	− 4
France	− 6	+10
Increase in production	+ 6	+ 6

These gains from specialization where each country has an absolute advantage in one product are fairly easy to understand, but they occur even where one country is better at producing both commodities as long as one country has a greater advantage in one product than in the other. Suppose England increased its efficiency fivefold and, as a result, production figures are as follows:

	Mushrooms	Courgettes
England	60	20
France	6	10
Comparative advantage	10 X	2 X

If England transferred one-fifth of one unit of resources from courgettes to mushrooms and France transferred one unit to courgette production the gains would be as follows:

	Mushrooms	Courgettes
England	+12	− 4
France	− 6	+10
Gains from specialization	+ 6	+ 6

(To ensure you understand the concept of *comparative advantage* see what gains from specialization would be if the production figures were

	Mushrooms	Courgettes
England	20	12
France	5	3

and one unit of English resources were transferred to mushroom production and four French units to courgette production. In this case

England has the same *absolute advantage*, four times, over France in both products.)

Now such gains from specialization will not be realized unless the two countries trade, providing each with a bigger market for its products. To the transport economist this is where the importance of transport lies. In our example, improved means of carrying perishable goods across the English Channel would enable trade to take place and specialization to occur. The essence of the argument then is that *if individuals, communities or societies specialize and then trade the well-being of society as a whole will be increased*. Transport, in bridging the producer—consumer gap, plays an important role. The increase in specialization and efficiency through economies of scale (see Chapter 3), will be constrained by the size of the market. Transport will extend that market.

Evidence of such a chain of events abounds. It was the railways in Britain that changed local markets into a national one. Goods produced in Birmingham could reach London in less than eight hours; fruit produced in the south-east could be sold in Glasgow; the advantage to the newspaper industry was obvious. This meant that industries had greater choice in location and were able to exploit economies of scale in greater concentration. Cotton textile production, for example, previously found throughout the country was concentrated in Lancashire as was wool in Yorkshire; cotton hosiery became associated with Nottingham and woollen hosiery with Leicester. Heavy engineering became concentrated in a few areas such as the Midlands, south-west Yorkshire, Clydeside and Tyneside.

1.5 Transport and economic development — interpretation of economic history

The changes outlined above do show that transport helps to (a) extend the market (b) to increase specialization, and (c) to increase productivity and efficiency (subject to qualifications outlined in Chapter 3). But does economic history tell us that transport is really of paramount importance to economic growth? Several studies suggest this to be the case. M. W. Flinn, for example, who studied early industrial development in the United Kingdom wrote: 'A . . . major field of change essential as a prerequisite to the Industrial Revolution was transport'[4]. Rostow[5] in his major study of economic growth refers to the 'take off' encouraged by leading sectors. He includes rail in this category which he suggests (a) lowered internal transport costs (b) encouraged exports and the availability of new capital, and (c) helped create modern coal, iron and engineering industries. Youngson[6] is equally confident: 'most people would agree that improved transport plays a key role in economic development. This, indeed, is one of the few general truths which it is possible to derive from a study of economic history'. Such evidence must be an important guideline to those wishing to encourage economic growth in the developing countries. The World Bank, established in 1945 and owned by the governments of 139 countries, exists to help raise standards of living in developing countries by channelling financial resources from developed countries to the developing world. In 1972 it set out the rationale for transport investment: 'Transportation is a necessary concomitant of the exchange economy and is indispensable to economic growth. Where there is no transportation, economic activity is restricted to hand-to-mouth subsistence levels'.

'Specialization and the generation of surplus for exchange on the basis of comparative advantage are not possible without the capability to move resources and goods from one place to another. The demand for transport services increases with extension of the input—output relationship of the economy and the provision of transportation services can be an important determinant of the pace and locational pattern of development'[7].

There are some good examples where transport investment has made a vast improvement in the distribution of particular sectors. In Nigeria, railway development in the twenty-five years prior to the Second World War encouraged a marked increase in the efficiency of groundnut and fish production. This was almost entirely due to the shortening of journey time and lowering of cost. Those trips from the Jos Plateau to the coast were reduced on average from 35 days to less than 35 hours and the cost fell from £29.10 per ton to £8 per ton[8]. There was also evidence of progress towards regional specialization and the creation of national markets, two of the important factors outlined in the theoretical analysis above. The regions in the north and south concentrated on export products whereas the middle area provided for domestic consumption as Figure 1.1 shows.

There seems then to be a strong economic case for transport investment. However, a closer look at economic history does not suggest such a clear positive relationship between transport and economic growth. For example, canals and railways in fact lagged behind growth periods in the United Kingdom and the United States, and one researcher in Russian and Chinese development concluded 'the transport sector as a whole is a handmaiden, and not a prime-mover in the process of development'[9]. This second view of transport's importance emphasizes its *permissive role*. Transport is just one of many necessary inputs which must interact with each other. Transport may offer opportunities for developing other resources but scope for development must be there in the first place.

Not only is it possible that transport plays a passive role in economic development but in some circumstances it may be positively harmful to growth as resources devoted to transport could have been better used elsewhere. Might this not be seen in the duplication in railway investment

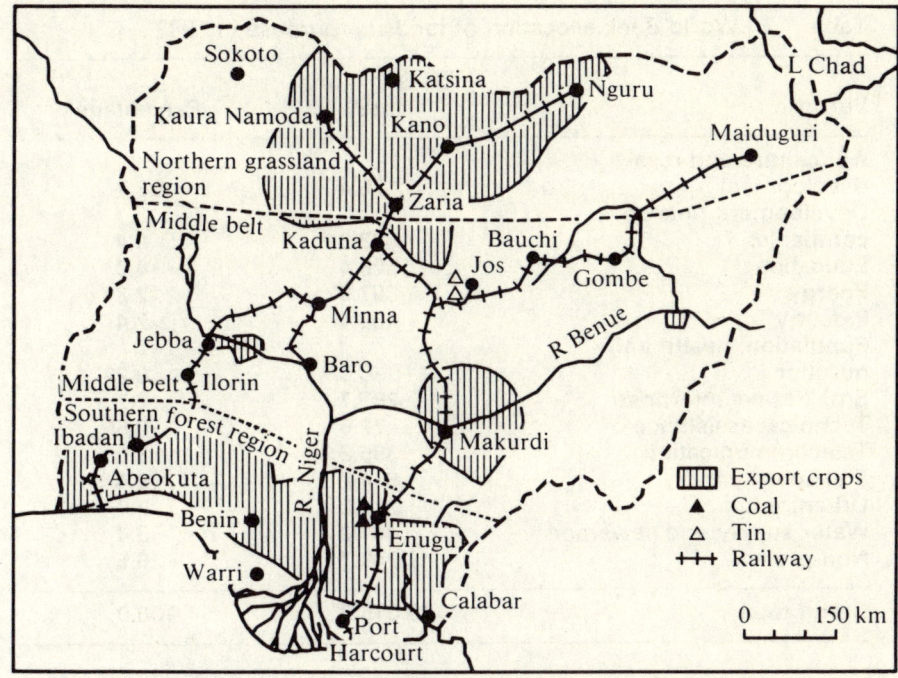

Figure 1.1 Nigeria—example of specialization.

in the United Kingdom in the nineteenth century, the building of Concorde and possibly the projected construction of the Third London Airport? It is significant that World Bank funds devoted to the transportation sector have declined in relative terms. In the period up to 1968, 32% of funds were spent on transport projects. Table 1.2 shows that in 1982 the corresponding figure was only 12.4%. This is partly explained by the fact that much basic infrastructure are now complete but it also reflects the new perception about the development of the member countries.

If many observers are sceptical of the importance of transport in developing countries they are even more aware of its limitations in a developed economy even in a regional context. The Leitch Committee Report[10] observed that in a developed economy transport costs are a very small proportion of total production and distribution costs. It was estimated that the M62 motorway in the United Kingdom reduced the total production costs in the region at the most by 0.33%[11]. Professor Gwilliam from his work at the Institute of Transport Studies in Leeds concluded: 'There is neither theoretical nor empirical reason to suggest that investments in transport infrastructure will cause radical changes in the level and location of activities'.

Table 1.2   World Bank allocation of funds by purpose in 1982

Purpose	US $ millions total	Percentage
Agriculture and rural development	3,078.4	23.7
Development finance companies	1,093.3	8.4
Education	526.4	4.0
Energy	2,897.5	22.3
Industry	959.4	7.4
Population, health and nutrition	36.0	0.28
Small-scale enterprise	285.7	2.2
Technical assistance	72.5	0.56
Telecommunication	395.8	3.0
Transportation	1,614.2	12.4
Urbanization	374.8	2.9
Water supply and sewerage	441.2	3.4
Non-project	1,240.7	9.5
Grand total	13,015.9	100.0

1.6   A policy for development?

The picture then, is one of confusion. Some observers see a strong positive relationship between transport and economic growth with transport playing a leading role. Some see transport playing a passive role, others a positively harmful one. What is the prescription, therefore, for the government of a developing country or an investment agency like the World Bank which must decide how much and what kind of investment will do the most to encourage economic growth? Sophisticated appraisal techniques, described in Chapter 6, are unable to assess development effects with sufficient accuracy and there is a great need for further research. The World Bank takes a pragmatic approach: 'The safest strategy of investment institutions is to wait until increases in production or captive productive schemes signal clearly the infrastructure requirements'[7].

The development of the Nigerian ports after the Civil War shows clearly the benefits from clearing bottlenecks and in many developing countries where a few products dominate the economy and where transport constitutes a large part of total production costs, e.g. maize in Kenya and iron ore in Brazil, such a policy will have immediate benefit. However, the World Bank still believes in the value of strategic planning, although it admits that it does not fully understand the wider development effects. It states: 'While the Bank can be fairly satisfied with the assessment of individual projects, the analysis of intrasectoral and perhaps more important, intersectoral priorities within a development strategy remains weak'[7].

It is obvious from what we have seen so far that a definite conclusion has not been reached on whether we should invest in transport or other sectors of the economy in order to encourage growth. In Appendix A.1 we describe an economic concept, *the multiplier*, that may hold the key to the answer. If the multiplier effect resulting from transport investment is greater than that from other sectors then a good case can be made in its favour.

Unfortunately, evidence in this area is rather scarce but it is significant that when economists, in describing the Keynesian approach to national economic management advocate the injection of Government funds to stimulate growth, the example they often use is the building of new motorways or railways! Is it likely that the multiplier is relatively higher in transport investment? Certainly, it is often labour-intensive and, therefore, increases the incomes of those with a high propensity to consume (see Appendix A.1). By its very nature it is usually geographically dispersed thus affecting many communities. Similar arguments could be made in favour of widespread agricultural and other investment areas seen in Table 1.2 but transport also involves high expenditure and capital. The impact on suppliers is important as evidenced by the impetus the United Kingdom railway network gave to the brick and iron and steel industries and to financial systems and institutions, such as the regional stock exchanges.

Related to this is a very persuasive argument put forward by Professor G. W. Wilson[12]. He suggests the important thing is to encourage entrepreneurial activity in developing countries. We have already seen that the World Bank is very skilled in assessing the direct costs and benefits of projects but it admits that the wider or *spillover* effects are difficult to judge accurately. Wilson considers it a question of changing peoples' attitudes. Therefore, projects must be considered not only in the light of their direct economic effects but also against their impact on the way people respond economically. He gives as examples a number of projects and places them on a scale with the two criteria at opposite ends, as Figure 1.2 shows.

We can see that investment in education or health will have little impact on direct productive activity but will have a marked effect on peoples' attitudes. The building of a steel mill on the other hand, while having direct benefits, will probably be seen by a small proportion of the population and so will have a negligible direct effect on peoples' entrepreneurial activity. Examine once again Table 1.2 and decide how closely World Bank spending reflects this approach to investment strategy. Transport, as you

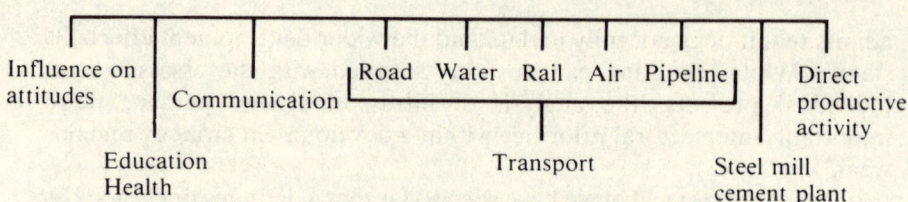

Figure 1.2 Investment projects — attitudes or production?

can see from Figure 1.2, comes between these two extremes, and we can also see that some modes are more in harmony with Professor Wilson's approach than others. This is quite obvious. If you wish to change people's attitudes then improving their access to new transport infrastructure is paramount. Investment in local roads would be more suitable, therefore, than in a pipeline or international airline, notwithstanding the promotional effect of a nation's flag carrier. The World Bank would appear to agree with this view and is placing greater emphasis on road programmes. Of the transport budget of US $1,062.8 million for the fiscal year 1981, 52.5% was spent on highway projects, many of which were intended to increase accessibility in rural areas[13]. In Benin, for example, $8.7 million was allocated for a three-year programme of feeder-road construction and maintenance to enable farmers to have year-round access to markets. In Chile, 250 kilometres of badly deteriorated sections of the country's only north—south trunk road was reconstructed to provide access for about 950,000 people, most of them rural and urban poor. In Colombia, emphasis was again placed on feeder roads in a $63 million project and, in Honduras, about 350 kilometres of feeder roads were built in selected agricultural valleys and 115 kilometres of secondary roads. In India, in the late sixties, only 11 per cent of the 646,000 villages were connected to the rest of the country by all-weather roads and one-third were further than five miles from dependable road connections[13]. To meet this problem US $52.9 million was allocated by the World Bank to a project to construct and improve 700 kilometres of rural roads in Bihar State to permit all-weather transport between farms and markets. About 2 million people were expected to benefit.

Of course, local roads are not the only infrastructure which provide greater accessibility for a majority of the, mainly rural, population. Improving local waterways would do just as well in some cases, although the opportunities for such investment are more limited. Most investment in this area has been in the context of main channels, as in Bangladesh, or ports (in Haiti and Thailand). Local railway networks, too, play an important role. In Yugoslavia, a three-year project costing US $67.5 million includes the reconstruction of an important junction, the installation of modern signalling and the purchase of rolling stock for the rail network in Kosov, the weakest part of the country's rail system.

1.7 Conclusions

Having examined the views of various historians and economists, outlined the relevant parts of economic theory and considered the work and views of the World Bank we must now arrive at conclusions on the following questions, relating to developing countries:

1 In terms of encouraging economic development how important is investment in transport compared with other areas?
2 What is the best form of transport investment for encouraging economic growth?
3 What is the best investment strategy?

1 Transport investment?
The answer to the question will depend on the stage of a country's economic development and the particular needs at the time. However, in general terms much will depend on the value of the multiplier effect and the way in which a particular investment changes peoples' attitudes in terms of entrepreneurial activity. Certain kinds of transport investment are favourable in this respect but then so are other investment areas, particularly agriculture, health and education.

2 Which mode of transport?
Accessibility would seem to be the key consideration. Although there are obvious promotional benefits from national airlines, prestigious airports and advanced urban transport systems, those investments which give greater access to local markets would seem to demand greatest attention. Thus, projects which improve communications for the mass of rural poor, whether it be road, rail or water, should be given priority.

3 The best strategy?
Ideally, long-term planning would be the best strategy. However, the World Bank which has carried out much research in this area, remains unsure how to forecast accurately the development effects of transport investments. Given this uncertainty and the large sums involved, the approach at the present time appears to be to take a pragmatic approach and attempt to clear bottlenecks in production and to solve particular accessibility problems on a piecemeal basis.

Examination questions

1 Examine carefully the relationship between improvements in transport facilities and the economic development of a region. Illustrate your answer with some specific examples.

2 Is there any reason to suppose that transport investments are more conducive to economic growth than investments of similar magnitude in other sectors?

3 To foster economic development, the 'World Bank' (International Bank for Reconstruction and Development) advances loans for the finance of projects in the less developed countries, and about one-third of the value of these loans is spent on transport investment. Why is so much importance attached to transport in this respect, and to what extent is the investment expenditure achieving the desired result?

4 Outline the role of transport investment in economic development. How does the experience of developing countries today compare with the experience of countries in Western Europe and North America in the nineteenth century?

5 Are transport networks mainly a cause or mainly an effect of patterns of economic development?

6 'The role of transport investment in economic growth is not unique. Transport investment is no more an indicator of growth than any other form of investment or deliberate policy', (G. W. Wilson, *The Impact of Highway Investment on Development*, Brookings Institution, 1966). Discuss.

7 'A transportation infrastructure is a prerequisite — though by no means a guarantee — of economic development.' (H. A. Adler, *Economic Appraisal of Transport Projects*, Indiana University Press 1971.) Discuss.

8 Consider the contribution which investment in transport facilities can make to the economic growth of developing countries. Discuss the major problems which such countries face in undertaking investment in transport.

9 Analyse carefully the relationship between improvements in transport facilities and the economic growth of a country.

10 Explain the economic function of transport.

2

The Demand for Transport

2.1 Introduction

In this chapter we analyse the nature of the demand for transport services. We begin by examining the usage of the various modes of transport in Britain and the way in which usage is changing over time. We then consider what factors influence demand and cause demand levels to fluctuate, and introduce the important concept of *elasticity of demand*. Finally, we look at some of the problems of actually measuring demand with particular reference to market research techniques in the bus industry.

2.1.1 Measures of usage

Two basic measures of usage are in common use in transport, those of quantity and of movement. Thus we can examine the number of passengers or the tonnage of freight carried, both of which describe quantity; or we can examine passenger mileage or ton mileage, which are measures of movement. A passenger travelling ten miles therefore counts as one passenger or ten passenger/miles. Similarly ten tons shipped a distance of 100 miles equals 1000 ton/miles of movement. Measures of movement measure both quantity and distance and trends therefore warrant careful interpretation. For example an increase in rail passenger mileage from 200 to 250 million passenger miles could mean 25% more passengers are travelling, alternatively it could demonstrate that average journey length has increased by 25%, or a combination of increasing passenger numbers and journey length.

2.1.2 Passenger usage

The pattern of passenger usage in Britain is shown in Table 2.1. Within the period 1960 to 1980 total passenger movement has increased from 268 to 528 billion passenger kilometres, a doubling of passenger movement within

Table 2.1   Passenger transport: by mode: 1960–1980

Billion passenger kilometres/percentage

	Road								Rail		Air (including N. Ireland and Channel Islands)		All modes	
	Buses and coaches		Private transport		Pedal cycles		All road							
1960	71	*27*	144	*54*	12	*5*	227	*85*	40	*15*	0.8	*0.3*	268	*100*
1961	69	*25*	161	*57*	11	*4*	241	*86*	39	*14*	1.0	*0.4*	281	*100*
1962	68	*24*	172	*60*	9	*3*	249	*87*	37	*13*	1.1	*0.4*	287	*100*
1963	67	*23*	186	*62*	8	*3*	261	*88*	36	*12*	1.3	*0.4*	298	*100*
1964	65	*20*	212	*65*	8	*3*	285	*88*	37	*11*	1.5	*0.5*	324	*100*
1965	63	*19*	231	*68*	7	*2*	301	*89*	35	*10*	1.7	*0.5*	338	*100*
1966	62	*17*	255	*71*	7	*2*	324	*90*	35	*10*	1.8	*0.5*	361	*100*
1967	61	*16*	271	*73*	6	*2*	338	*90*	34	*9*	1.9	*0.5*	374	*100*
1968	59	*15*	286	*74*	6	*1*	351	*91*	34	*9*	1.9	*0.5*	387	*100*
1969	58	*15*	292	*75*	5	*1*	355	*91*	35	*9*	1.9	*0.5*	392	*100*
1970	56	*14*	309	*76*	5	*1*	370	*91*	36	*9*	2.0	*0.5*	408	*100*
1971	56	*13*	330	*77*	5	*1*	391	*91*	36	*8*	2.0	*0.5*	429	*100*
1972	55	*12*	347	*78*	4	*1*	406	*92*	35	*8*	2.2	*0.5*	443	*100*
1973	54	*12*	364	*79*	4	*1*	422	*92*	35	*8*	2.4	*0.5*	459	*100*
1974	54	*12*	350	*79*	4	*1*	408	*92*	36	*8*	2.3	*0.5*	446	*100*
1975	54	*12*	352	*79*	4	*1*	410	*92*	35	*8*	2.2	*0.5*	447	*100*
1976	53	*12*	367	*80*	4	*1*	424	*92*	33	*7*	2.3	*0.5*	459	*100*
1977	53	*11*	387	*81*	4	*1*	444	*92*	34	*7*	2.1	*0.4*	480	*100*
1978	52	*10*	412	*82*	4	*1*	468	*93*	35	*7*	2.4	*0.5*	505	*100*
1979	52	*10*	416	*81*	4	*1*	472	*92*	36	*7*	2.8	*0.5*	511	*100*
1980	51	*10*	433	*82*	5	*1*	489	*93*	36	*7*	2.8	*0.5*	528	*100*

Source: *Transport Statistics Great Britain 1970—1980* (HMSO: London, 1981)

two decades. Within this global figure use of the various modes has exhibited significantly different trends. In absolute terms, road passenger transport has experienced a significant decline in usage of 28% and an even larger fall in its market share from 27% to 10%. No single factor accounts for this, although the increase in car ownership within the period is a significant factor together with real increases in fares and service reductions. Private road transport usage has trebled between 1960 and 1980 and this provides the major explanation for the overall increase in passenger movement. Private transport provided broadly half of passenger movement in 1960 and 82% in 1980. Rail transport shows an absolute decline of only 10% despite a substantial contraction in the rail network during the 1960s although its market share has halved. Domestic air travel represents a small proportion of total usage reflecting the relatively short distance between cities in Britain. It does show a substantial increase of 350% between 1960 and 1980.

The overall pattern therefore is of a major increase in passenger movement within which there is a major move from public to private transport.

2.1.3 Freight movement

Data for goods uplifted and goods moved are shown in Table 2.2. The total amount of goods uplifted has declined by 12.5% between 1970 and 1980. This reduction of approximately 250 million tonnes reflects the decline of basic industries such as steel making and of sections of manufacturing industry. Thus, the amount of iron and steel materials and products moved has declined from 155 million tonnes in 1968 to 78 million tonnes in 1980 whilst coal moved has declined from 266 to 161 million tonnes in a similar period. The relative shares of the various modes show a slight decline for road transport and a relatively larger decline for rail with increased usage of coastal shipping and pipelines. These changes in shares reflect the dependence of certain modes on certain industries. Within rail's 154 million tonnes, 94 million tonnes are coal and coke, 15 million tonnes are minerals, earth and stones, and 13 million tonnes are iron and steel and other metals. The demand for rail freight is therefore heavily dependent on primary industry and heavy engineering, sections of the economy which are in relative decline. Road freight demand is more broadly based reflecting its role in distributing finished goods as well as moving raw materials. The breakdown of tonnage by types of goods is shown in Table 2.3.

2.2 The problem of the peak

Figure 2.1 shows the pattern of demand through the day for bus travel in an

Table 2.2   Usage of freight transport

	Goods lifted				Goods moved			
	1970		1980		1970		1980[3]	
	Million tonnes	%	Million tonnes	%	Billion tonne/ km	%	Billion tonne/ km	%
Road[1]	1,610	84.1	1,373	81.9	85.0	61.5	95.7	77.6
Rail[2]	209	10.9	154	9.2	26.8	19.4	17.6	14.3
Coastal shipping	51	2.7	62	3.7	23.2	16.8	—	—
Inland waterways	6	0.3	5	0.3	0.1	0.1	0.1	0.1
Pipelines	39	2.0	82	4.9	3.0	2.2	9.9	8.0
Total	1,915	100.0	1,676	100.0	138.2	100.0	123.3	100.0

[1] Includes all carriage of goods on public roads by British registered vehicles but excludes work done by foreign goods vehicles.
[2] Excludes freight by passenger trains.
[3] Coastal shipping data not available. Total tonne-kilometre and percentage figures not comparable with 1970.
Source: *Transport Statistics Great Britain* 1970—1980 (HMSO: London, 1981)

urban area. You will notice that there are two distinct periods of peak demand, 0700 to 0900 and 1600 to 1800 hours. These peaks are caused by travel to and from work and school – these journey purposes accounted for over 96% of peak journeys in the area shown in the example, compared with 44% of journeys in the interpeak period. The other major journey purpose in the interpeak period is shopping, which accounted for 37% of journeys. After 1800 hours travel is primarily for leisure purposes. Half the total daily journeys are concentrated within the four peak hours, and within these periods there are further fluctuations in the level of demand so that the maximum demand is typically concentrated into a very short period – perhaps fifteen minutes.

Why should these peaks in demand cause operators problems? After all, supply can be expanded to meet the additional demand, and surely the extra business should be welcomed? The answer is that, for a number of reasons, peak services cost substantially more to provide and require a disproportionate amount of management attention compared to off-peak services. Why should this be so?

Figure 2.2 shows the pattern of supply of buses throughout the day in the same urban area as in Figure 2.1. The first thing to notice is that the supply

Table 2.3   Goods lifted road freight 1980

	Million tonnes	Percentage (%)[1]
Food, drink, tobacco and agricultural products	288	21.0
Minerals, earths and stones	333	24.3
Building materials, wood, timber and cork	167	12.2
Coal and coke	67	4.9
Iron, steel and other metals	65	4.7
Chemicals and fertilizers	56	4.1
All other commodities (inc. mixed loads)	322	23.5
	1,373	

[1] Percentage rounded
Source: *Transport Statistics Great Britain* 1970–1980 (HMSO: London, 1981)

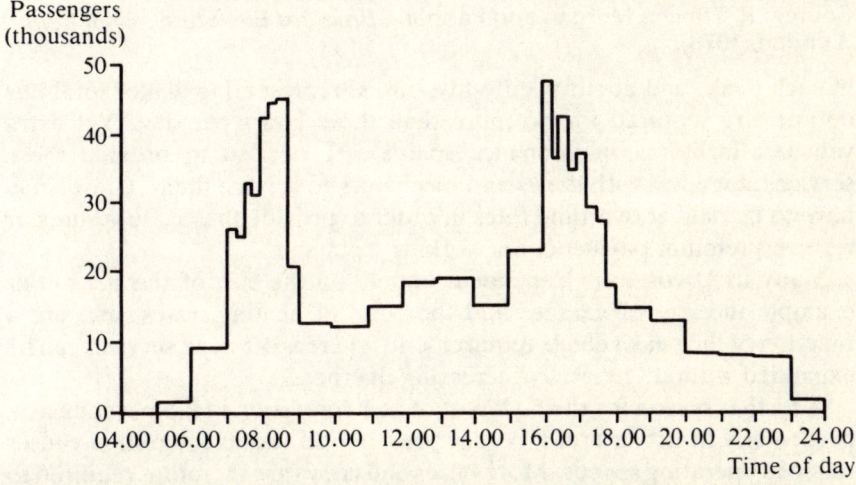

Figure 2.1 Bus passenger demand by time of day, Bradford.
Source: R. Travers Morgan and Partners, *Bradford Bus Study, Final Report* (London, 1976).

peaks last longer than the demand peaks – roughly from 0630 to 0930 and from 1530 to 1830 hours. This reflects the time taken to get buses out of garage and into position to meet the demand peaks, and the time taken at the end of the peak periods to run down to a lower level of service. Load factors during the 'shoulders' of the peak are therefore relatively low. The second point to notice is that the last few buses are in service for much less than the full four-hour peak. Some buses are required for only half an hour

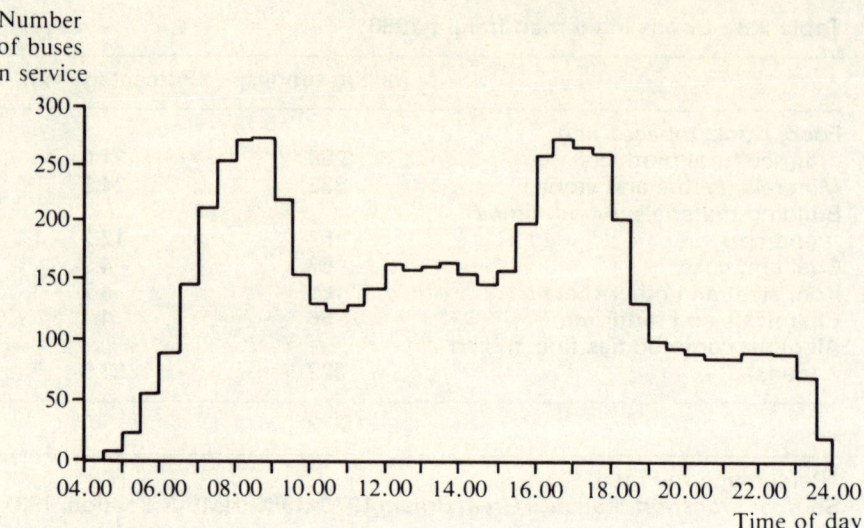

Figure 2.2 Buses in service by time of day, Bradford.
Source: R. Travers Morgan and Partners, *Bradford Bus Study, Final Report*
(London, 1976).

in each peak, and about twenty-five buses, representing 9% of total bus
output, are required for no more than three hours per day. Yet extra
vehicles, including maintenance spares, are needed to provide these
services, together with crews and mechanics to service them. Crews may
have to be paid at overtime rates in order to provide the last few buses or
receive premium payments for working 'split shifts'.

Many fixed costs are dependent largely on the size of the peak. For
example the size of garages and the costs of heating, rates, etc. are a
function of the peak vehicle requirement, whereas off-peak services can be
expanded without generally increasing overheads.

A further reason for the high cost of peak provision in the bus industry,
particularly in urban areas, is that peak period traffic congestion causes
reduced operating speeds. More buses and crews are therefore required to
operate a given service headway.

There are a number of ways in which peak problems might be alleviated
as follows.

(a) The *economic* solution would be to charge fares according to marginal
costs, which would generally imply increasing fares at peak periods
and reducing them at off-peak times. This approach might not be
appropriate however if marginal *social* costs are taken into account,
particularly in urban areas, where lower peak fares might be justified
in order to attract car users to public transport, giving benefits to other
road users from reduced congestion.

(b) Although bus operators do sometimes charge higher fares at peak periods, particularly for children's travel, it is more common to find special discount fares at off-peak periods in an attempt to boost off-peak travel.

(c) Peak demand may be reduced by boarding restrictions. For example, concessionary travel for pensioners is often confined to the off-peak. A special kind of restriction is often implemented to help long distance passengers at peak periods, with certain buses reserved for passengers travelling beyond a certain point on the route.

(d) Operators can sometimes increase off-peak demand by seeking special contract work, e.g. buses taking schoolchildren to playing fields or swimming baths.

(e) Restrictions in peak supply can bring large savings in costs. This can be achieved by altering standards of service – for example having an aim that peak passengers should be able to board the second bus to arrive at their stop, instead of the first bus to arrive.

(f) Labour costs could be reduced by employing part-time labour to operate additional peak services.

(g) Bus priority measures and other forms of traffic management or traffic restraint, by increasing operating speeds, can help to reduce peak costs.

(h) Staggering of work and school hours can make a substantial contribution to solving the problem of the peak. This has been adopted to some extent – the introduction of 'flexitime' in many offices has helped, while some schools within the same area have staggered starting and finishing times. Maximum demand is now often determined by schools traffic, so further staggering of school hours would be desirable.

2.3 Seasonal variations

These present similar problems to the peak with concentrated demand requiring investment in fixed assets which have low utilization. Prior to nationalization, the number of vehicles in the Great Western Railways carriage fleet was primarily determined by peak holiday demand during a dozen or so summer weekends. Stock was therefore retained, together with siding capacity, for use on perhaps thirty days a year. Similarly, signalling sections and signal boxes were provided to ensure sufficient capacity to work holiday trains. The trend from public to private transport has shifted the peak holiday demand problem from rail to road. Spectacular traffic jams on roads to Devon and Cornwall during summer weekends have resulted in the provision of additional road capacity which is under-utilized for the bulk of the year. Similar problems of concentrated

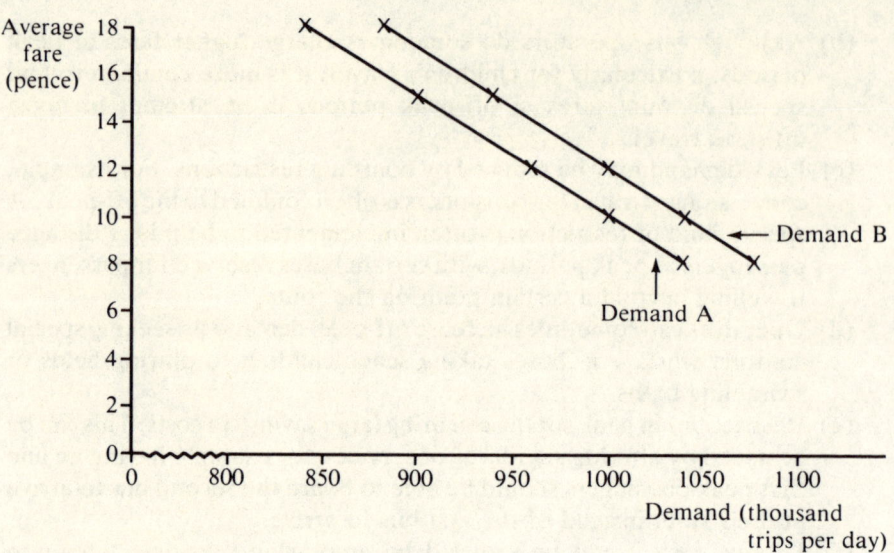

Figure 2.3 A demand curve for bus travel.

holiday demand are experienced at ferry ports and the extra port capacity provided does not necessarily lend itself to alternative uses. However, when extra vehicles are provided then these may be leased out during off-peak seasons. An example of this is an aircraft exchange agreement between Air Europe in Britain and the American airline Air Florida. Two Air Europe Boeing 737's are leased to Air Florida during the autumn and winter when British demand for inclusive tour flying is less and two Air Florida Boeing 737's are provided for Air Europe's use during the British summer holiday season. This ingenious exchange permits both operators to match their capacity to demand at different times of the year and to ensure good asset utilization. Other operators may resort to leasing in peak capacity whilst leasing out aircraft off-season.

2.4 Factors affecting demand

We have seen how the demand for transport fluctuates and how it has changed over the years. We now want to look a little more closely at the factors affecting demand for transport as a whole and for particular modes.

Price is an obvious factor affecting demand and in most cases the higher the price the lower the demand will be. This has been clearly illustrated in some large cities in the UK where low fare public transport policies have resulted in increases in demand which has fallen off when the policies have been abandoned. The way that demand varies with price is shown as a *Demand Schedule* in Table 2.4, and as a *Demand Curve* in Figure 2.3. On the graph price is always shown on the vertical axis and the amount demanded (or supplied) on the horizontal axis. You can see quite clearly that as price falls demand increases, and vice versa. We have taken as an example a theoretical demand for bus travel.

Table 2.4 A demand schedule for bus travel

| Year | Average fare per trip (p) | Passenger Journeys | | | |
		Demand A (000)	Revenue £(000)	Demand B (000)	Revenue £(000)
1	8	1,040	83.2	1,080	86.4
2	10	1,000	100.0	1,040	104.0
3	12	960	115.2	1,000	120.0
4	15	900	135.0	940	141.0
5	18	840	151.2	880	158.0

2.4.1 The basis of demand — marginal utility

In Chapter 1 we stated that society has unlimited wants and limited resources with which to satisfy those wants. The same applies to the individual who usually has a finite income. We assume he aims to achieve maximum satisfaction or *utility* with his income. At this point we must distinguish between *total utility* and *marginal utility*. Total utility is the total satisfaction we derive from the consumption of a commodity. We would expect in most cases that this would increase as we obtain more of the same product, although of course there will be some, like alcohol, where it might eventually decrease!

2.4.2 The concept of the margin

One of the most important, and most difficult, concepts in economics is that of marginality. It is important because we are concerned with decisions about consumption and production which involve questions like 'Shall I purchase one more of that item?' or 'Shall we produce a few more of that product this month?'. In other words, they are decisions at the margin. *Marginal utility is the satisfaction we derive from possessing one extra unit of a commodity, or the satisfaction we lose if we give up one unit.*

We are always making choices between commodities and often about extra consumption: 'Shall I buy an extra can of fruit or some more cakes?'. An important factor in this choice is the fact that *the more we consume of something the lower will be the utility of an extra unit*. The first cigarette or pint of beer usually provides greater satisfaction than subsequent ones. This is the hypothesis of *diminishing marginal utility* which can be stated as:

'The utility that any individual obtains from successive units of a particular commodity will diminish as total consumption of the commodity increases, the consumption of all other commodities being held constant'.

We assume that the individual will try to maximize his satisfaction in his choice of commodities within the constraints of his finite income. It can be shown mathematically that he will achieve this when the ratios of the marginal utilities of all the commodities to their respective prices are equal. That is: $MU_x/P_x=MU_y/P_y=MU_z/P_z$ where MU_x, MU_y and MU_z are marginal utilities for commodities x, y and z and P_x, P_y and P_z are their respective prices per unit.

This can be illustrated with the help of Figure 2.4. It shows the diminishing utility for three items of expenditure, electricity, bus travel and telephone calls in relation to their unit price. With his fixed income the consumer allocates his expenditure until the marginal utility:price ratios for the three items are equal. In this case:

$$\frac{15 \text{ units of satisfaction}}{15 \text{ pence per unit}} = \frac{10 \text{ units of satisfaction}}{10 \text{ pence per unit}} = \frac{5 \text{ units of satisfaction}}{5 \text{ pence per unit}}$$
$$\qquad\qquad Electricity \qquad\qquad\qquad Bus\ travel \qquad\qquad Telephone\ calls$$

To show that the consumer has in fact maximized the utility imagine he decides to give up one unit of electricity consumption and to spend the 15 pence saving on bus travel and telephone calls. Because diminishing marginal utility means that marginal satisfaction decreases with increased consumption, for that extra one unit of bus travel he obtains only 5 units of satisfaction and for the extra telephone call only 4 units of satisfaction. He therefore gives up 15 units of satisfaction and for the same expenditure gains only 9 units.

Transferring expenditure in turn from both bus travel and telephone calls will produce similar results.

We can use this analysis to show how demand varies with price. Using the figure from the previous example assume the price of bus travel increases to 15 pence per unit. Then the marginal utility:price ratios will no longer be equal i.e.

$$\frac{10 \text{ units of satisfaction}}{15 \text{ pence per unit}} \neq \frac{5 \text{ units of satisfaction}}{5 \text{ pence per unit}}$$
$$\qquad\qquad Bus\ travel \qquad\qquad\qquad\qquad\qquad Telephone\ calls$$

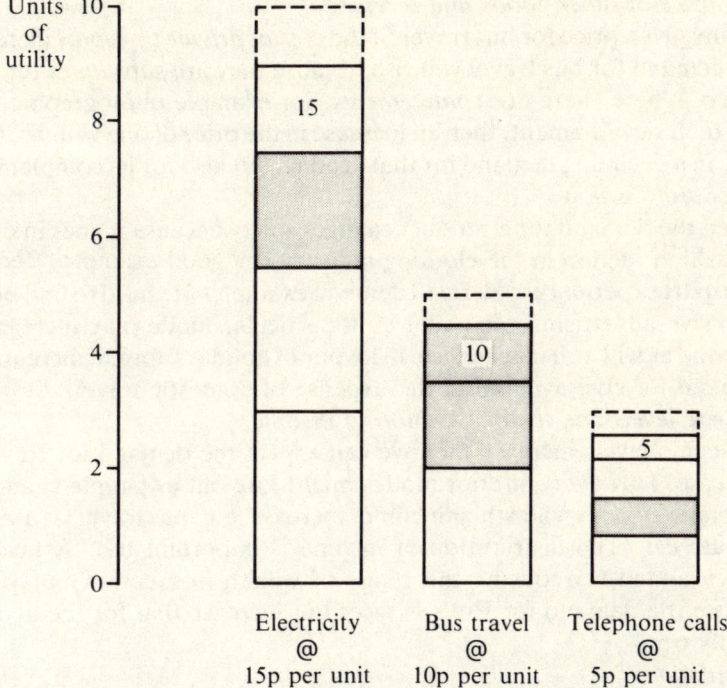

Figure 2.4 Price and utility for a consumer in relation to three services.

If marginal utility decreases with increased consumption then conversely reduced consumption will raise marginal utility. So to maximize his satisfaction in the face of the price increase the consumer will reduce bus travel (say giving up his least important trip) until the marginal utility rises to 15 units and the equation becomes,

$$\frac{15 \text{ units of satisfaction}}{\underset{Bus\ travel}{15 \text{ pence per unit}}} = \frac{5 \text{ units of satisfaction}}{\underset{Telephone\ calls}{5 \text{ pence per unit}}}$$

Therefore, as the demand curve in Figure 2.3 shows when price increases demand will fall, giving the normal downward sloping shape.

2.4.3 Conditions of demand

There are other factors affecting demand in addition to price and these we call *conditions of demand*. These will determine the demand for a product *at any given price*. They include:

1 *The price of other goods and services*
   At any given price for bus travel, if the cost of *private transport* increases
   the demand for bus travel will rise because they are *substitutes* for each
   other. Where there are *complements*, for example photographic films
   and their development, then an increase in the price of one will result not
   only in a declining demand for that product but also for its complement.
2 *Taste and fashion*
   Often the demand for a product changes solely because it goes in or out
   of fashion; denim in the clothing industry is a good example. Because
   transport experiences a derived demand examples are hard to find but an
   intensive advertising campaign by a particular mode may increase its
   demand as will a change in taste in favour of holidays abroad increase the
   demand for civil aviation at the expense of domestic travel.
3 *Income levels and the distribution of income.*
   If income levels increase then we can expect the demand for travel to
   increase. However, inferior modes might lose out as people change to
   the *superior* ones when their incomes increase, e.g. bus travel vis a vis the
   private car. The distribution of income is important too. A taxation
   policy aimed at reducing the range of wealth in a country may well
   reduce the demand for Rolls Royces but increase that for the average
   family car.
4 *Population.*
   Obviously a growth in population will encourage an increase in demand
   but a change in the age structure will have a more complex impact.

   The important distinction to make between price and conditions of
demand is that the former determines the *shape* of the demand curve (and
we will return to this later) whereas the conditions determine the *position*
of the demand curve. If we suppose that the price of petrol rises and
therefore the cost of private motoring increases, we would expect the
demand for bus travel to rise at any given price. The demand schedule
might shift from A to B in Table 2.4, and we can see in Figure 2.3 that the
demand curve has shifted to the right.

2.5 The factors affecting the demand for transport

We shall now examine factors which affect the demand for both freight and
passenger transport looking at factors affecting demand as a whole and
then those factors influencing modal choice.

2.5.1 The demand for freight

The demand for freight is very much a derived one depending on the level
of output in the economy and the location of producers and consumers. We

shall see in Chapter 8 that forecasting demand is very difficult as the relation between Gross Domestic Product (a measure of the level of output) and freight mileage is a rather complicated one and forecasting GDP itself is an uncertain exercise. It has been observed that there is a close relationship between the two but that the ratio of tonne-miles to GDP is falling over time[1].

It is suggested that there are three reasons for this:

1 There is a trend towards the production of lighter products;
2 Changes in the degree of specialization have reduced the need for the movement of semi-finished goods; and
3 Producers are moving closer to the consumer[2].

Price does not appear to be a major influence on freight demand. This is mainly due to the fact that transport costs (at about 10%) constitute quite a small proportion of total manufacturing costs.

For this reason price does not seem to play a large part in modal choice either. Producers choose rather more on the basis of *quality of service*. This would include reliability, flexibility and protection from damage or theft. These factors have in the past favoured road freight rather than rail and own account operation rather than general road haulage, although the development of containerization has reduced rail's disadvantage regarding damage or loss. Speed is, of course, an important factor. Road haulage has always had a significant advantage over rail in this respect because it can offer door-to-door service. This avoidance of transhipment has a large impact on time and cost on all but the longest of domestic journeys.

2.5.2 The demand for passenger travel

The analysis and therefore the forecasting of passenger demand is easier in some respects than for freight and it is due largely to the fact that there are published charges and timetables and many thousands of customers making individual decisions. Therefore, if there are any changes on the supply side their magnitude will be known and customer response is usually quantifiable.

There are many factors influencing the total demand for passenger transport:population and real income levels are obvious ones. We shall see in Chapter 8 that forecasting on the passenger side is not without its problems largely because factors like population and income are themselves difficult to predict. However, we do have a wealth of information on which to analyse historic demand patterns.

Factors which influence the individual's decision are numerous. Price is one of the most important but then so too are levels of service, convenience and flexibility, comfort and journey time. Transport economists soon realized that price was only one factor which made up what the passenger considered to be the total cost of a journey so the concept of '*generalized cost*' was introduced. What should be included in such a composite cost? Imagine all the steps involved in taking a journey by bus. We have to walk to the bus stop, wait for the bus to arrive, hoping it will be on time, pay the fare, hope we can get a seat and that the journey will be quick and comfortable and then walk to our final destination, or change to another bus or other mode of transport. All these things represent a deterrent to our trip making and can be described as costs. They may be summarized as:

1 Fares
2 Journey time
3 Ease of access to the system
4 Reliability
5 Probability of getting a seat
6 Comfort in the vehicle and in gaining access to it
7 Number of interchanges.

In practice only those which are quantifiable are included and generalized cost is normally made up of fare, walking, waiting and in-vehicle time and some kind of interchange penalty. In order to analyse demand it is then necessary to determine a monetary value of time so as to relate fares to other components of generalized cost.

2.5.3 The value of time

Imagine you live on one side of an estuary and work on the other and it takes you over an hour to drive to work. When a bridge is built it saves you an hour's driving but costs you £1 in toll fees. You decide to continue going the long way round. What does that tell us about your value of time? Well, it must be less than £1 per hour otherwise you would have used the bridge and paid a pound to save an hour. Equally, if you did decide to use the bridge we can deduce from your behaviour that you value your time at least as great as £1 per hour.

Why is knowledge of people's value of time important in demand theory? Quite simply, it enables us to forecast the impact of changes in journey time. One of the chief selling points with Concorde is its speed. But how many more passengers will travel because the journey time across the Atlantic is reduced to three hours and fifty-five minutes? We need to be able to place a value on those time savings to estimate their impact and eventually to determine whether the project is worthwhile. In Chapter 6 we shall look at time values in more detail paying particular attention to methods of their determination.

2.6 The elasticity of demand

2.6.1 Introduction

Suppose you worked in a bus company and the average fare went up last year by 25%, from 8 pence to 10 pence and as a result the number of passenger journeys went down from 1,040 thousand to 1,000 thousand. One day the General Manager announces he is considering increasing the fares and poses the question 'If they went up to 12 pence, how many passenger journeys would the company lose?' To answer that question you might look at what happened last time the fares went up. They were increased by 25% and passenger journeys went down by about 4%. This time fares are going up by 20% so demand should fall by just under 4%. If you followed this line of thinking you would be using the concept of *elasticity*. In this case it is price elasticity but it can be applied to all those factors which affect demand. *Elasticity merely exresses the rate of change in demand in response to a rate of change in a factor which affects demand.* Let us look at price elasticity a little more closely.

2.6.2 Price elasticity

If you had to travel to work by train because, say, there was no alternative means of public transport and you could not afford a car, then if price went up you would have little alternative, unless you changed your job or moved nearer to work, but to continue to use the train. We would describe your demand curve for that particular rail travel as being *inelastic*. In other words, you are fairly unresponsive to price change. If there were many rail commuters in your position then the rail company would face an inelastic demand curve. Leisure trips by rail are considered to be relatively elastic, and the demand curve in relation to price for such leisure travel can be compared with the demand curve for commuters in Figure 2.5.

Notice that the curve for leisure travel is much flatter, illustrating that a price increase of, say, £1 will cause a larger fall in demand $(Q—Q_2)$ than for the 'captive' commuter market $(Q—Q_1)$. To be accurate, if there is an 'inelastic' demand the figure is less than one which has the effect of increasing revenue if price goes up. Conversely, an 'elastic' demand means that the proportional change in demand is greater than the proportional change in price so in the case of a price increase revenue will fall.

Mathematically, price elasticity can be expressed as: $[(Q_2—Q_1)/Q_1]/[(P_2—P_1)/P_1]$ where Q_1 and Q_2 are quantity demanded before and after a price increase, and P_1 and P_2 are price before and after. Thus, if we take as an example the demand schedule shown in Table 2.4, the price elasticity when the price is raised from 8 to 10 pence can be calculated as follows: $[(1000—1040)/1040]/[(10—8)/8]=(—40/1040)/(2/8)=—0.038/0.25=—0.15$, where $Q_1=1040$, $Q_2=1000$, $P_1=8$ p, $P_2=10$ p. This figure means that if the

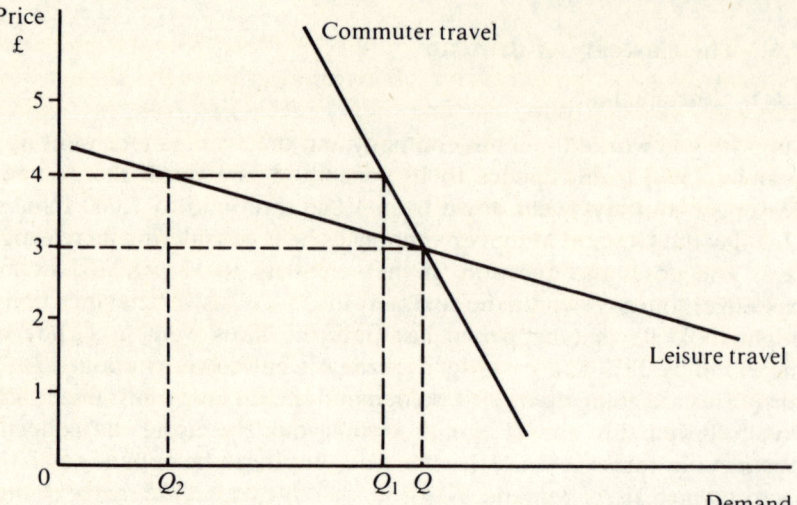

Figure 2.5 The differing demand curves for commuter and leisure travel.

price is increased by, say, 10% then demand will fall by 1.5%. The price in this case in fact went up by 25% so demand fell by 0.15×25=nearly 3.8%. Notice from Table 2.4 that because the demand is inelastic (less than one) revenue has increased, in this case from £83200 to £100,000 even though demand has fallen. If price then goes up by 20% we would expect demand to fall by 3%.

2.6.3 Some complications

In practice most operators will be content to use these simple calculations to forecast the effects of price changes but there are circumstances where they are not sufficiently accurate. If we look at the demand schedule in Table 2.4 we can see that when price was increased by 20% from 10 to 12 pence demand actually fell by 4%. Why is this? Calculations show us that the elasticity has changed from -0.15 to -0.2: $[(Q_2—Q_1)/Q_1]/[(P_2—P_1)/P_1] = [960—1000)/1000]/[(12—10)/10] = -0.04/0.20 = -0.2$. This can be explained by examining the demand curve in Figure 2.3. It shows in fact that the elasticity will change continuously from the lowest prices to the highest. Although there is the same absolute decrease in demand as price increases by one pence the *rate* of change becomes greater as the original quantity becomes smaller. At the same time the rate of change in price falls as the original price increases. This is a serious obstacle to predicting what will happen when prices change; if we cannot use past trends to help us predict with any confidence what is the alternative? A particular problem in passenger transport is that price changes tend to be large and the elasticity which relates to the old price is inappropriate for the change to the new one when, as we have seen, elasticity is changing all along the demand curve. We can partly solve this problem by replacing the *point* elasticity by a *mid-point* elasticity. This in effect takes the elasticity figure half-way between the old and new prices and can be expressed mathematically as: $\{(Q_2{-}Q)/[(Q_2{+}Q_1)/2]\}/\{(P_2{-}P_1)/[(P_2{+}P_1)/2]\}$ where Q_1 and Q_2 are the quantities demanded before and after and P_1 and P_2 the prices before and after the change.

Thus the corresponding figures to those for point elasticity are: When price changes from 8 p to 10 p $\{(1000{-}1040)/[(1040{+}1000)/2]\}/\{(10{-}8)/[(10{+}8)/2]\}=({-}40/1020)/(2/9)={-}0.04/0.22={-}0.18$. When price changes from 10 p to 12 p $\{(960{-}1000)/[(960{+}1000)/2]\}/\{(12{-}10)/[(12{+}10)/2]\}=({-}40/980)/(2/11)={-}0.04/0.18={-}0.22$. To be even more accurate we should use calculus to express the equation of the curve for its whole length but even then you would have to assume that the equation of the curve remains the same.

Estimating demand elasticity from past events is beset with problems, not the least of which is the difficulty of isolating the effect of one factor, say price, from the effects of all the other factors, such as service level and income changes. Many studies have been carried out with regard to bus transport and there seems to have been a consensus for accepting a price point elasticity in the region of −0.3. Such a universal figure may not always be very useful. You really need to break down trips by journey purpose at least. One recent study estimated[3] fare elasticity for shopping trips to be in the range −0.58 to −0.80. For other purposes (mostly work and education trips) fares elasticities were found to be between −0.32 and −0.46. Another recent study[4] found the fares elasticity for weekday travel to be −0.2. In recent rail travel research[5], mean fare elasticities for second class travel were estimated to be −0.50±0.07 for season tickets, −0.65±0.06 for cheap-day tickets and −0.20±0.04 for full-fare tickets. (The authors of this report are careful to point out that the possible presence of systematic errors suggests that the relatively small standard errors on the mean are likely to overstate the accuracy of these estimates.)

We made the distinction earlier between the slope of the demand curve and its position, and we said that conditions of demand determine the position at any given price. However, there will be a rate of change in demand in response to a rate of change in conditions of demand as there is with price. Obviously, it is difficult to determine the relationship between, say, comfort and demand but we are able to quantify the effects of changes in service levels such as frequency and journey time.

2.6.4 Service level elasticities

Service level changes appear to cause a greater passenger response than fares changes. The Gosport and Fareham case study above found a value of bus-kilometres elasticity of 0.6 for the week (0.81 for weekends and 0.55 for Mondays—Fridays). This means that for weekday travel a 10% increase in bus-kilometres will increase demand by 5.5%. The Telford study found shopping trips to be fairly insensitive to changes in service frequency, but elasticities with respect to a weighted combination of walking, waiting and in-vehicle time were estimated to be in the range −0.55 to −0.71. The corresponding range for non-shopping trips is −0.43 to −0.76. The rail study described above estimated journey-time elasticities for two stations in the BR Western region served by the High Speed Train. Values for off-peak travel were found to be about −0.7 but mean journey time differences in the peak were too small for analysis. A service frequency elasticity of 0.6 was obtained for season ticket travel from one of the stations.

The effect of changes in fares and service levels can be estimated within the framework of generalized cost. The change in service frequency for example can be translated into a change in waiting time which after applying values of time will be reflected in a change in generalized cost. This used in conjunction with generalized cost elasticity will give expected change in demand.

As an example, suppose the generalised cost of one journey by bus is made up of:

Fare	20p
In-vehicle time	30p
Walking time	10p
Waiting time	20p
Total	80p

If the service frequency is improved so that waiting time is halved, the new generalized cost will be reduced to 70p. There is, therefore, a 12.5% change which if applied to a generalized cost elasticity of, say, −0.7 will give an increase in demand of 8.75%. You can then translate it into revenue terms and compare that with the cost of increasing the service.

2.6.5   The price or quality of substitutes

Another condition of demand is the price or quality of other goods and services. Operators are concerned with the degree to which transport demand is affected by changes in price or service levels of other modes, particularly if they are in competition (i.e. are close substitutes). We are therefore concerned with *cross-elasticity* and for price the equation will be (in its simplest form): $[(Q_{2x}-Q_{1x})/Q_{1x}]/[(P_{2y}-P_{1y})]$ where P_{2y}, P_{1y} are price before and after for mode y, and $Q_{2x}Q_{1x}$ are quantity demanded for mode x before and after price change in mode y.

London Transport has pioneered much of the work in demand analysis and the results of some of its recent research[6] is summarized in Table 2.5. It shows how fares and service elasticities for individual modes (bus and underground) can be broken down into components that represent transfers to other public transport modes (assuming their costs are unchanged) and a conditional component that will occur even if all public transport costs by all modes move in concert.

2.6.6   Income elasticity

Income elasticity is another important tool for the transport economist. The relation between income and demand can be expressed as follows: $[(Q_2-Q_1)/Q_1]/[(Y_2-Y_1)/Y_1]$ where Q_2 and Q_1 are quantity demanded before and after, and Y_1 and Y_2 income before and after.

The elasticity can be either positive or negative depending on the nature of the mode. We should expect the superior modes such as car, train (vis a vis bus) or air travel to have positive elasticities. Inferior modes such as bus and coach might be expected to experience negative elasticities as people switch mode (particularly to car) when their income rises. However, most studies have found that even for bus travel there is increased travel with a raising of income. One study[7] suggested that the effect of earnings on bus travel can be represented by a positive elasticity but one which is probably very small and with upper limits of 0.4. The London Transport study used consumer spending as a proxy for income and in relation to retail sales found an elasticity of 0.2 for bus, and for rail 0.45 on weekdays and 0.5 on weekends.

There is finally the impact of population changes, changes in conditions and locations of employment and in leisure and shopping trend patterns. These, of course, are factors beyond the control of an operator and ones which are not subject to rapid and significant change. London Transport includes these in the *secular trend* and estimates an annual reduction in demand due to these factors of 2.5% for bus and 2.0% for the underground.

2.7   Demand measurement and market research

We have implicitly assumed in this chapter that the transport operator has knowledge of the demand curve which he faces. In order to obtain this information in practice, it is necessary to devote quite a lot of effort into researching the market, and this is particularly the case with public transport operation. A common criticism levelled at bus operators is that in the past they have spent insufficient attention to demand and have concentrated their efforts on the supply side of the market. We therefore

Table 2.5   Demand research by London Transport

(a) *Summary of fares elasticities*

	Weekday	Off-peak	Peak	Total
Bus				
Conditional component	−0.33	−0.38	−0.28	−0.34
transfer to Underground	−0.17	−0.17	−0.17	−0.17
transfer to BR	−0.02	−0.02	−0.02	−0.02
Total	−0.52	−0.57	−0.47	−0.53
Underground				
Conditional component	−0.18	−0.26	−0.15	−0.19
transfer to bus	−0.15	−0.15	−0.15	−0.15
transfer to BR	−0.07	−0.07	−0.07	−0.07
Total	−0.40	−0.48	−0.37	−0.41

Notes: 1 Weekday results are taken directly from the statistical analysis.
Other results are a synthesis of these and the weekend results.
2 Standard errors of co-efficients are typically in the range 0.02 to
0.04.

(b) *Service elasticities estimated for the period*

	Weekday	Off-peak	Peak	Total
Bus				
Conditional component	0.33	0.35	0.31	0.34
transfer to Underground	0.33	0.19	0.47	0.30
Total	0.66	0.54	0.78	0.64
Underground				
Conditional component	0.1	0.06	0.12	0.09
transfer to bus	0.1	0.24	0.04	0.12
Total	0.2	0.30	0.16	0.21

Notes: 1 See note 1, (a).
2 Standard errors are typically of the order of 0.1.
3 No BR transfer components were isolated.

consider in this section some of the recent developments in demand studies
in the bus industry, and the way in which they can be used for marketing
public transport.

In the past, bus operators commonly measured the existing demand for their services by reference to ticket sales. This was perfectly adequate so long as each ticket sold represented a single bus journey. There are two reasons why this is not usually the case nowadays.

1 Many of the ticket machines in common use are capable of issuing only a limited number of ticket values. One, two or more tickets may therefore be issued per journey, the precise number depending on the length of journey. The total number of tickets issued is not a very helpful indicator of demand in these circumstances.
2 The growing use of system-wide season tickets ('travelcards') and other forms of passes means that the only way of measuring the number of journeys being made is to physically count them.

In order to measure existing demand it is therefore necessary to undertake surveys. The West Midlands Passenger Transport Executive, for example, carry out a regular programme of Continuous On-Bus Surveys (COBS) to enable them to measure changes in demand over time for the whole undertaking and to provide information about demand for individual routes. The surveys are based on samples of bus journeys selected so as to give a representative picture of patronage by day of week, time of day, district, and type of passenger. The information collected includes details of the journey being surveyed and, for each passenger, the fare stage in which they board the bus, the fare stage at which they alight, and the type of ticket which they hold[8].

Another example of surveys carried out to determine existing demand patterns is the Market Analysis Project (MAP) carried out by various National Bus Company subsidiaries[9]. MAP surveys are more comprehensive than COBS in the sense that they include more details about passenger journeys—for example the *actual* origin and destinations of journeys, rather than just the bus stops—but they are not designed to provide information over time.

On-bus surveys are a good means of measuring existing demand levels. In rural areas, where buses tend to be more lightly loaded and where passengers' journeys tend to be longer, it is also possible to use on-bus interviews to obtain more details about passenger characteristics such as age, level of car ownership, and attitudes to bus services. This information is of great value in marketing, which involves tailoring the service to meet identified passenger requirements. The MAP surveys are used in this way. In urban areas it is not possible to obtain as much information from on-bus interviews because bus loadings are generally higher and journeys shorter—in these circumstances it is usually best to use household surveys to complement the on-bus surveys. Household surveys also enable the operator to collect information about people who do not use his services, and this can be of as much value as the information on bus-users—for example, it can highlight areas where the bus share of the travel market is below average, and where marketing efforts might usefully be concentrated.

In addition to their COBS system, the West Midlands Passenger Transport Executive have for some years carried out household surveys in connection with their Area Studies programme[10]. The studies, based on areas with a population of between 50,000 and 100,000 are aimed at establishing the pattern of movement by all modes, establishing the public's attitudes to public transport services, and discovering changes which the public would like to see. A sample of 1 in 20 households is selected from the electoral register, and trained interviewers are used for the household surveys. The questionnaires seek details on:

— The journey to work and school (destination, means and time of travel)
— Journeys made the previous day (for all purposes)
— Improvements sought to existing services
— Areas difficult to reach by bus
— Profile information (age, sex, car ownership, etc.).

Following the surveys, the data are analyzed, and proposals for network changes are formulated. At this stage the on-bus surveys become important because they can be used to show the effect of any proposed changes on existing passengers. Local councillors and the general public are also consulted before changes are implemented. Finally, following implementation a further household survey is carried out in the area some 9—12 months later, primarily to determine residents' attitudes to the changes which have been made.

Marketing covers the whole range of means available for matching the product to a customers requirements. Some aspects of marketing, such as pricing, are considered elsewhere. A public transport operator having set his fares and designed his service network according to the results of market research and forecasting studies might turn to promotional activity in order to increase patronage and revenue. In some cases this promotional activity may simply be bringing services (or service changes) to the attention of existing or potential passengers. Alternatively, the operator may promote particular attractions and their accessibility by public transport. For instance, two Passenger Transport Executives have recreational transport officers, jointly appointed by the Countryside Commission and the PTE's, to promote access to the countryside by public transport.

An example of the effects of promoting public transport can be found in a TRRL study on information leaflets[11]. This study considered the cost-effectiveness of promoting public transport through leaflets giving timetable and route network information. The study area covered a network of rural services in South and West Yorkshire. The services operated through several interchange points, and through-tickets were available permitting interchange between routes at these points. Some of these facilities were reasonably well known whilst others were both little publicized and little used. An information leaflet was prepared and distributed on buses and through enquiry offices, sub post offices and libraries. Distribution was quite effective and an on-bus survey two weeks after the leaflet distribution found that 71% of passengers had obtained a copy of the leaflet.

A before and after study of patronage and revenue on the promoted services was conducted and the results compared with those on a control group of services operating in a similar area. The overall results can be seen in Table 2.6.

Table 2.6 Survey results of TRRL Leaflet experiment

Survey date	Passengers, promoted services	Passengers, control services	Ratio	Index	Effect of leaflet
14 May (before)	12,791	1,037	12.33	100	—
20 June (after)	12,730	918	13.87	112.4	+12½%
19 Sept (after)	11,970	944	12.68	102.8	+3%

Source: *TRRL Laboratory Report* 825 TRRL 1978

Patronage on both groups of routes declined but less so on the promoted group. This relative improvement was attributed to the effects of the leaflet distribution. However, these effects were relatively short-lived and the second after study, taken less than four months after the leaflet distribution, found only a 3% improvement compared to the earlier 12½%. The scheme was judged cost effective since revenue was estimated to have increased by broadly £4,000 whilst the leaflet itself cost £1,000.

Further studies have now been conducted on the cost effectiveness of information leaflets but in an urban area[12]. These also found that the promotional effect was of a relatively short duration but despite this the information leaflets were cost effective yielding an increase in revenue between three and ten times the cost of the leaflets.

Examination questions

1 Why do economists often refer to the demand for transport as being largely a 'derived' demand? What is meant by this, and why is it important?

2 What methods can be employed in the estimation of passenger demand elasticities?

3 Analyse the factors which affect the magnitude of price-elasticities of demand for transport services. For what reasons would you expect short-run price-elasticities to be different from long-run price-elasticities?

4 Distinguish between 'own-price elasticity of demand' and 'cross-price elasticity of demand'. In relation to the demand for transport services, indicate how these elasticities might be estimated and discuss the factors which affect their magnitudes.

5 Assess the effects of 'real' increases in energy prices on patterns of passenger transport demand.

6 Define the term 'price-elasticity of demand'. In relation to the demand for transport, discuss the problems involved in estimating price-elasticities and examine the factors which affect their magnitudes.

7 Why does the 'problem of the peak' tend to be more serious in transport than in most other industries? How might the incidence of the problem within the transport sector be reduced?

8 Define what is meant by the term 'cross-elasticity of demand', and analyse the factors which affect its magnitude. Illustrate your answer with reference to demand for passenger transport.

9 'In relation to the overall demand for passenger transport, the magnitude of income elasticity is relatively large'. Explain the meaning of this statement.

10 Explain why economists refer to the demand for transport as a 'derived' demand. Examine the implications of this characteristic in relation to the problems of forecasting traffic and measuring elasticities.

3

The Supply of Transport

3.1 Introduction

This chapter contains descriptive and theoretical elements relating to the supply of transport. The structure of an industry is the result of the interplay of economic forces and the presence, or otherwise, of legislative controls. The structures of the main British transport industries are described although these should be seen as an illustration since similar modes elsewhere may have significantly different structures. The economic significance of a particular structure can be analyzed by using a range of market models. Students new to economics may find these models unsatisfactory because they seem too abstracted from reality and therefore it is difficult to find an industry which completely demonstrates the characteristics of a particular model. This is to misunderstand the model's purpose which is to demonstrate a specific set of characteristics rather than describe the entire workings of an industry. We will use them in this chapter to demonstrate the impact of market structure on costs and profits and in Chapter 4 to consider the interaction of market structure and pricing policy. We will examine economic theory relating to transport costs and illustrate its application to the bus and railway industries. The relative cost advantages of small or large scale operation will be considered with reference to the bus industry. Finally, the two themes of demand, from Chapter 2 and supply will be combined into a consideration of the price, introducing pricing in Chapter 4.

3.2 The structure of the road passenger industry

The British bus and coach industry can be divided into five basic groups:

(a) The nationalized companies comprising the National Bus Company (NBC) and the Scottish Bus Group (SBG)

(b) The Passenger Transport Executives (PTEs)
(c) The London Transport Executive (LTE)
(d) Municipal operators
(e) Privately-owned bus and coach companies

The first four of these are within the public sector and are subject to varying degrees of central and local government control. Much of this structure can be attributed to the 1968 Transport Act and the 1972 Local Government Act. The first created the National Bus Company from the already nationalized Transport Holding Company's operations and newly acquired former British Electric Traction (BET) companies. It also created the first four PTEs (Merseyside, SELNEC, Tyne and Wear and West Midlands) with dual responsibilities as public transport co-ordinating bodies and as the operators of substantial bus fleets from former municipal operators, expanded subsequently by purchases from NBC and private companies. The 1972 Act produced the 1974 local government re-organization which brought the establishment of six metropolitan counties in England each with a PTE. This led to some boundary re-organizations of existing PTEs, recognized by the name change from SELNEC to Greater Manchester Transport for example, and the creation of new PTEs in South Yorkshire and West Yorkshire. A PTE was also established in Glasgow known originally as Greater Glasgow PTE and now known as Strathclyde PTE. The Act also brought changes to district council areas and consequent mergers of some smaller municipal operators, for example the Haslingden and Rawtenstall fleets combined under the Rossendale name. Consequently, the numbers of municipal operators were further reduced. The declining profitability of stage carriage bus services has resulted in a reduction in numbers of private bus companies and major companies, such as Lancashire United Transport (LUT) have been sold, LUT now forming part of Greater Manchester Transport. However, there are substantial numbers of private contract, express, excursion and tours and private hire operators.

Table 3.1 shows the principal statistics relating to the main bus operating groups. Care must be taken in interpreting these, for example the passenger receipts figures reflect not only usage but also fares policies pursued in various areas. Ratios of staff employed to vehicles measure not simply productivity but also the nature of operations. The largest single operator is London Transport with a fleet exceeding 6,000 vehicles. The larger NBC fleet is subdivided into 37 operating subsidiaries ranging from small coaching units to fleets of 700 or 800 buses. There has been a trend of unit mergers, such as Devon General with Western National but latterly the large Midland Red company has been subdivided. The PTE fleets range from Tyne and Wear, the smallest with 550 vehicles to Greater

Manchester with 2,400. Since the larger municipals were absorbed into the PTEs the municipal operator group has declined in numbers and average fleet size. The largest fleet is the 380 vehicles of Nottingham and most fleets have some 50 to 100 vehicles. The private sector represents 39.6% of the vehicle fleet and 31.1% of the vehicle mileage despite employing only 17.1% of road passenger staff. This reflects the concentration of the private sector on contract hire and coaching work.

Table 3.1   Road passenger public transport 1980

Operator group	No. of fleets	Vehicles	Staff employed	Vehicle kilometres million/ km	Passenger receipts £ million
London Transport Executive	1	6,185	33,954	279	206.9
Passenger Transport Executives	7	10,356	45,111	510	314.7
Municipal operators	51	5,677	19,213	241	160.4
National Bus Company	37	15,981	57,704	1,026	491.4
Scottish Bus Group	7	3,631	10,755	203	108.8
Private operators	5,504	27,375	34,290	1,020	341.8
All operators	5,607	69,205	201,027	3,280	1,624.1

Source: *Transport Statistics Great Britain 1970—1980* (HMSO: London, 1981)

The trends then within the industry have been an increase in public ownership combined with amalgamations into larger companies. The full impact of the licensing relaxation in the 1980 Transport Act has yet to be seen but at present it has tended to allow existing operators to expand into new activities rather than encourage new entrants into the industry.

3.3   Railways

The main national rail network is operated by the nationalized British Railways Board (BRB). The three other public sector railway operators are the London Transport Executive, which operates the extensive Underground network, Strathclyde PTE operates a small electrified underground railway in Glasgow and Tyne and Wear PTE which operates the Light Rapid Transit Metro. There are also a variety of privately owned railways operating primarily as tourist attractions often using steam traction. These can be classified into former British Railways standard gauge lines, former mineral-carrying narrow gauge lines and purpose-built narrow gauge lines. The principal statistics for these operators are shown in Table 3.2. A commentary on trends in rail usage can be found in Chapter 2.

3.4 The structure of the road haulage industry

The road haulage industry like road passenger operators experienced partial nationalization following the 1947 Transport Act. Subsequently, parts of the industry were denationalized following the 1953 Transport Act and more recently with the staff buy-out of the National Freight Corporation in 1982. Thus, little of the industry remains within the public sector. Operators can be divided into two groups, those carrying their own goods who are known as *own account operators* and those available to carry anyones' goods known as *hire and reward operators*. The industry is now subject only to quality licencing (see Section 7.4.3) and quantity licencing no longer applies. Principal statistics for the industry are set out in Table 3.3 and an analysis of vehicles in fleet size in Table 3.4.

Whilst the two sectors account for similar proportions of total goods moved own account operators use relatively fewer large vehicles and carry the bulk of their goods (85%) on journeys under 100 kilometres. This reflects the role of own account operators as distributors of finished

Table 3.2 Railways in Britain 1980

	BRB	LTE	Strathclyde	Other[3]
Route kilometres	17,645	388	11	227
Of which electrified	3,718	388	11	na
Locomotives	3,379	—[2]	—[2]	230
Multiple unit carriages	11,475	4,353	33	9
Freight wagons	138,600	—[2]	—[2]	—[2]
Staff employed	214,626[1]	25,498	na	na
Stations	2,366	248	15	87
Passenger journeys millions	760	559	6.8	3.3
Passenger movement millions/km	31,700	4,253	18.8	44.5
Passenger receipts £ million	954	253.7	1.2	2.3
Freight carried million	154			
Freight movement	17,640			
Freight receipts £ million	451.3			

Source: *Transport Statistics Great Britain 1970—1980* (HMSO: London, 1981)

[1] Includes 36,567 with British Rail Engineering Ltd.
[2] Locomotives and freight stock used for maintenance purposes only
[3] Comprises those lines offering a regular passenger service over a route of not less than 5 kilometres
na – not available

Table 3.3 Road freight transport 1980

	Mainly own account (million tonnes)	Mainly public haulage (million tonnes)	Total (million tonnes)
Goods lifted	672	677	1,349[1]
In vehicles 16 tonnes gross weight and under	153	48	201
In vehicles over 16 tonnes gross weight	519	628	1,147
On journeys of 100 km or less	570	495	1,065
On journeys over 100 km	102	182	284

Source: *Transport Statistics Great Britain* 1970–1980 (HMSO: London, 1981)

[1] Includes 1 million tonnes unclassified by vehicle size

Table 3.4 Road freight fleet sizes 1980

	Thousand vehicles
1 vehicle	67.7
2—5 vehicles	118.2
6—50 vehicles	199.1
51—100 vehicles	43.0
101—200 vehicles	31.6
Over 200 vehicles	42.1
Total	501.7

Source: *Transport Statistics Great Britain 1970—1980* (HMSO: London, 1981)

Table 3.5 United Kingdom airline operations 1980

	Passengers (million)	Passenger movement (million/km)	Aircraft kilometres (million)	Average distance per passenger (km)
International scheduled services	14.964	47,393	326.7	3,167
Domestic scheduled services	7.199	2,770	57.7	385
Inclusive tours	9.663	17,113	147.1	1,771
Other charters	1.161	2,942	21.8	2,534

Source: *Transport Statistics Great Britain* 1970–1980 (HMSO: London, 1981)

products. The hire and reward sector with its greater involvement in 'trunk' operation carries a higher proportion of goods over long distances and in larger vehicles. Table 3.4 can be interpreted to give an analysis of the structure of the industry. Analysis is complicated by the collection of data by licencing area and one operator may operate in several areas. However, we can estimate that there are some 108,000 operators of which single vehicle operators account for 67,700, operators of two to five vehicles 33,000 and larger fleets the remaining 7,300. Many of the single vehicle operators will be owner drivers operating within the hire and reward sector and encouraged by the absence of capacity restraints under the quality licensing system. However, this ease of entry has taken its toll on rates and profitability within the industry, particularly in times of recession.

3.5   The structure of the British airline industry

Airline operation, particularly international operation of schedule services, is subject to a variety of forms of quantity licencing together with quality or operator licensing. The structure of the industry is moulded by the licensing system which can be used variously to encourage mergers, promote competition or protect monopolies. Which aim is paramount depends up which governments are in power and in Britain this also determines the view taken of the role of state enterprise in Britain. The principle statistics relating to British airline operators are shown in Table 3.5.

The structure of the British airline industry reflects the impact of these changing views on monopoly, competition and licensing and the legislation enacted to implement these. It also shows the development of airlines catering for package tour holidays. The cost of new aircraft has also affected the industry's structure.

In 1967, a committee of inquiry into civil air transport was established under the chairmanship of Sir Ronald Edwards charged with considering licensing and competition in the British airline industry. The report of the committee was published in 1969[1]. Legislation to implement some of its recommendations was overtaken by a change of Government and the new legislation introduced by the Conservatives, the 1971 Civil Aviation Act reflected their own view on the balance between the public and private sectors of the industry. Two changes foreseen by Edwards were rationalization among the independent airlines and a closer relationship between the publicly owned British European Airways, BEA, and the British Overseas Airways Corporation, BOAC. The first of these occurred through a series of mergers which created the independent British Caledonian Airways, BCAL as a 'second force' airline with a network including some former BOAC and BEA services. BEA (including its charter subsidiary, British Airtours) and BOAC were indeed brought closer together and finally merged into British Airways in 1972. This merger of airlines with dissimilar fleets, route structures and operating practices was not entirely successful and in 1982 the airline was subdivided into three divisions: Intercontinental, European and Gatwick (which includes charter flying). This suggests a partial reversion to the former BOAC, BEA, British Airtours structure although many facilities and services remain shared. The subdivision has also been seen as a preliminary to the sale of part or all of the airline as part of the Conservative government's policy of 'privatization'. Despite recent losses and consequent cutbacks British Airways in 1982 remained a major airline with 42,000 staff and 146 aircraft.

In 1982, BCAL was the only private operator of long-haul scheduled services following the collapse of Laker Airways which operated the 'Skytrain' North Atlantic services. In the domestic and short haul sector the withdrawal of British Airways from some routes and the policy of promoting competition has provided new opportunities for independent airlines. In consequence, new airlines have been created and existing ones expanded. Not all of these have been successful and a number of operators of minor domestic and cross-Channel routes have either merged or gone out of business. Thus new and larger groupings have come into existence, for example Air UK (formed in 1980 from Air Anglia, British Island Airways, BIA/Air West and Air Wales) and the merger in 1982 of Eastern Airways, Casair and Genair. The promotion of competition has allowed airlines like British Midland to expand its network and operate on major domestic routes, for example, London to Glasgow, in competition with British Airways and BCAL. We could therefore see the growth of airlines specifically geared to domestic and shorter European routes supplementing existing major airlines whose cost structures are unsuited to this form of operation. British Midland has already enjoyed some success at converting loss-making former British Airways routes to profitable operation.

There has been a major expansion in the sector of the industry catering for inclusive tour holidays. Passengers uplifted have increased from 4.903 million in 1970 to 9.663 million in 1980. In the 1960s much of the inclusive tour flying was done by specialized charter airlines using relatively cheap, obsolescent equipment. More recently the inclusive tour industry has seen a form of vertical integration with major operators such as Thomsons, Intasun and Horizon establishing their own airlines (Britannia, Air Europe and Orion respectively). These airlines have all purchased new fleets of Boeing 737 aircraft and in 1982 each had plans to introduce new fuel-efficient aircraft with Britannia buying Boeing 767s, Air Europe involved with lease/purchase of Boeing 757s and Orion ordering Boeing

737–300s. This has reduced the market available to existing charter airlines and required them to invest in newer equipment to remain competitive. Over-capacity in the charter market combined with the cost of financing new equipment was one cause of the Laker Airways crash.

3.6   The economics of market structures

In Sections 3.2 and 3.5 we have considered the structure of various parts of the British transport industry and commented on why these structures have evolved. We can consider their significance for the operation of transport firms by using economic models of various market structures. You will recall from the introduction to this chapter that the purpose of these models is to examine the interplay between firms within an industry rather than to describe the total operation of a firm. The models may show an extreme or pure form of the market structure compared to real firms. The significance of market structure for pricing policy is considered in Chapter 4.

3.6.1   Perfect competition

The characteristics of this market are that there are a large number of small producers all producing a similar (homogeneous) product. Within the market all buyers and sellers know the prevailing price (often described as 'perfect knowledge') and new firms are free to enter the market, there being no barriers to entry (such as quantity licensing for example). The essence of this market is that a single price prevails determined by the overall level of demand and supply. The individual firm can sell as much as it makes at the prevailing price but any attempt to raise the price, to increase profits, will result in all customers switching to another firm selling at the prevailing price. In this case the firm faces a totally elastic demand curve. A price cut would offer no advantage. Free entry to the market ensures that firms earn only normal profits (i.e. a just adequate rate of return to keep those factors of production in their current use). In the event that abnormal profits are earned new firms enter the market and supply increases and prices fall until only normal profits are earned and the market returns to equilibrium. A price cut therefore in a market equilibrium will result in a loss to the firm cutting its price. (You should be able to deduce how the market will return to equilibrium). Thus the firm in a situation of perfect competition is a price taker.

3.6.2   Imperfect or monopolistic competition

The essential difference from perfect competition is that each firm is presumed to be selling a product which is slightly different from its

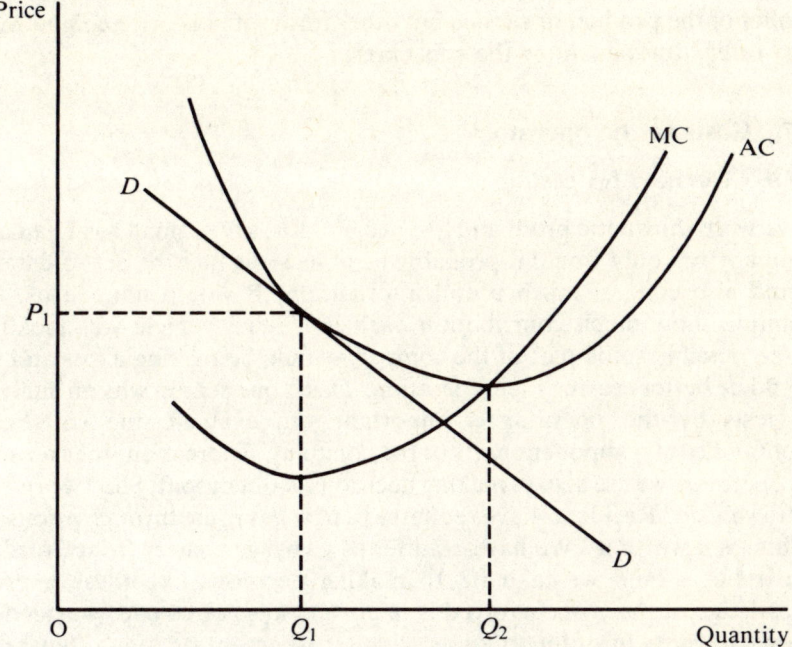

Figure 3.1 Long-term equilibrium for a firm under imperfect competition.

competitors. As a result the firm can charge a price above the market price and retain some buyers whilst an unmatched price reduction will attract some, but not all, the customers of competitors. The firm thus faces a downward sloping demand curve rather than the horizontal, totally price-elastic, demand curve of perfect competition. New firms will again enter the industry if existing firms are earning abnormal profits and in consequence there will be a leftward shift of the demand curve for existing firms. The industry will eventually settle into equilibrium with only normal profits being earned. However, in contrast to perfect competition the equilibrium position is not efficient. Referring to Figure 3.1 which depicts the long-run equilibrium for a firm under imperfect competition you will note that equilibrium is where price equals average cost of output OQ_1. However, the firm is not producing at its lowest cost output of OQ_2. Thus, firms within this market structure can be described as having excess capacity. Since under perfect competition long-run equilibrium is reached at minimum average cost we can therefore state that under imperfect competition prices will tend to be higher and output lower than under perfect competition. A further consequence is that firms may prefer to compete not on price but on differentiating their product from that of their competitors. Some of this may be done by genuine improvements in the quality of the product or service but other forms of non-price competition may offer little benefit to the consumer.

3.7   Costs to the operator

3.7.1   The need for costing

If we were shown the profit and loss account for, say, a small road haulage company not only would it probably be at least six months out of date, it would also conceal much useful information. It would not tell us, for example, how much contribution each individual vehicle was making. Quite possibly some part of the company would be making a loss and we would be better ceasing their operation. This is one reason why an analysis of costs by the operator is important—to evaluate the costs and profitability of component parts of the company. There is another reason. As operators we are always making decisions about output. Shall we run an extra vehicle? Residents have requested a new bus route through a housing estate; is it worth it? We have an offer of a voyage charter from Brazil to Australia; should we take it? In making decisions like these a prior knowledge of the costs involved is important and, of course, we need to know the costs in order to know whether to accept or reject that price offered.

3.7.2   Some definitions of costs

Let us stay for the moment with the road haulage company. What kind of costs are incurred by the firm? First of all there are those costs incurred before a wheel is turned—rent and rates on the buildings, wages and salaries, office charges such as those for telephones and typewriters, depreciation, licences and insurance for vehicles and time-related maintenance. In the transport industry these are usually called *standing charges*, for obvious reasons. Then there are costs incurred when the vehicles are operating—wear and tear, maintenance, fuel, oil and tyres—*running costs*. In economics, standing charges are generally referred to as *fixed costs*, i.e. those that do not vary with output; running costs, on the other hand, are termed *variable costs* because they do vary with output. It is important to make this distinction. Suppose the weekly standing costs for a road haulage company were £300, i.e. £60 a day and that the firm is offered a load to London, which takes a full day and is a round trip of 400 miles, running costs will be at, say 32 pence per mile £128. The price offered by the customer is £170. Should the firm accept the contract assuming no other work is forthcoming for that vehicle that day? The answer is that it will meet the variable costs and make some contribution towards those fixed costs which have to be met anyway. If the operator had not made this distinction between fixed and variable costs and instead had added up all his costs and divided them by the expected mileage to get average mileage costs he would have found the price offered to be too low and might have rejected it. In this way he would have foregone the opportunity of meeting some of his overhead costs.

This is necessarily a simple example but cost analysis is a complicated area of transport economics and must be examined more closely. First of all, we want to allocate our costs to a *cost centre*. This might be a vehicle, a workshop, a company or indeed a particular route or service. Then we must decide how to allocate those costs. In the example above, it was fairly simple. Our cost centre was the vehicle and we allocated costs such as vehicle licensing and insurance to it as *direct* costs. However, we had to make some important decisions regarding costs such as office expenses and salaries and rent and rates on the buildings. These had to be divided in some way between the vehicles in the fleet. The most obvious way would be to divide those overhead costs by the number of vehicles equally. But what if the vehicles were of different sizes? Should the bigger vehicles be allocated more of these costs on the grounds that they involve more office time? What if the larger vehicles were primarily involved in international work? The allocation of these *indirect costs* is a difficult problem, particularly in larger organizations with significant overheads and many cost centres. These will be examined further below.

So far, four types of costs have been identified — individual costs items can be allocated to these catagories as shown in Table 3.6. Can you think of any examples to place in Box C?

Table 3.6   The categorization of costs where the vehicle is a cost centre

	Fixed	Variable
Indirect	A. Rent and rates Office salaries Workshop expenses	C. ?
Direct	B. Vehicle insurance Vehicle licence Driver's wages	D. Fuel Oil Tyres

Table 3.6 illustrates another difficulty in cost analysis. Driver's wages are described as fixed costs. This is true if we are considering whether to accept that load down to London tomorrow. But if we are considering whether to accept a new contract for the next month driver's wages become a variable cost as a new driver will need to be employed. *Thus, whether a cost is fixed or variable depends on the time period under consideration. It also depends*

on the scale of output. If the new contract was large enough to warrant the purchase of new vehicles then many costs become variable. We may need, for example, another workshop for the maintenance of those new vehicles. So the choice of cost category depends on what kind of decision regarding output is made.

3.7.3   Escapability and opportunity cost

To help in the difficult task of allocating costs to particular activities the economist uses two concepts — *escapability* and *opportunity cost*. Escapability, used in identification, involves asking the question 'what costs will be escaped (or saved) if this particular activity is not undertaken?' British Rail, as we shall see below, make much use of this concept in their cost analysis. Opportunity cost, or *resource cost*, helps to calculate the value of an identified cost by asking the question 'what would be the next best alternative use of those resources?' Thus, the opportunity cost of the time you spend reading this book would be the value you get from the best alternative use of your time. The cost of building the Channel Tunnel could be expressed in terms of the alternative uses those resources could be put to. Often the opportunity, or resource cost, is reflected in its price. Thus, the labour costs are expressed as wages but often prices are not available or sufficiently accurate and *shadow prices* have to be used (see Chapter 6).

3.7.4   Joint and common costs

In relation to Table 3.6 above you were asked to give examples to place in Box C — indirect/variable costs. These would be costs which do vary with output but cannot be directly allocated to a particular cost centre. Suppose the cost centre was a trip to London. Costs would be allocated to it as described above, and if the customer is offered a load back from London it could be carried almost for nothing (ignoring loading and unloading costs). On the other hand if the haulier knew beforehand he was getting a return load he could divide the costs between the two customers thus offering the first one a lower price. Therefore if the cost centre were a journey rather than a vehicle, we could place in Box C the variable costs involved in the London trip which have to be allocated between the two activities. Rather than indirect costs, we would call them *joint costs*. These occur where it is technically impossible to produce one thing without producing another and the problem is how to allocate the costs between them. An oft-quoted example in economics is the production of mutton and wool and in transport, the return journey. This is particularly relevant to the pricing policies in passenger transport.

There is another form of joint costs which some economists call common costs. This occurs where equipment, for example railway track, signalling systems and terminals which once installed can provide a range of services and, therefore, different products within their capacity at little extra cost. Thus, just as the return load from London could be provided at almost nil cost if a railway track was laid down for passenger services, it could also carry freight at night for little extra cost. The dilemma is how much of the total cost to allocate to each service and therefore what price to charge.

This problem is made worse because often the unit of demand, e.g. passenger-mile or tonne-mile for which a charge is made, is smaller than the unit of supply, say, vehicle-mile, on which costs are based. The avoidable cost of one passenger or tonne-mile is negligible if the vehicle with spare capacity is already running. However, we could hardly expect the operator to charge the first customer the whole cost of the journey and provide a free service to the rest because 'he was going that way anyway'! In practice there are bound to be joint costs which must be averaged between the customers and we must be realistic about what our marginal product is. There are many examples in freight transport where goods are carried in bulk and, therefore, joint costs are small but the problem is a real one in, say, parcels traffic. Even in services where trains are made up of complete wagon loads like the British Rail Speedlink service these are the joint costs of locomotive and crew in addition to infrastructure costs. The problem is most acute, of course, on the passenger side where a great deal of averaging between customers is required.

3.8 The firm's costs in relation to output

So far we have looked at cost analysis in order to help us determine the costs of particular activities within an organization and decide whether it is worth cutting down on other activities or taking on extra work. It is now necessary to see how a firm's costs vary with its output, with the aim of determining the 'best' output. In Chapter 4 we suggest that in some cases what is best for the firm may not be best for society, so the term is left undefined for the present.

3.8.1 Time horizons

Consider the following decisions that a transport manager might take.

(a) Can we get an extra load per week out of our six vehicles?
(b) Shall we purchase another five vehicles and increase the size of our workshop?

There is a major difference between them. The first concerns the level of output with the existing fixed resources. This is defined as a *short-run decision*. The second is concerned with changing the amount of fixed resources used and is a *long-run decision*. There is also the very long-run in which decisions concerning the introduction of new technology are made. The building and use of the Channel Tunnel would be a good example. In this chapter we are concentrating on the first two.

3.8.2   The production function

The relation between the inputs to a firm (usually described as land, labour and capital) and the output from the production process is called *the production function*. The relation is an interesting one and can be looked at in three ways, as shown in Table 3.7. This might be an example of farm labourers planting rice in a paddy field or lumberjacks felling a forest. Their product is, therefore, the number of seedlings planted or trees cut down. The area of land is fixed and the variable factor is labour. As the number of workers is increased we might expect them to work more efficiently as they form a team or divide the area so each has less ground to cover. Thus, two workers may produce more than twice as much as one, or three produce more than 50% more than two. However, it might be that as the number is increased further they get in each others way (certainly a problem in tree felling!) and the *total production* may increase less or even fall. This relation can be seen in Table 3.7 and Figure 3.2. We can also see how *the average product* (i.e. product per worker employed) varies and how much more production is achieved by adding one extra worker. This is *the marginal* product. Notice that both curves in Figure 3.2(a) rise and then fall. They illustrate the *hypothesis of diminishing returns* which states:

> If increasing quantities of a variable factor (say labour) are combined with a given quantity of fixed factors (say land), the marginal product and the average product of the variable factor will eventually decrease.

Table 3.7   Output variation with one factor fixed and one variable

(1) Quantity of labour L	(2) Total product TP	(3) Average product AP	(4) Marginal product MP
1	5	5.0	
2	11	5.5	6.0
3	18	6.0	7.0
4	28	7.0	10.0
5	36	7.2	8.0
6	42	7.0	6.0
7	47	6.7	5.0
8	51	6.4	4.0
9	54	6.0	3.0
10	56	5.6	2.0

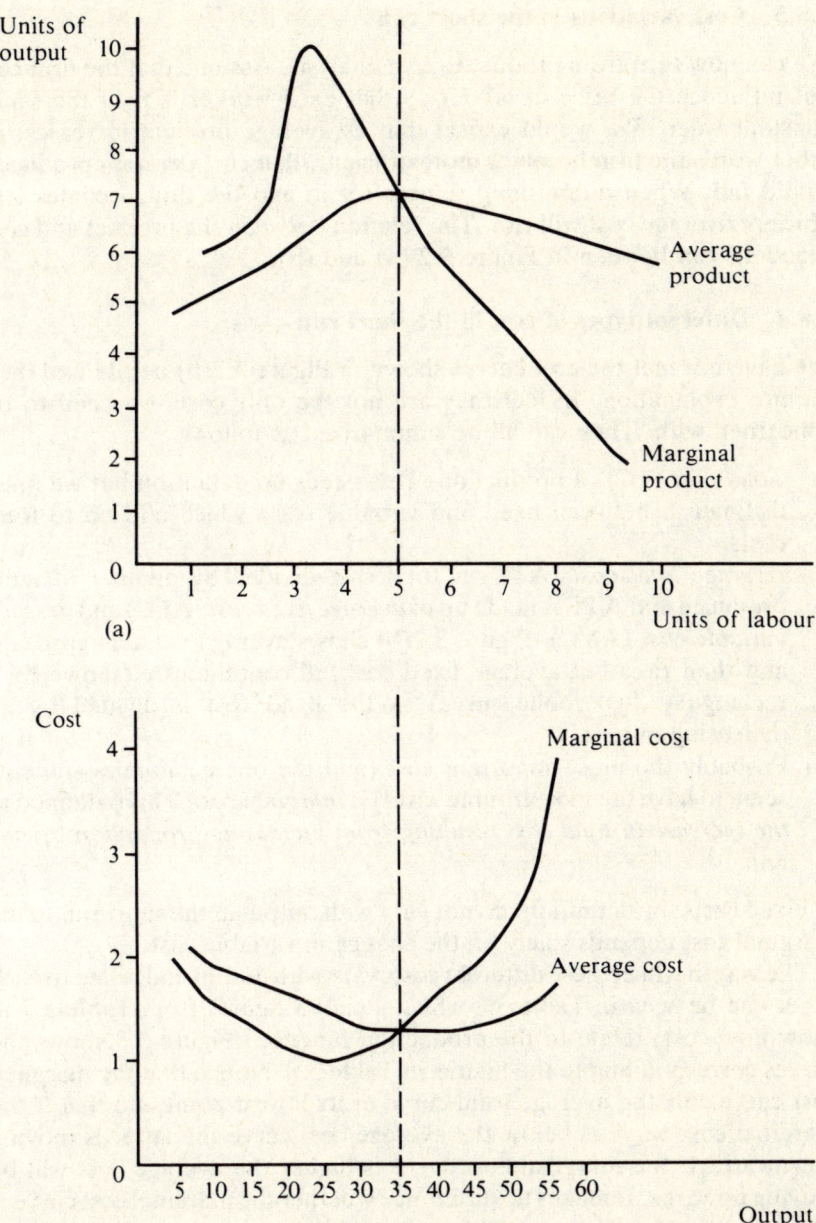

Figure 3.2 The relationship between production and cost in the short run.
(a) Variations in average and marginal product with the supply of one factor
of production fixed.
(b) Variations of costs with output in the short run.

3.8.3   Cost variations in the short run

We can now turn from product to cost analysis. Assume that the firm can not influence the price of labour so that each worker is paid the same constant wage. We would expect that as average product increases, in other words the firm becomes more efficient, that cost per item produced would fall. When diminishing returns set in and the firm becomes less efficient average cost will rise. The relation between the product and cost functions can be seen in Figure 3.2 (a) and (b).

3.8.4   Different types of cost in the short run

We have not met the cost curves shown in Figure 3.2(b) before and they require explanation. In fact they are not the only costs we need to be concerned with. They can all be summarized as follows:

(a) *Total cost* (TC) of production. This needs no definition but we must distinguish between fixed and variable costs which add up to total costs.

(b) *Average total cost* (ATC) is total cost divided by number of units produced and ATC is made up of *average fixed cost* (AFC) and *average variable cost* (AVC). Figure 3.2(b) shows average variable cost falls and then rises but average fixed cost fall continuously (shown by a rectangular hyperbolic curve) as the fixed cost is divided by an increasing output.

(c) Probably the most important cost (and the one economics students seem to have the most trouble with!) is *marginal cost*. This is defined as *the increase in total cost resulting from increasing production by one unit.*

Fixed costs, by definition, do not vary with output in the short run so the marginal cost depends solely on the change in variable cost.

The way in which these different costs vary with output and relate to each other can be seen in Table 3.8 which includes figures from Table 3.7 to show how costs relate to the production function. Figure 3.3 shows the curves corresponding to the figures in Table 3.8. Notice that the marginal cost curve cuts the average total curve at its lowest point and that if the marginal cost curve is below the average cost curve the latter is moving downward. If the marginal cost curve is higher the average cost will be moving upwards. It makes no difference whether the marginal cost curve is sloping upward or downward. Looking at the cost curves it seem quite obvious what the 'best' short run output for the firm is. It is working at its most efficient where the average total cost curve is at its minimum i.e. at about fifty-two units (employing nine persons) when the cost per unit is £3.52. However, this does not necessarily mean that the firm will make the

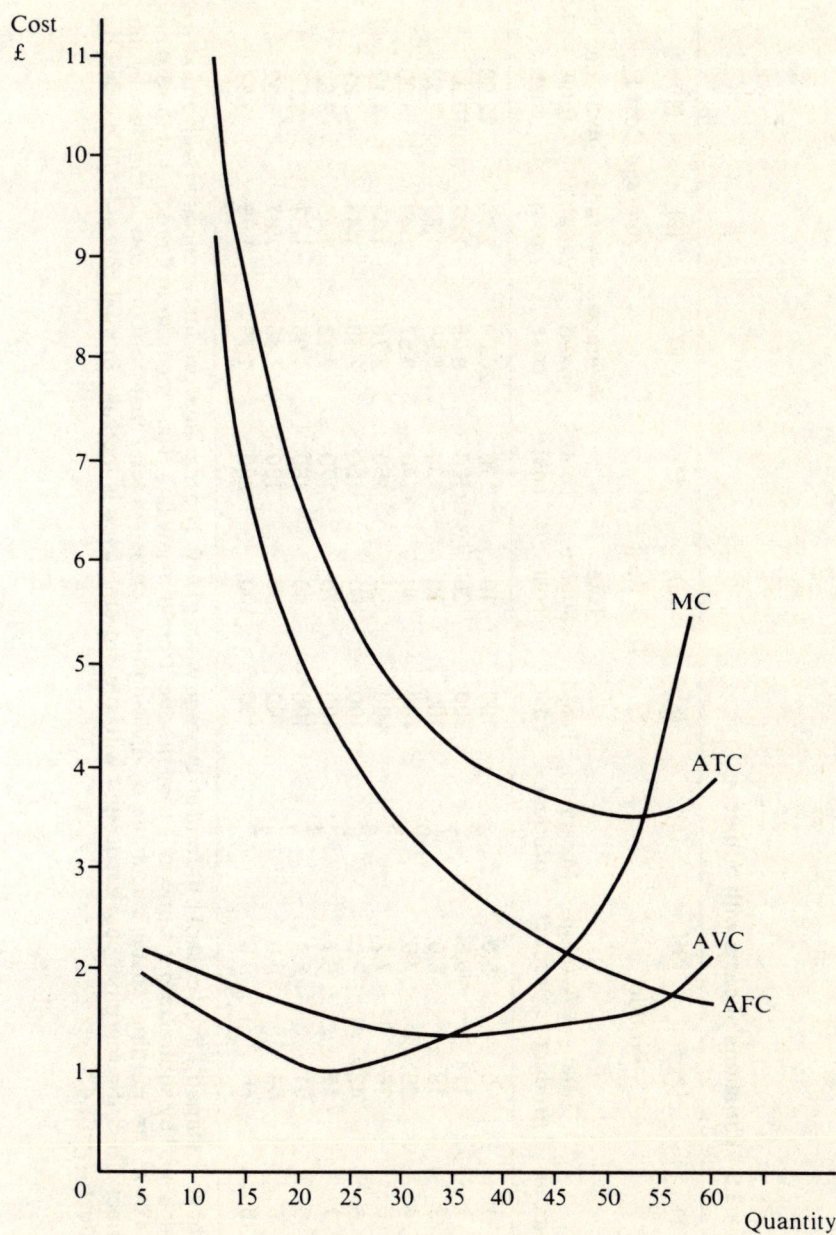

Figure 3.3 How costs vary with output.

Table 3.8 Variations of costs with output

(1)	(2)	(3)	(4)	(5)	(6)	(7)	(8)	(9)	(10)	(11)
	Product			Total Cost £			Average Cost £			
Labour	Total product	Average product	Marginal product	Fixed cost	Total variable cost	Total cost	Average fixed cost	Average variable cost	Average total cost	Marginal cost
1	5	5.0	6	100	10	110	20.00	2.00	22.00	1.67
2	11	5.5	7	100	20	120	9.09	1.82	10.92	1.43
3	18	6.0	10	100	30	130	5.55	1.67	7.23	1.00
4	28	7.0	8	100	40	140	3.57	1.43	5.00	1.25
5	36	7.2	6	100	50	150	2.78	1.39	4.17	1.67
6	42	7.0	5	100	60	160	2.38	1.43	3.81	2.00
7	47	6.7	4	100	70	170	2.13	1.49	3.62	2.50
8	51	6.4	3	100	80	180	1.96	1.57	3.53	3.33
9	54	6.0	2	100	90	190	1.85	1.67	3.52	5.00
10	56	5.6		100	100	200	1.79	1.79	3.58	

We have assumed a fixed cost of £100 and an average wage of £10. The marginal product associated with an extra employee is calculated by subtracting the previous total product from the new one. Thus the marginal product of the 3rd employee is 18−11=7. The marginal cost is calculated by dividing the increase in total cost from one row to the next by the marginal product. Thus the marginal cost associated with the 3rd employee is increase in total cost —(£10) divided by marginal product (7)=£1.43.

most profit at this output. This is why we did not define 'best' and we shall explain this further in Chapter 4.

This section has, of course, used simplified figures in order to illustrate the basic measures of costs and important concepts, such as avoidability and jointness. We can now use these to examine costing in practice within the bus and railway industries.

3.9   Costing in practice

3.9.1   Bus costing — the CIPFA system

The traditional practice in the bus industry was to estimate the operating costs associated with any particular route by calculating the average cost per mile operated for the undertaking as a whole, and applying this average rate to the number of miles operated on the route in question. This method is acceptable only if all miles operated are comparable. Many costs — the obvious example is crew wages — depend on time rather than distance travelled, and allocation of these costs on a mileage basis will be inaccurate if operating speeds vary from route to route. The need to make significant economies as a result of drastically reduced demand in the last 20 years or so, led to the development of a more sophisticated costing methodology. Following research by a number of organizations, the Chartered Institute of Public Finance and Accountancy (CIPFA) produced recommendations for a standard system in 1974[2] with further refinements in 1979[3].

In the CIPFA system, costs are allocated to routes in three ways

(a) *Time basis*   Costs are allocated in proportion to the 'standard time' on a route. Standard time includes time when the bus is actually in service on the route, running time from completion of a previous journey on another route, time spent at terminal points, and travelling time to and from the depot.
(b) *Mileage basis*   Some costs are allocated in proportion to bus miles operated on each route.
(c) *Peak vehicle requirement basis*   The peak vehicle requirement is defined as the maximum number of buses required at any one time, calculated for the period of time, which is the maximum for the cost centre. (A depot, or a group of depots, or the whole undertaking, may be classified as a cost centre).

We have already explained the reason why some costs should be allocated on a time basis. There remain some categories of costs which are still best allocated in proportion to mileage — for example fuel and tyres. The third basis for allocation reflects the fact that some costs are dependent on the overall size of the undertaking and that this is governed by the needs of the peak — examples are vehicle depreciation and rent/rates on buildings.

CIPFA further classify costs into 'variable', 'semi-variable' and 'fixed'. Variable costs respond rapidly to changes in service levels and are therefore important if economies are needed quickly. Semi-variable costs respond more slowly, perhaps over a period of a year after a change has been introduced. Fixed costs may change over a period of years, but usually only when large changes have been made.

The CIPFA's classification of cost is shown in Table 3.9, together with an indication of the relative importance of each cost category in a typical bus company. The system is based on full cost allocation, i.e. it includes all the costs incurred by the undertaking, including general overheads. The system therefore reflects the long-run marginal costs facing the bus operator.

The CIPFA system was refined in 1979 to give an improved treatment of crew costs and a method of calculating the differing costs of operation at peak and off-peak periods. The problem with the original method of allocating crew costs — the standard time basis — was that it did not allow for the widespread practice of premium payments made to bus crews for work at different times of day: these payments may be made for work early in the morning, in the evening, at weekends, or for working split-shifts (where a day's work involves a few hours in the morning peak, and a few hours to cover the evening peak). Full details of these revised methods are contained in the CIPFA report, but it essentially involves calculating the number of hours paid to çrews for each hour of standard time in the different time periods under consideration. The report also highlights a problem associated with calculating peak and off-peak costs, namely what do we actually mean by the peak? Do we mean all operations at the period of maximum supply, or just the *additional* operation needed to cover the peaks?

3.9.2   Rail costing

In principle the costing of rail services can be carried out using methods similar to the CIPFA system. In practice rail costing is far more complex than bus costing. British Rail for example is divided into six business sectors each containing a wide range of services, and with a high degree of sharing of facilities. Moreover, a high proportion of British Rail's costs can not be directly attributed to any particular measure of output — the classic example being expenditure on track and signalling.

The main cost elements arising in the railway industry are listed in Table 3.10. The table makes a distinction between *direct costs* which can be directly related to output and *indirect costs* which do not vary with output.

Table 3.9 Suggested cost allocations (from *Passenger Transport Operations*) and proportions of total cost which are typically attributable to each item

Basis of allocation of cost	Variable costs (respond rapidly to changes in service) %	Semi-variable costs (respond only slowly to changes in service, over period of months) %	Fixed costs (do not respond in the short-term to changes in service: if at all, changes accrue over period of years) %
Time (standard bus-hours operated)	Wage costs and expenses One man drivers Crew drivers Conductors Vehicle servicing — **40**	Traffic operational staff Maintenance supervisory staff Vehicle maintenance (PSV's) Miscellaneous traffic expenses ⎱ 15 Miscellaneous garage expenses ⎰ 5 Training board levy/grants — **20**	Administration staff — 11 Education, medical and welfare benefits ⎰ 4 — **15**
Mileage (standard bus-miles operated)	Fuel oil and duty — 6 Tyres — 2 Hire charges for manned vehicles Third party insurance, compensation ⎰ 2 — **10**	—	—
Peak vehicle (maximum number of buses on road during peak)	—	Tickets, ticket machines and equipment Publicity expenses Vehicle licence duties and fire insurance Leasing/renting unmanned vehicles Vehicle depreciation — **5**	Rent, rates, building insurance Maintenance, power, light, heat for buildings ⎰ 3 Depreciation of buildings Staff vehicles ⎰ 2 Telephone, postage, stationary Fees, bank charges and miscellaneous general expenses ⎰ 5 — **10**
Total	**50**	**25**	**25**

Source: *Passenger Transport Operation Peak/Off peak cost and revenue allocation* (Chartered Institute of Public Finance and Administration: London, 1979)

Table 3.10   Main cost elements in the railway industry

Direct costs
Provision of locomotives
— depreciation and interest
Maintenance of locomotives
— including stabling and servicing
Fuel, power, lubricants
Train crew
Shunting and marshalling
Provision of rolling stock
— coaches, DMU/EMU sets or freight wagons
— depreciation and interest
Maintenance, stabling, servicing and cleaning rolling stock and wagons
(including DMU/EMU sets)
Terminal costs
— Provision and maintenance — buildings and equipment and track within
terminal, amortization, interest
— Terminal staff
— Power, lighting, heating, etc.
— Provision and maintenance — freight handling equipment
— Road collection and delivery facilities

Indirect costs
Infrastructure (track and signalling)
General administration

N.B. In practice these main elements are extensively sub-analysed.

Source: *Measuring Costs and Profitability in B.R.*, (British Railway Board:
London, 1978)

Costs are further classified according to whether they are *specific,
common* or *joint*. Specific costs are those which are uniquely associated
with one service. Common costs are shared between services in a
well-defined way (e.g., train crew costs) so that it is possible to trace them
to individual services. Joint costs are the costs involved in providing two or
more services, whose production can not be separated for physical reasons,
so that provision of one service automatically makes the facility available
for other services. Some examples will help to make these categories clear.

The costs of shunting and marshalling in a marshalling yard are direct and
specific to the freight business.
Terminal staff costs are direct and common to the various train services
using the terminal, but terminal buildings costs are joint.
Main line track and signalling costs are joint, indirect costs, but track and
signalling on a branch line used by a single passenger service are specific to
that service.

The method of costing adapted by British Rail is to use these various cost categories to assess the *avoidable costs* associated with individual services and business sectors, that is those costs which would definitely be avoided if that service/sector ceased to exist. Costs which can not be allocated to individual services/sectors — which will generally be the indirect joint costs — are shown separately in balance sheets as a 'basic facility cost'.

3.10   Economies of scale

In the short term the supply of at least one of the factors used by a firm is fixed. Thus a railway may be able to increase its capacity by using extra tracks or additional staff, but can not increase track capacity by doubling a single line in the short term. If the firm has already reached the output of minimum average cost, then an increase in output results in higher average costs caused by using a relatively inefficient combination of factors. In the long run, the quantity of all factors of production can be varied and a more efficient combination selected.

3.10.1   Long-run average costs

A long-run average cost (LRAC) curve can be constructed from all available least cost factor combinations for given outputs. In Figure 3.4 the average cost of producing output Q_1 is C_1 using the combination of factors represented by short-run average cost (SRAC) curve $SRAC_1$.

Using the factor combination represented by $SRAC_2$ the average cost for this quantity, Q_1, is higher at C_2. Thus to produce Q_1, the factor combination $SRAC_1$ is preferable. If the larger quantity Q_2 is required the cost is lower with factor combination $SRAC_2$, at C_3, than $SRAC_1$ at C_4, and thus $SRAC_2$ is prefered for output Q_2. Thus in the long-run when the quantity of all factors of production can be varied, a firm would choose factor combination $SRAC_1$, for output Q_1 and $SRAC_2$ for Q_2 and these would represent points on the firm's long-run average cost curve. Thus the LRAC is constructed from the least-cost factor combination on any available SRAC curve for a given output.

Initially, the LRAC curve is downsloping with average costs decreasing as output increases. This indicates the existence of *economies of scale*. If average costs remain the same, irrespective of output, no such economies exist and the firm is described as experiencing *constant returns to scale*. In Figure 3.4. average costs on $LRAC_1$ increase beyond output Q_3, indicating the existence of *diseconomies of scale*. Thus, economies of scale refer to the effects on average costs of changes in output. It is important to note that economies of scale, resulting from the ability to do things, whether producing, marketing or managing in a different and lower cost way, vary at larger outputs. They do not arise simply from the ability to spread fixed

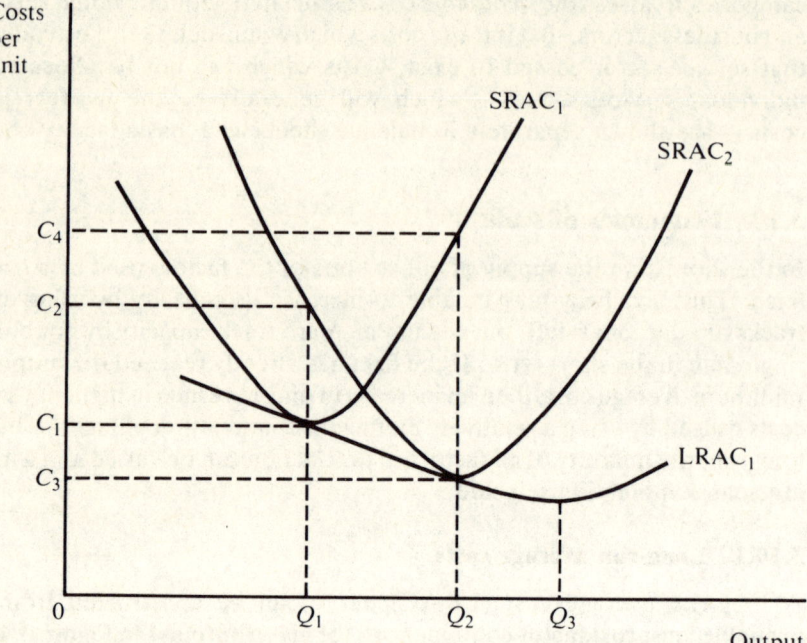

Figure 3.4 The relationship between short-run and long-run average costs.

costs over a larger number of units. Thus economies of scale relate essentially to the long-run rather than short-run average cost curve.

3.10.2   Sources of economies of scale

These can be classified thus,

1 Technical economies
2 Marketing economies
3 Financial economies
4 Managerial economies

3.10.2.1   Technical economies
These arise from the ability to use different equipment or processes for larger outputs. For example, components for a prototype aircraft are often 'handmade' at considerable expense whilst those for production aircraft are batch or mass produced at lower cost using sophisticated machine tools. Livesey[4] notes that the relationship between area and volume causes the capacity of a vessel to increase faster than its area and hence its cost. So the cost per tonne of a 200,000 tonne vessel is 75% of that for a 100,000 tonne vessel. Similarly, the sailing cost per day *per container* for a 1,250 TEU

vessel is 70% of that for a 200 TEU vessel. Larger outputs may permit new technology to be exploited, linked processes to be adopted and progression along the 'learning curve' (which relates time taken per operation with output). This is illustrated in the extract below concerning production of the Lockheed P-3C Maritime patrol aircraft.

'The Navy now expects to buy six P-3C's a year into the forseeable future. By the mid 80's Orion production may drop below the slowest rate of 11 aircraft a year and thus is bound to increase costs', says Lloyd Graham (Vice-President for Government Programmes) — 'When the production line is moving slowly people only come back to a job once in two months and tasks take longer to complete'.
Flight International, 10 July 1982

Another source of economies is the so called 'law of large numbers' which can be applied to aircraft utilization. This suggests that the allowance of spare aircraft to cover maintenance, unserviceability and delay, does not increase with fleet size. 'Thus the larger the fleet the lower, normally, the ratio of reserve aircraft. From this it follows that it will be easier, other things being equal, to achieve higher utilization rates with a large fleet than with a small[5].

3.10.2.2   Marketing economies
These existing both in buying and selling. Larger outputs may permit bulk-buying savings to be made. In selling, the marketing costs per unit of output may decrease with output and certain media appropriate only to larger volumes used.

3.10.2.3   Financial economies
With larger scale a wider range of sources of funds become available. In road haulage an owner-driver may be restricted to relatively expensive bank loans and hire-purchase whilst a national fleet operator may raise capital through a share-issue. Within share issues, economies of scale may exist since costs do not increase proportionately with the amount to be raised.

2.10.2.4   Managerial economies
These include the ability to use equipment such as computers or word-processors and to recruit quality staff, employ specialists and promote internally. The firm may also be able to undertake it's own research and development.

3.10.3   Diseconomies of scale

These have proved difficult to measure or categorize, however a possible source is managerial diseconomies arising from the bureaucracy of large organizations. Poor communications, departmentalization and 'empire-building' may cause an increase in management costs per unit of output. Lipsey[6] suggests that diseconomies may actually be due to hidden fixed costs or rising factor prices. In theory, diseconomies could be avoided by expanding output until all economies of scale have been exploited and then establishing another production unit rather than expanding the existing one. However, institutional factors may prevent this solution being adopted. The boundary between economies and diseconomies of scale may exist only at a given time and be changed by new circumstances. For example, despite thoughts that the ultimate size had been reached there have been significant jumps in tanker size, despite restrictions on routes and parts.

There are three areas in which economies of scale are important besides their significance to international trade mentioned in Chapter 1.

1 Barriers to market entry
2 Monopoly versus competition
3 Protection of 'infant industries'

In an industry where there are no absolute cost advantages (arising from patent processes, access to factors of production etc.) but economies of scale exist, these can deter entry to the market. A new entrant with a small market share would be at a cost disadvantage compared to existing firms. In industries where the output threshold for achieving economies of scale is low, existing firms can increase it by additional marketing expenditure as a means of deterring new entrants. Where there appear to be significant economies of scale, these can be advanced as a justification for reducing competition or permitting monopoly, since the larger firms will be able to exploit the economies of scale. There is no guarantee that these benefits will be passed on to the consumer, however. The third argument is that where economies of scale exist in an internationally traded good then countries seeking to enter that market are at a cost disadvantage. Thus tariff, protection, or other non-tariff barriers may be sought to protect the infant industry until it is of sufficient size, or admits that it is, to cope with competition. This argument may apply in the development of airlines or the establishment of aircraft production.

Having considered the economic theory of economies of scale, we now consider the evidence for their existence in various sectors of the transport industry. Some comparisons can be made concerning vehicles, like the relative costs of tankers mentioned earlier. Alternatively, studies can be based on variations in cost and size for a single firm, as in the Bradford Bus Study, or by comparing firms of different sizes in the same industry.

3.10.4 Air

Economies of scale can be shown to exist in aircraft size. It is common for aircraft to be designed with the potential for the design to be 'stretched' to give additional payload or range, usually by increasing fuselage length and engine power whilst retaining other features of the existing variant. Stretched variants demonstrate lower seat mile costs than their smaller brothers and thus the unit costs for a DC-9 80 series are significantly lower than for the earlier DC-9 30 series. However, when making such comparisons it is important that similar technologies are compared, otherwise the cost difference noted may be due to technical change rather than scale. Thus the improvement in seat/mile costs of a Boeing 757 or 767 compared to a 727 are essentially the result of technical change.

The advantages and disadvantages of scale for airlines were considered by the Edwards Committee[1], which saw advantages to scale if a standardized fleet is operated in markets where the operator had a large market share and where a widespread route and marketing network is required. However, size was seen to be a disadvantage in particular markets including inclusive tours, charter operation and freight. Edwards recommended that the two state-owned airlines BEA (primarily a domestic European operator) and BOAC (a long-haul operator) should be brought together under a joint Airways Board rather than a merger. Subsequently, the two were merged to form British Airways and there has been considerable doubt whether overall economies of scale have been achieved. However, in May 1982 it was announced that British Airways was to be split into separate divisions, European, International and Gatwick, although sharing central engineering, personnel and other services.

3.10.5 Infrastructure

Where economies of scale exist in transport infrastructure, such as roads or runways, these are not always realizable. Thomson[7] points to the problems of indivisibility or 'lumpiness' in infrastructure and to the difficulties of realizing economies of scale if scale is increased in stages rather than a single increment. Thus, there could be economies of scale comparing a single track and a four track railway, but these will not necessarily be realized if a single line is doubled, then quadrupled rather than built as four track initially since the costs of phased construction may outweigh the economies of scale. Indeed Thomson noted, concerning infrastructure costs 'Despite the inherent economies of scale, therefore, the dominant factor is often the diseconomies of growth and of unplanned growth in particular. The infrastructure component in the long-run cost structure of transport tends to be, therefore, a steeply rising one'.

3.10.6   Road haulage

Prior to the introduction of the Operator Licence system studies of road haulage in Britain showed a trend of increasing size of firm. However, removal of quantity restriction has had an impact on the structure of the industry. It is possible to suggest that larger firms may be able to consolidate loads or match a range of vehicles to specific tasks. However, smaller operators may have lower overheads, perhaps resulting from undervalued work by the operator's family. Studies by Harrison[8] and Edwards and Bayliss[9] suggested constant returns to scale although larger firms may be more able to survive cyclical downswing.

3.10.7   Road passenger

There appears to be some potential for economies of scale in vehicles through the use of higher capacity including articulated vehicles. The

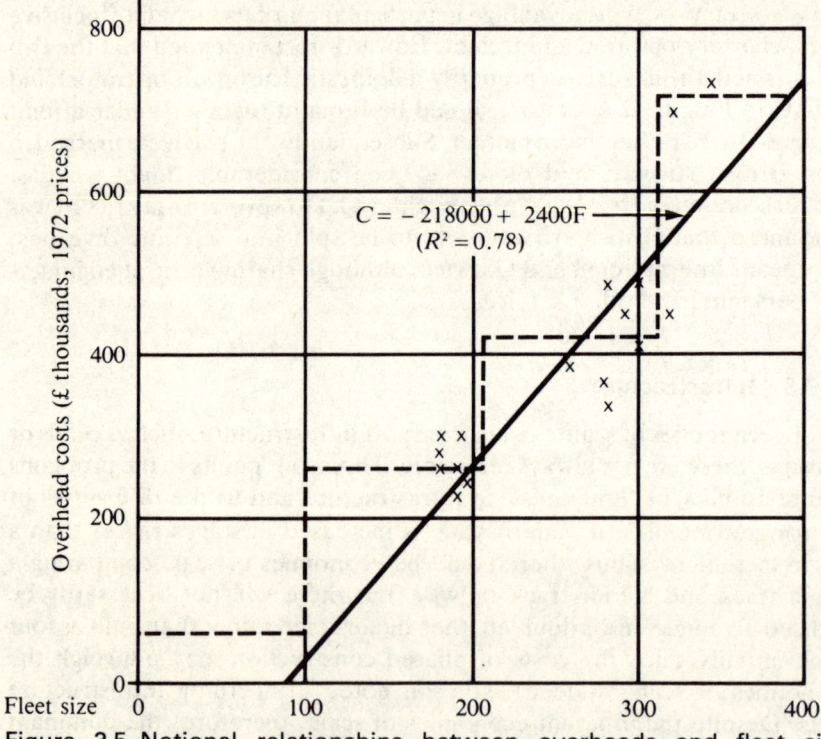

Figure 3.5 Notional relationships between overheads and fleet size, Bradford City Transport motor buses, 1956–1973.
Source: R. Travers Morgan and Partners, *Bradford Bus Study, Final Report* (London, 1976).

ability to realize these depends upon adequate demand however. A study by Lee and Steadman[10] considered British Municipal Fleets and concluded 'the weight of our evidence supports the hypothesis of constant returns to scale'. However, significant differences in costs were found between fleets of similar size, possibly due to labour cost variations. Studies for the Bradford Bus Study[11] of municipal operators' costs 'gave no indication of a curved or stepped relationship between costs and fleet size'. A further analysis, based on the expansion of the Bradford City motorbus fleet between 1956 and 1973, suggesting the possibility of a step function relating overheads and fleet size is depicted in Figure 3.5.

The evidence for British operation therefore, does not convincingly demonstrate the existence of economies of scale and it is noteworthy that some larger operators, e.g. London Transport and National Bus Company, have adopted decentralization to smaller operating units.

3.11 The interaction of supply and demand

In Chapter 2 we considered how the demand by individual consumers for goods at a range of prices could be combined and depicted as a demand

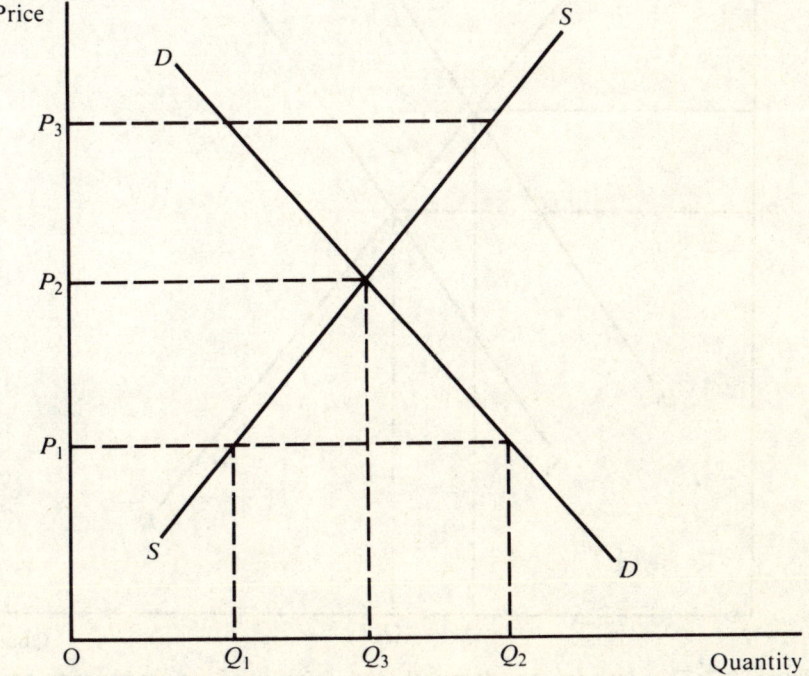

Figure 3.6 The interaction of supply and demand.

curve for a particular service or product. Given that the price elasticity of demand is greater than zero but less than infinity this curve will be down-sloping indicating that a decrease in price will result in an increase in demand. We have also considered the costs facing individual producers. These too can be aggregated into a single curve depicting supply. This however exhibits the characteristic that an increase in price will result in an increase in supply whilst a decrease in price will result in a decrease in supply. This reflects the costs facing individual firms and changes in the number of firms in the industry.

These two elements of demand and supply can be combined into a simple model depicting a market. If we assume that there is no government intervention then we can use the model to make simple predictions about price. Figure 3.6 shows the demand and supply curves for a product.

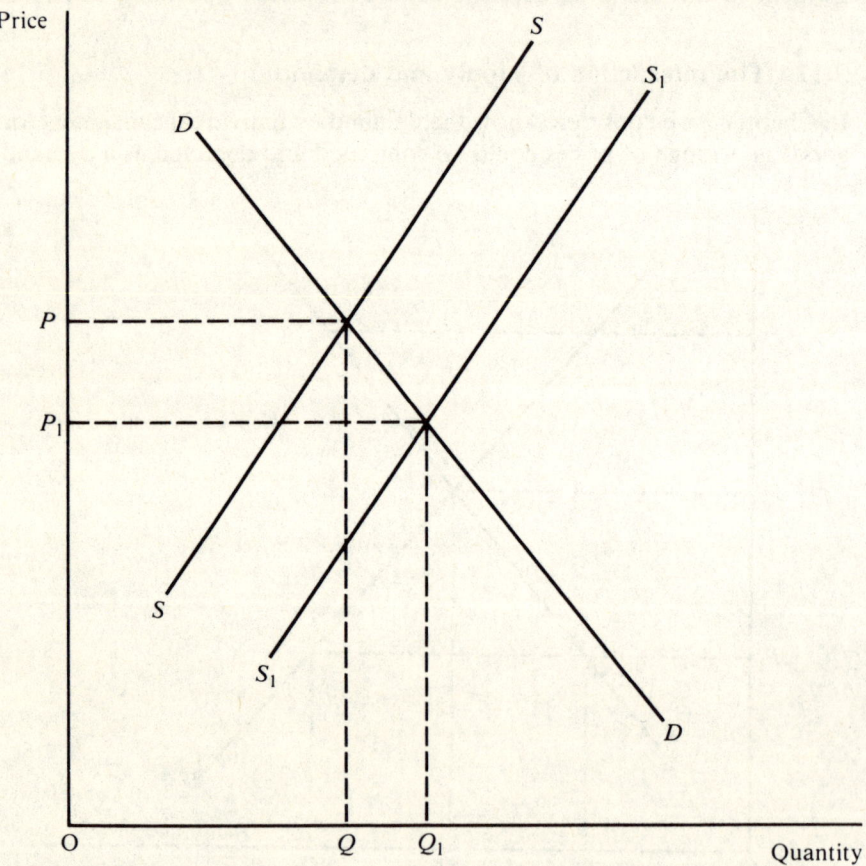

Figure 3.7 The impact on demand and supply of an improvement in technology.

Consider the situation if the product is being sold at price OP_1. Quantity OQ_2 is demanded but only quantity OQ_1 is supplied. There is an excess of demand over supply. The demand curve shows that some, but not all, buyers are prepared to pay more for the product. If price is allowed to rise demand will be reduced. The increase in price will also bring forth additional supply. This process continues until equilibrium is reached at price OP_2 when the quantity demanded, OQ_3, is the same as that supplied. (You should test your understanding of this by considering how equilibrium is reached from OP_3.)

Changes in demand or supply as a result of price changes are shown as movements *along* the relevant curve. However, entirely new circumstances may apply such as new technology which alters the cost structure of an industry or an increase in peoples' income. These changes are shown by movements in the *position* of supply or demand curves since different quantities would be demanded or supplied at the same price. Thus figure 3.7 depicts the situation of improved technology with a resultant shift in the supply curve. The original equilibrium in the market is at price OP with quantity OQ demanded and supplied. The effect of the improved technology is that producers are willing to supply a larger quantity than OQ at this price and consequently an excess of supply over demand exists. This causes a fall in price and equilibrium is re-established at the lower price of OP_1 with the larger quantity OQ demanded and supplied. (Consider how an increase in income would be depicted and its impact on the equilibrium price and quantity.)

This simple model therefore enables us to explore the interaction of demand and supply. The theme of pricing is considered in more detail in the next chapter. The model does have certain limitations. A firm may be unsure of the demand for its product over a wide range of prices. Supply is depicted as being continuous and thus any quantity can be produced. In practice, supply may be available only in discreet steps. Thus for a shuttle type airline operation using 170 seat aircraft you cannot produce just 172 seats. If 172 passengers present themselves you can either disappoint 2 passengers or supply 340 seats. The introduction of the Boeing 747 brought significantly lower costs per seat/mile but these benefits could only be achieved in steps of 400 to 500 seats. The airlines were then faced with the problem of whether sufficient demand existed at prices which would cover both the operating and capital costs of the new equipment. Some of the pricing practices adopted are considered in the next chapter.

Examination questions

1 A major difficulty in the costing of transport services is that many costs are jointly incurred. Explain the nature of this difficulty and illustrate with

examples how the prevalence of joint costs can influence the commercial policies of transport undertakings.

2 To what extent are transport undertakings subject to economies or diseconomies of scale? Compare the importance of these effects in different modes of transport.

3 Outline the structure of costs in road freight transport. To what extent is the road haulage industry one in which economies of scale are likely to accrue?

4 Explain the nature and significance of the distinction which economists draw between 'fixed' and 'variable' costs. Illustrate your answer with reference to one particular mode of transport.

5 A major characteristic of supply in the transport industry is that output cannot be stored. Examine the effects of this on the economics of operating passenger and freight services.

6 In relation to one or more modes of transport, explain in some detail the extent and manner in which unit operating costs vary with sector length.

7 Compare the importance of economies of scale in different modes of transport.

8 Discuss the influence of the technical characteristics of the operating unit used in different forms of transport on the level of costs.

9 What is meant by 'economies of scale'? How important are they in the transport industry?

10 Outline the structure of costs incurred in bus transport. What factors affect the level of costs per bus-mile?

4

Pricing in Transport

4.1 Introduction

The Government wishes the nation's resources to be used efficiently. To this end it offers guidelines to state industries on how to price for their services. Within these constraints the national railway organization naturally wishes to obtain as much revenue as possible. What pricing techniques will help achieve this? The American airline recently freed from price fixing agreements might reduce its fares to increase custom but what will its competitors do? At the other end of the scale there is the road haulage owner driver who depends on a large customer for his business, and the customer decides the rate for the job. Can the haulier afford to accept the contract?

These are examples of the kinds of pricing problems that have to be dealt with in transport. Economic theory can help us to analyse them.

Economic theory is very much concerned with how efficiently the resources described in Chapter 1 are allocated, and the prices charged for goods and services play a significant role in this allocation process. The pricing policies adopted by transport organizations are therefore important. This chapter will examine the policy suggested by economic theory paying particular attention to the difficulties involved. It will then look at the way market structures affect pricing policies and go on to examine some practical considerations taking the bus industry as an example. Finally, there will be a section on one aspect of pricing that is very important in transport economics — that of charging for the use of road space — and this will be compared with existing methods of restraining private vehicle traffic.

4.2 Pricing theory

4.2.1 Profit maximization and resource allocation

The resource allocation process described in economic theory depends on the assumption that firms aim to maximize their profits. This assumption does have its critics but for the moment we would ask you to accept it in order that the basic economic model can be dealt with more easily. How does a firm achieve profit maximization? Table 4.1 shows the demand schedule, cost structures and profit margins for the CARRIO General Haulage Company, which we will assume is a firm in a perfectly competitive market and as such is a price taker facing a horizontal demand curve. The table shows that the firm achieves normal profits (which in a perfectly competitive long-term situation is equivalent to profit maximization) where the firm's marginal cost (Column 4) is equal to its marginal revenue (Column 7), i.e. where the firm produces 50 loads per week (Row 5).

Marginal revenue is simply the extra revenue the firm obtains from selling one more unit of its product in this case measured in loads per week. From this observation we might suggest a simple rule for a firm to follow if it wishes to maximize its profit—the amount it produces should be such that the cost of producing an extra unit equals the extra revenue which will be gained, that is, where marginal cost equals marginal revenue. The logic of this can be seen quite clearly in Figure 4.1 which shows the demand and cost curves for the company. If the firm reduces or increases its output from 50 loads per week then average costs will increase while average revenue stays the same and it will therefore lose money.

Would this rule apply for a firm in a near-monopoly situation like a large municipal bus operator or a tanker operator? In Table 4.2 we show the demand schedule and the cost structures for the OILY Road Tanker Company. Quite clearly, profit maximization occurs where marginal cost equals marginal revenue. Output would be 20 loads per week, price would be £72.20 per load and marginal revenue and cost would be £44.50. So the rule is still valid for firms outside a perfectly competitive market. *Profit maximization is achieved when the firm adjusts its price and output to make marginal revenue equal to marginal cost.*

Although this rule achieves profit maximization for firms working under perfect and imperfect market conditions, its adoption does not mean that resources are necessarily efficiently allocated in both types of market. Consider Table 4.1 and Figure 4.1. When the CARRIO General Haulage Company operates at 50 loads per week and the price is £48 per load its profits are maximized. It is also working at its most efficient, that is at minimum average total costs, £48 per load. The OILY Tanker Company, on the other hand, when maximizing its profit is operating at an average cost of £48.50 per load, which is above the minimum average cost of £48.00 (see Figure 4.2). So it is not working at its most efficient and resources are being wasted or misallocated.

There is another reason why in imperfect market conditions resources might not be allocated efficiently if the pricing policy adopted is designed to pursue profit maximization. Economic theory assumes *consumer sovereignty*. The customer knows best and it is not for the economist to judge how much value a consumer places on the good or service he has purchased other than by observing the price he has paid for it. If someone pays 100 pence for a packet of cigarettes the economist merely says their

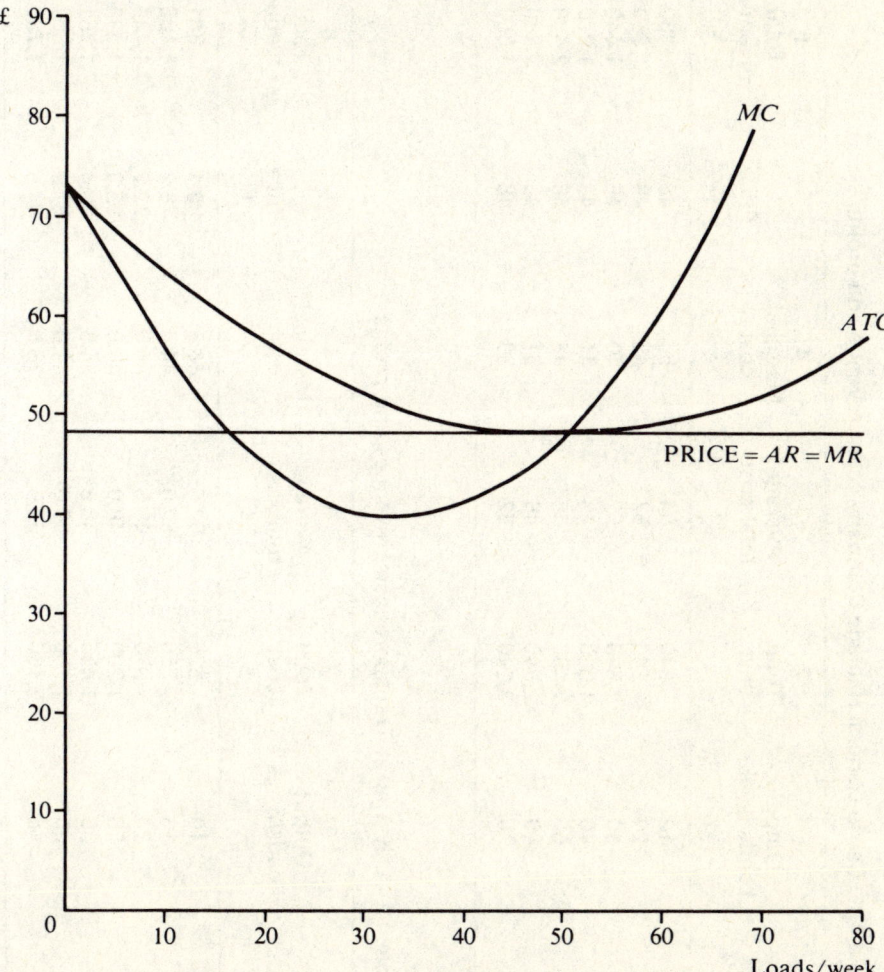

Figure 4.1 General haulage company, costs and revenues.

Table 4.1   Carrio General Haulage Company costs, revenue and profits

	1 Output Loads/week	2 Total cost £	3 Average total cost £	4 Marginal cost £	5 Price £	6 Total revenue £	7 Marginal revenue £	8 Profit £/week
1	10	640	64	56	48	480	48	−160
2	20	1,140	57	45	48	960	48	−180
3	30	1,560	52	40	48	1,440	48	−120
4	40	1,960	49	41	48	1,920	48	−40
5	50	2,400	48	48	48	2,400	48	0
6	60	2,940	49	61	48	2,880	48	−60
7	70	3,640	52	80	48	3,360	48	−280

Table 4.2   Oily Tanker Transport costs, revenues and profits

	1 Output Loads/week	2 Total cost £	3 Average total cost £	4 Marginal cost £	5 Price £	6 Total revenue £	7 Marginal revenue £	8 Profit £/week
1	10	525	52.5	46.5	86.1	861	72.2	336
2	15	750	50.0	44.0	79.2	1,188	58.4	438
3	20	970	48.5	44.5	72.2	1,445	44.5	475
4	25	1,200	48.0	48.0	65.3	1,633	30.6	433
5	30	1,455	48.5	54.5	58.4	1,751	16.7	296
6	35	1,750	50.0	64.0	51.4	1,800	2.9	50
7	40	2,100	52.5	76.5	44.5	1,780	−11.0	−320

value to the smoker is at least 100 pence and forms no further opinion on their benefit to him.

We can see from the demand curve in Figure 4.2 that some customers are willing to pay £85 per load to have their traffic carried while others are prepared to pay less right down to the last customer who is willing to pay an amount only just greater than zero. The benefit to each, as far as the economist is concerned, is represented by the price each is willing to pay.

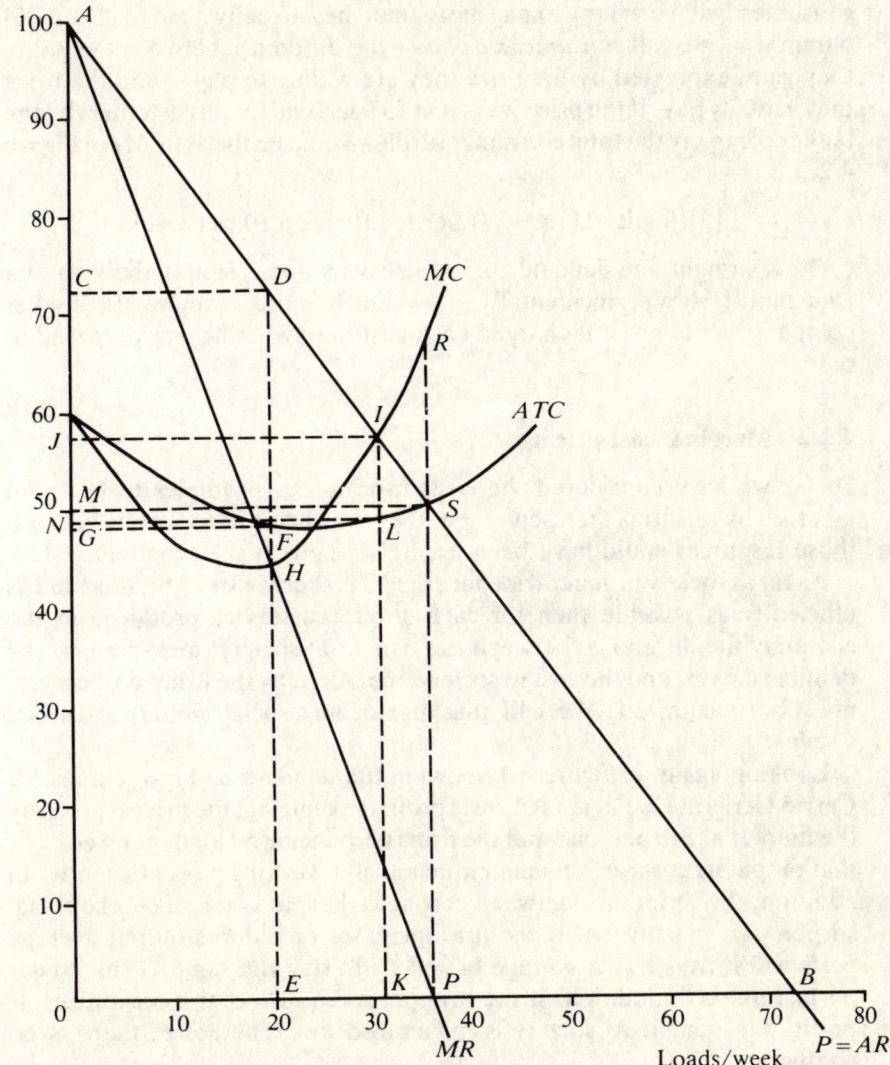

Figure 4.2 OILY Tanker Company, costs and revenues.

The benefit to them all of the bulk haulage service offered can be found by adding the number willing to pay £85 to those willing to pay £84 and so on down to zero. It is equivalent then to the area under the demand curve OAB. We can expand this to suggest that the benefits to users (and therefore society) of a particular good or service is represented by its demand curve.

The user, of course, will most likely have to pay for the good or service he consumes. If the producer charges a *uniform* price for his product, some consumers will be willing to pay more than they actually need to. They will obtain what we call *consumer surplus* — the difference between the utility they gain, expressed by the price they are willing to pay — and the price they actually pay. If the price was set at £57 per load for all customers by the tanker company the total consumer surplus would be the area *AIJ* in Figure 4.2, i.e.

$$\tfrac{1}{2} [31 \text{ loads} \times £(100-57) \text{ per load}] = £666.50 \text{ per week.}$$

(With a straight line demand curve the calculation is simply the area of a triangle. It shows, incidentally, how much more revenue the tanker company would get if it charged each customer what he was prepared to pay).

4.2.2 Marginal cost pricing

So far we have considered the costs used in our examples to be those incurred by the firms themselves, but they are also costs to society because those resources could have been used elsewhere in the economy.

As far as society in general is concerned if resources are to be allocated as efficiently as possible then for each good and service produced in the economy the difference between the benefit to society, measured by the demand curves, and the cost to society, measured by the firms' cost curves, must be maximized. We call this maximizing social welfare or social surplus.

Looking again at Figure 4.1 showing the demand and cost curves for Carrio General Haulage, the firm is profit maximizing, the price is given by the market at £48 per load and the firm is producing 50 loads per week. At that output its costs are at a minimum and it is working most efficiently. In addition, the difference between consumer benefit and costs — the social surplus — is maximized. If the firm increases or reduces output average costs will increase and average benefits will stay the same. Thus, under perfect market conditions if the firm produces such that it maximizes its profits the benefit to society is maximized too. Therefore, there is no conflict.

This is not so if a firm under imperfect market conditions attempts to maximize profits. With reference to Figure 4.2, if the firm adopts a profit maximizing policy it will charge *OC* (£72) and produce *OE* (20 loads per week). Profit will be *CDFG* (£475) see Table 4.2. However, Figure 4.2 shows that there is an area *DHI* which represents potential benefit over cost. If the company reduces its price to *OJ* (£57) where the marginal cost curve cuts the demand curve, more customers, buying *EK* (11) extra loads, will use its services and the benefit to them *EDIK* will exceed costs to the company *EHIK* by *DHI*. So society will benefit if the company rather than setting its price to maximize profit sets its price equal to marginal cost. The company's profit will however fall from *CDFG* to *JILN*.

If the firm adopts an average cost pricing policy and reduces its price to *OM* (£50) it will encourage *KP* (5) extra loads demand. The firm will break even but society in general will suffer because as output increases the cost to society *KIRP* will exceed the extra benefits *KISP* by *IRS*.

In this monopoly situation, therefore, resources will be most efficiently allocated if the firm prices according to marginal cost. To remind you, the same applies to a firm in perfect competition but there is no conflict with a profit maximizing policy because with a horizontal demand curve marginal revenue is the same as average revenue.

We therefore have a general prescription for allocation of resources in the most efficient way—organizations should price according to the marginal cost of production. This is sometimes referred to as the Hotelling—Lerner pricing rule for public enterprises, the assumption being that Governments can lay down pricing rules only for those organizations in the public sector. The U.K. Government would appear to endorse this rule. In the 1976 Consultation Document *Transport Policy* it stated:

'The strict economic approach to pricing would be to ensure the user pays at least the full marginal resources costs of his transport; then there would (in theory) be no misallocation of resources.'

It recognized, however, that there are problems in pursuing such a policy. To these we now turn.

4.2.3   The problems with marginal cost pricing

4.2.3.1   *Determining marginal costs*

The most likely question the student will ask when presented with the marginal cost pricing rule is 'This sounds very straightforward, but do we know what the marginal costs are?' Having already examined costing problems he probably has a good idea how pertinent such a question is. We have already seen the problems with allocating joint and common costs in Chapter 3. There is also the question of the unit of output to be costed—should it be the cost per passenger-mile or bus-mile for example? These do appear to be important questions but, in practice, the quantitative implications are not significant. Most economists would be happy to see prices *reflecting* marginal costs as going someway to meeting the criterion. There are more fundamental difficulties to be examined.

If we do agree that prices need only to reflect marginal costs then the first problem we are faced with is that long-run marginal costs may differ greatly from short-run marginal costs. Which should be used? The argument in favour of long-run marginal costs is that the consumer should pay costs sufficient to enable the operator to invest in new facilities. Short-run pricing however ensures that the best use is made of existing resources. If consumers are prepared to pay a price equal to their short-run marginal costs then benefits will be lost if they are excluded from consumption.

Gwilliam and Mackie[1] illustrate the problem with three examples. The

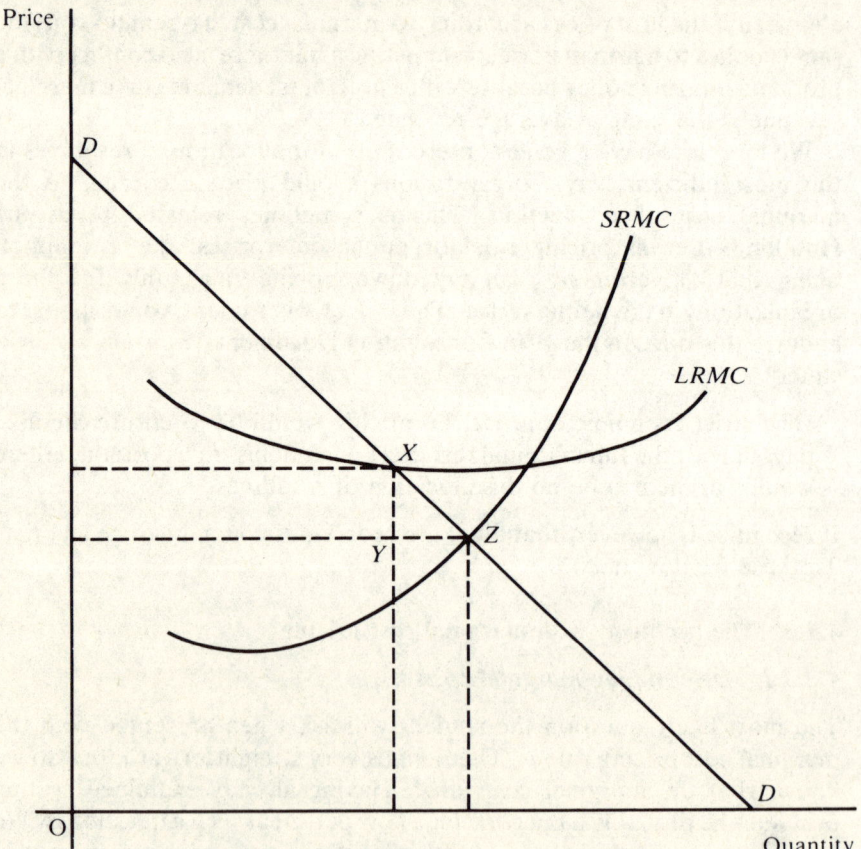

Figure 4.3 Short- or long-run marginal cost?

first is where there is an under-utilized facility where the short-run is less than long-run marginal cost, and when present assets are exhausted there is no intention of replacing them. An example might be a rural rail service due for closure. The costs to take account of here are those which will be incurred in the future. The costs of past investments cannot be recovered and there is no intention to aim for an economic return on future investments. Short-run marginal cost is, therefore, the appropriate one and in the case of the rail service would be those of, say, fuel, maintenance and crew costs and not those of infrastructure and rolling stock.

The second example is that of a well-used facility requiring regular major re-investment and maintenance. The problem can be discussed with reference to Figure 4.3.

If long-run marginal cost pricing is adopted then the area XYZ represents the loss of user benefit to those who are prepared to pay the lower SRMC but not the LRMC. On the other hand if short-run marginal cost pricing is adopted how are future investments to be paid for?

Finally, there is the congested facility where short-run marginal costs are rising steeply. The cross harbour tunnel in Hong Kong is a good example. Facilities cannot be expanded quickly and the scarce resources must be rationed in some way. Short-run marginal cost pricing will do this most efficiently in ensuring that no one receives a benefit lower than the SRMC he imposes.

For most situations and with some qualifications the Government appears to support long-run marginal cost pricing for Nationalized Industries[2,3].

Another difficulty in determining marginal costs concerns shifts in the demand curve which will cause changes in the marginal cost. Most passenger operators are aware of this problem and we see many examples of differential peak/off peak pricing. This only presents a problem where the demand curve shifts unpredictably.

The final complication under the heading of cost determination is most important to the transport economist. So far in the analysis we have argued that if producers and consumers base their decisions on their marginal costs and benefits then society's welfare will be maximized. Consider, however, the following example.

It is not uncommon for oil tankers to have their tanks washed at sea. The oil released often pollutes shorelines and the cleaning costs have to be met by the governments of countries affected. That is a cost to society which normally will not be met by the producers of that cost — the parties to the transport contract, i.e. the shipowner and the shipper. Their decision is made, therefore, on the basis of private costs but not the true social costs. Those governments paying for the cleaning-up operations are third parties affected by that contract and suffering what we call an external cost. If it was possible to make shipowners pay for those pollution costs and they become part of the operating costs which are passed on to the customers we would say that the external cost is internalized. These higher true costs faced by oil consumers might then lead to some reduction in demand.

The essential point in economic theory is that there are social as well as private costs which should be taken into account when decisions are made about production, pricing and consumption. The most discussed example in transport economics is probably the social cost imposed by a motorist (for example by delays to other motorists) which he may not consider when he decides to make a journey. We will return to this in Section 4.5. There are, of course, external benefits too. When considering whether to close a rail service the decision maker will need to take account of the benefits to

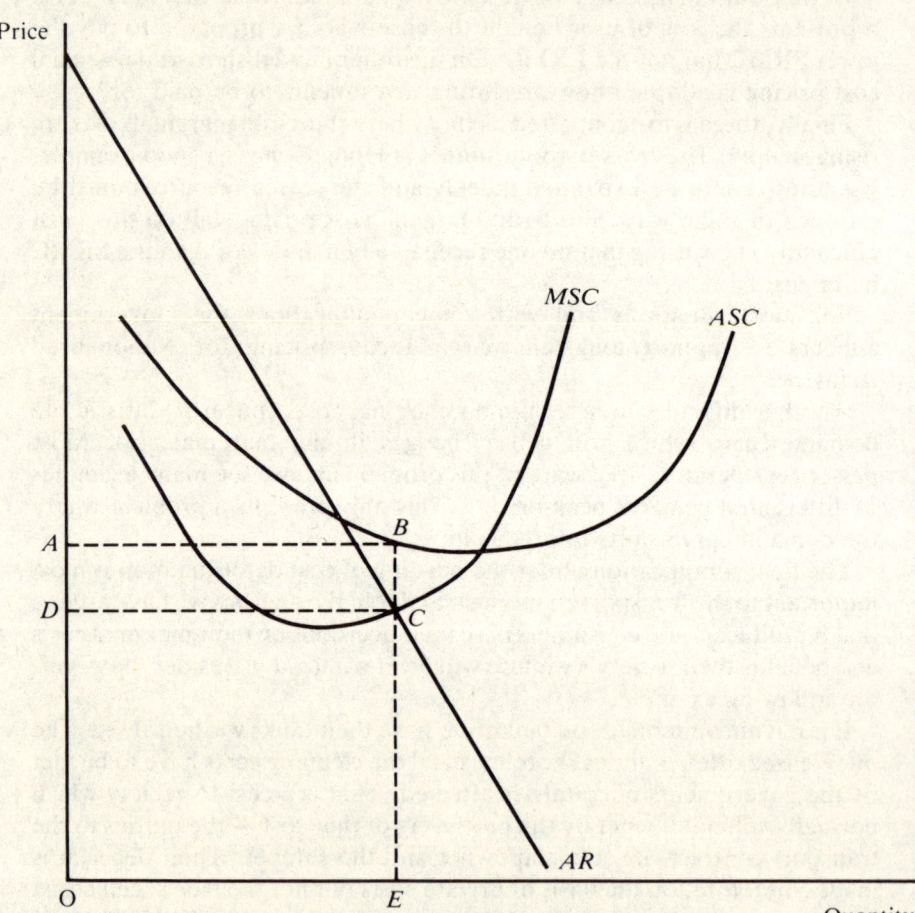

Figure 4.4 Loss-making with marginal cost pricing.

the community served over and above the benefits expressed by the prices users are willing to pay. The prescription is, therefore, for marginal *social* cost pricing rather than marginal *private* cost pricing, the difference being that social costs include externalities.

4.2.3.2 *Loss making through marginal social cost pricing*

There are going to be cases where if an operator adopts marginal cost pricing it will make a loss. Consider Figure 4.4. In this example the operator is faced with decreasing average costs. Pricing at marginal cost will result in output *OE* and price *OD*. There will be a loss equivalent to *ABCD*. One way of meeting this loss is by financing from other sources such as general taxation. Many economists argue against this solution on equity grounds emphasizing the point that economic efficiency hinges on users paying the full marginal costs they impose on society.

There is a solution however, which conforms to the principle of marginal cost pricing and covers the loss in this kind of situation. It is called the two-part tariff charging system. All consumers pay a fixed charge to meet the loss but still make decisions about consumption on the basis of the marginal costs. This is a simple matter in the case of, say, electricity supply or the telephone system where almost all households are consumers, but in an industry or service where there are many casual users it would be rather difficult to impose a fixed charge in the same way.

Another problem faced by an operator attempting to adopt this pricing system is that if he faces competition (i.e. there are close substitutes) the high fixed charge might persuade customers to change mode even though they are willing to pay the marginal costs. British Rail might be in this situation in the face of competition from coach operators in the inter-city market.

Price discrimination (described in Section 4.3) is another means of reducing deficit or increasing revenue and it still gives the operator the flexibility to relate prices in some way to marginal costs, but as we shall see other factors play significant roles in the consequent pricing structures.

4.2.3.3 *Welfare implications*

The final question marks against the marginal cost pricing principle are based in economic theory[4] and we consider these are fundamental criticisms difficult to dispute.

The first theoretical question mark concerns the implications if marginal social cost pricing is not adopted throughout all sectors of the economy. Some observers feel that although resource misallocation will occur it is still better to pursue the principle in the transport sector. This view is not supported by a famous, highly technical and formidable analysis by Lipsey and Lancaster (1956) called *The General Theory of Second Best*. They showed that if all the necessary conditions for a first-best optimum allocation could not be met then it is possible that adopting a piecemeal approach, i.e. at least optimize in those sectors where you can, will not necessarily improve social welfare. This might be particularly true for the transport sector which cannot be isolated from other sectors. For example, consider the implications of transport costs on land-use.

Finally, the arguments in favour of marginal cost pricing outlined above depend on a very important assumption — that the demand curve reflecting willingness to pay also reflects user benefits and, therefore, benefits to society. This implies that willingness to pay should not be distinguished from ability to pay. It also implies that the economist accepts the distribution of income in society as given and ignores the distributional effects of pricing policies geared to optimal resource allocation. This is based on the view that the elected government is responsible for redistributing income through the tax/transfer system and that this can be done effectively. Many economists are unhappy with this. Millward[5] argues that perhaps economists should not accept that individuals are the best judge of their own well being and quotes education and health as examples. He gives two examples in the transport field where distributional implications might be considered and some departure from marginal cost pricing pursued.

(a) The introduction of pricing to goods and services previously subject to some kind of non-price rationing such as charging for parking or the use of road space.
(b) Major changes in pricing procedures such as switching from average cost pricing to peak/off-peak pricing to reflect marginal costs.

These criticisms of the assumptions behind the use of the demand curve appear to us seriously to undermine the rationale behind the marginal social cost pricing principle. Foster appears to take this view[6].

'The conclusion seems that we cannot argue a case for MSC pricing on the grounds of allocation of resources . . .'

and he gives two reasons. The first is that 'The income distribution policies implied by it are politically unacceptable'. The second is one we have not referred to yet. It concerns the rate of return we need to guide us in decisions about investment problems where capital is scarce or capital investment is significantly indivisible. MSC pricing leads to a social surplus rate of return which is difficult to use and unfamiliar to those used to working in terms of profit maximization.

Do these criticisms mean that we should abandon the principle and look for something else? Foster feels we do not have sufficient knowledge to be able to say:

'On *a priori* grounds I challenge anyone to make a case for MSC pricing or indeed for profit or consumers surplus maximization in a mixed economy on the grounds of achieving a better allocation of resources and a higher rate of economic growth. At present there is equal though not invincible ignorance'.[6]

Millward feels there is still scope for using the MSC pricing principle in the public sector and emphasizes its advantages of being a decentralized but easily administered system. While recognizing the formidable problems of second best outlined above he suggests R. Turvey's prescription to be worth consideration[7]. It is:

(a) The public enterprise's product to be sold at a price whose relationship to marginal cost approximates to that in the competing private enterprise;
(b) Adjust taxes on the competing private sector group to ensure that the price/marginal cost ratio is broadly in line with the rest of the economy;
(c) General equilibrium policy weapons such as taxation and investment should be used to reduce the inefficiency in the private sector so that the partial equilibrium operation of the public sector could be replaced by general equilibrium operations using marginal social cost pricing.

It must be clear that the debate on this topic will be a continuing one for some time yet and the analysis required to help understand it is really beyond the scope of this book. We would recommend the references given[4,5,6,7], if you wish to go into the subject in more detail. It is fair to say that we are really at the frontiers of knowledge in welfare economics in this area and for our purposes, it is sufficient to adopt the marginal social cost pricing principle although we should be aware of its limitations.

4.3 Pricing and market structure

The practice of pricing policy depends on an individual company's relationship to the market as a whole. An owner driver in general road haulage constitutes a small part of the supply of road transport in his own market and locality. He thus has little market power and must accept the general market price. Attempts to obtain a higher price, unless as a result of offering a differentiated service, will result in loss of the business to a competitor willing to accept a lower price. This factor combined with an inadequate knowledge of costs and a ready supply of new entrants may explain the poor profitability of small road haulage operators. Larger undertakings with a larger share of a market are in a better position to set the market price. Indeed as we have seen a sole supplier (monopolist) can fix the market price. Alternatively, a number of firms can join together to regulate the market by establishing a cartel. Thus an agreement can be made to set prices collectively or to allocate shares in the market in order to restrict competition. This mechanism has long been a feature of shipping (through liner conferences) and scheduled airline operation. The ability to control the market can permit excess (abnormal) profits to be earned, the protection of high cost operators and the restriction of consumer choice. These characteristics have been recognized in America where de-regulation of internal airline operation has made it easier for new airlines to enter the market and compete on price and service with existing operators. The attraction of this policy is that it may offer wider choice and, through competition, promote efficiency and cost effective operation. The 1980 U.K. Transport Act, which allowed new entrants into the markets for long distance coach travel and certain excursions and tours, was based on similar thinking. Although de-regulation may promote competition it does not necessarily enhance profitability and many established American airlines and new entrants are making losses in their attempts to retain a share of the market.

To summarize the pricing policy followed depends upon the aims of the company and its market power combined with the demand characteristics of the market. Chapter 3 examined the various market models. Students often regard these models with a degree of scepticism since they are too simplified to describe the real world accurately. This is to misunderstand the purpose of models which is to focus attention on the relationship being studied. By using these models it is possible to understand how the relationship between a firm and the overall market affects its pricing policy.

We shall now look at the implications for pricing of each market structure.

4.3.1 Perfect competition

We have already seen that a firm in a situation of perfect competition is a *price taker*. This may be the situation of owner drivers in the road freight market since they are obliged to accept the market rate. The substitution of quantity for quality licensing allows a steady stream of new entrants to the market which keeps prices down and prevents abnormal profits being earned. However, owner drivers may adopt other methods of pricing since it cannot be presumed that 'perfect knowledge' exists in this market. One method is a 'cost plus' approach which simply adds a fixed percentage on top of the direct costs for undertaking a particular journey. Thus direct cost $+X\%=$ price. Unfortunately, this method, although having the attraction of simplicity, does not guarantee profitability since the $X\%$ must cover overheads and unforseen expenditure as well as providing profit. If we take as an example a 21-ton articulated vehicle, running costs, based on 1981 Motor Transport cost tables are set out below:

Running cost per mile

	pence
Fuel	19.857
Oil	0.402
Tyres	5.721
Maintenance	16.352
	42.332

However, standing costs for this vehicle, including wages, amount to £19,500 per annum. Allocated on a mileage basis this would be equivalent to a further 64.497 pence per mile based on an annual mileage of 30,000 miles per annum. (This figure would decrease as annual mileage increased and would be 27.641 pence with a utilization of 70,000 per annum).

Thus operating a variable cost plus whatever contribution towards overheads can be obtained is unlikely to guarantee full cost recovery let alone profit. A more sophisticated method starts with a target rate of return on capital which can be translated into a profit target, thus:

Target rate of return 15%
Capital employed £200,000
Profit target (15% of £200,000) — £30,000
This can be related to target turnover £300,000 giving a 30,000/300,000=10% profit add on
Price then equals direct cost+overheads+10%

4.3.2 Imperfect competition

Within this market structure each firm aims to make its product different from that of its competitors. Examples of this can be seen amongst airlines with common routes who may differentiate by check-in arrangements, cabin layout and seat pitch, in-flight catering and entertainment or a variety of 'free' gifts. Each firm then has a monopoly of the supply of its own particular brand of the product and indeed some texts refer to this market form as monopolistic competition. Since the firm's product is somewhat different from that of its competitors it has greater pricing flexibility. Thus, if it increases its price it will lose some of its customers to its competitors but not all (unlike perfect competition). If it lowers its price it will gain some, but not all of the customers of its rivals. Thus, the firm faces a downward sloping demand curve rather than the perfectly elastic demand curve of a firm under perfect competition. The firm is thus no longer a price taker but can vary the price charged or the quantity sold in order to maximize profits. Further firms in this type of market do not compete on price alone but on the factors which help to separate or differentiate their product from that of their competitors.

4.3.3   Oligopoly

Oligopoly can be used to describe the situation amongst ferry operators from Britain to the Continent where there are a few large operators competing. The size and market power of existing firms makes it difficult for new firms to enter the market. Although firms in this market are less troubled by the prospect of new entrants their profitability (or fulfilment of other corporate aims) depends upon the actions of their competitors and their competitors' reaction to their own strategy. This interaction can be seen in the interaction of Aloha with Hawaiian Airlines in the case study below. The firms are thus not simply price takers or price makers but interact with each other according to their strategy.

The two airlines, Aloha and Hawaiian, fly between Big Island and Honolulu, in Hawaii. The 1978 U.S. Airlines De-regulation Act increased price competition between the two airlines as described by Aloha Airlines Vice-Chairman Kenneth Chan. 'For Aloha he says the great battle began in September 1979 when the airline's market share crept up to a record 48% in competition with Hawaiian operating DC9's (Aloha used Boeing 737 aircraft): 'To celebrate its 50th anniversary our competitor announced a 50% discount coupon plan, very similar to that started by United Airlines earlier in the year. A few days later we announced the temporary suspension of all our full fares ($63) and the 25% discount on all our flights'. Aloha's reasoning, says Chan, was basically very simple: 'Passengers on our competitor were being asked to fly one round trip at full fares to obtain a 50% discount on a subsequent trip. We could obtain the same yield by offering an immediate 25% across-the-board discount. Hawaiian promptly matched this, simultaneously giving away 50% coupons. We rejected the idea of coupons allowing our competitor in December to take the lion's share of the market by refusing to honour his coupons. Aloha's market share dropped to 35% though yield per passenger climbed from $23 to nearly $25' But for the fourth quarter of that year Aloha made an $875,000 loss while Hawaiian reported a $2.8 million loss. Early in 1980 Aloha introduced new promotional family, group and excursion fares and in September it launched inflight contests — immediately matched by Hawaiian — involving for Aloha $125,000 in prizes and for Hawaiian 100 free trips and a lifetime pass for one person. 'Then the fun began' says Chan. In February 1981 the two airlines saw the first advertizing of a new competitor. Mid-Pacific Airlines introduced 60 seat YS-11 (turboprop) aircraft and announced special introductory fares of $25. Hawaiian had already announced a $25 'Super Saver' fare for advanced purchase which Aloha had matched. But Mid-Pacific introduced coupon booklets ('Buy 10 to get one free, but 20 to get 3 free'). Aloha 'stayed put' but Hawaiian countered with a $20 standby fare on the newly introduced Dash 7 turboprop aircraft.'[8]

The case study above illustrates price competition at work in a dynamic market. Within two years prices have fallen, a new operator has entered the market (following the removal of barriers to market entry) and new, more fuel-efficient equipment has been introduced.

As we have seen in the airline example, competitive behaviour in this type of market does not guarantee profitablity and firms may be torn between attempting to drive competitors out of the market (at the expense of incurring short-term losses) and seeking to avoid the loss of profits incurred by price competition. Solutions to this dilemma may be to compete on factors other than price or to attempt to form a cartel. If a cartel is established then the operators effectively act together as if they were a monopolist and so are in a position to dictate the price in the market.

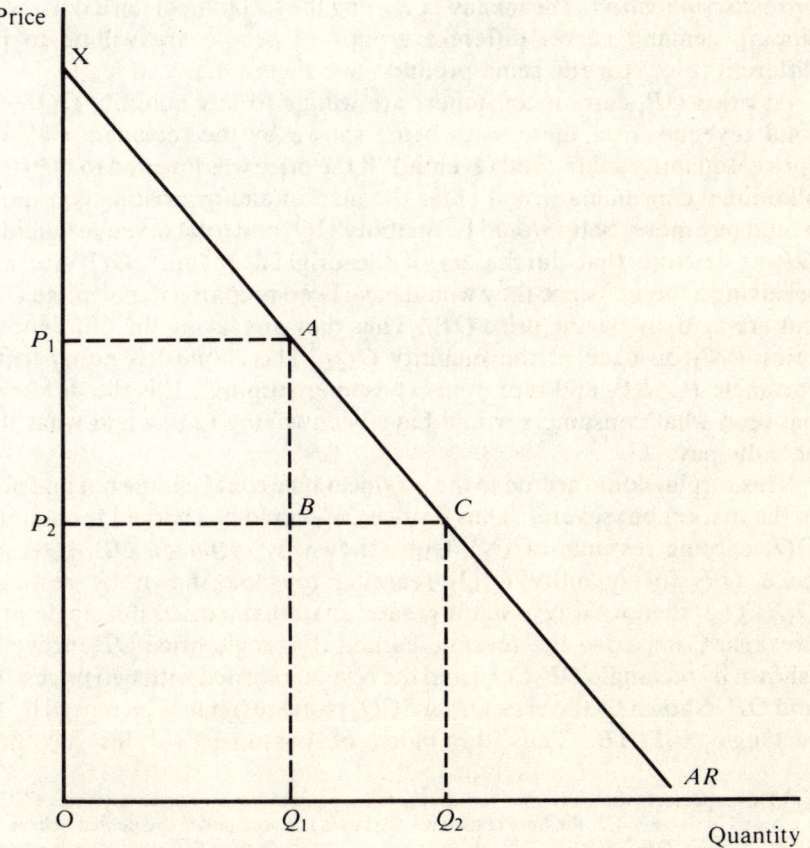

Figure 4.5 Price discrimination.

4.3.4 Monopoly

In the case of monopoly there is a single producer of the product. The demand curve for the firm and that for the market are the same. Thus the firm can choose the price or the quantity supplied to the market. If we assume that the aim of the monopolist is to maximize profits then the price solution will be that where Marginal Cost=Marginal Revenue.

If the additional revenue from producing one extra unit (MR) is greater than the cost of producing that extra unit (MC) then it is worth increasing production. However, if the additional revenue (MR) is less than the additional cost (MC) then production should be reduced. Thus the optimum output is where MC=MR and this maximizes profits, or minimizes losses (for there is no guarantee that a monopolist will earn profits).

Thus, a single price and a single level of profit (or loss) prevails. However, a monopolist can attempt to improve profitability by practising *price discrimination*. The means exploiting the fact that, given a downward sloping demand curve, different groups of people are willing to pay different prices for the same product. See Figure 4.5.

At price OP_1 certain consumers are willing to buy quantity OQ_1, the total revenue from these sales being shown by the rectangle OP_1AQ_1 (price×quantity sold=total revenue). If the price was lowered to OP_2 then additional consumers would enter the market and/or existing consumers would buy more. Sales would be quantity OQ_2 and total revenue would be OP_2CQ_2. Note that purchasers of the original quantity OQ_1 are now receiving a 'bonus' since they would have been prepared to pay price OP_1, but are actually paying price OP_2. Thus they are saving the difference in price P_1P_2 on each of the quantity OQ_1. This 'bonus' is equal to the rectangle P_1ABP_2 and represents consumer surplus*. It is the difference between what consumers would have been willing to pay and what they actually pay.

This surplus could accrue to the producer if he could charge not one price in the market but several. Thus if price OP_1 could be charged for quantity OQ_1 earning revenue of $OP_1.OQ_1$ (shown by rectangle OP_1AQ_1) and price OP_2 for quantity Q_1Q_2 (earning revenue shown by rectangle Q_1BCQ_2), then total revenue is greater than that earned if a single price prevails. Comparing the revenue earned if a single price OP_2 prevailed (shown by rectangle OP_2CQ_2) and the revenue earned with two prices OP_1 and OP_2 (shown by the area OP_1ABCQ_2) total revenue is increased by the rectangle P_2P_1AB. Thus the block of consumer surplus has been

---

* This represents the consumer surplus for those people only willing to pay price OP_1. As we noted in Section 4.2, the *total* consumer surplus is the area under the demand curve, i.e. P_2XC at price OP_2.

transferred from the consumer to the producer. (It should be noted that some consumer surplus remains shown by the triangles P_1XA and ABC.)

In order to succeed with price discrimination it is necessary to prevent consumers in higher price markets buying the product in lower priced markets. Thus in our diagram if all consumers had entry to the market with price OP_2 none would buy at the higher price of OP_1. Therefore the markets must be separated and barriers erected to prevent people from higher priced markets purchasing in lower priced markets. These barriers are not physical barriers but can be the various conditions imposed on ticket purchase for example. Airlines have long practised price discrimination attempting to maintain high price business travel whilst generating low price leisure travel. Conditions such as the advance purchase of an *APEX* ticket serve to divide the market. Thus the businessman who is unwilling to commit himself to longer term travel plans is prevented from enjoying the lower advance purchase fare.

It will be noted that price discrimination can only be successful in a controlled market (monopoly or cartel) otherwise other firms will seek to provide means for consumers to avoid the barriers separating markets.

Price discrimination need not be confined to the private sector: British Rail's pricing policy since the early 1970's has been based upon the principles of price discrimination. The previous system of pricing according to distance travelled has been abandoned in favour of market pricing. This has two aspects, different prices for different geographical markets and the price structure for different passenger markets.

Thus prices in a geographical market (for example London—Edinburgh) are established by considering the price of competitors (airlines and coaches), service quality and frequency, and the price sensitivity of the market. As a result, the rail fares for journeys of equivalent lengths are different in various parts of Britain. Different passenger markets are served by a range of discount fares often available only to holders of the appropriate railcards. These railcards serve to delineate and separate the various markets.

4.4 Practical considerations — the bus industry

Between 1964 and 1980, bus fares rose by 616%; during the same period retail prices rose on average by only 376%. It is not surprising therefore that public discussion of bus fares tends to concentrate on the *level* of fares and the question of whether bus services should be subsidized. The subsidy issue is dealt with in Chapter 5. In this chapter we are concerned with the more fundamental questions of how fares are *structured*, and the relationship between the structure and the supply and demand functions facing the bus operator. We shall assume therefore that the bus operator has a duty to break even.

We saw in Chapter 3 that bus operations display constant returns to scale in the long run, so that average costs are equal to marginal costs. In very general terms therefore a bus operator who has to break even would charge an average fare equal to the long-run marginal cost of carrying an additional passenger. The reason why pricing policy in practice is more complicated than this is that neither supply nor demand consists of homogeneous units.

On the supply side, some costs depend on the overall size of the undertaking and are fixed in the short run. Some costs vary with the number of hours of operation and some vary with mileage. The cost of supplying a given level of service varies according to time of day, day of week, route, type of operation etc. A bus operator tailoring his pricing policy to his cost structure would therefore charge fares on the following principles:

(a) The fare for any journey would consist of a two-part tariff, i.e. a fixed charge plus a charge varying with distance or time reflecting the short-run marginal costs.
(b) Differential fares would be charged at peak and off-peak periods to reflect the higher marginal costs of peak operation.
(c) Different fares would be charged on different routes, also to reflect cost differences.

On the demand side, the market is segmented into journeys of different lengths between different pairs of origins and destinations. Journeys are made by different kinds of people: some rich, some poor, some having alternative means of transport available. Journeys are made for different purposes, some of which are essential (e.g. travel to work) while others are optional (e.g. travel to the shops). The responsiveness of demand to changes in price, as measured by the fares elasticity, varies between market segments.

A bus operator tailoring his pricing policy to demand considerations would therefore attempt to discriminate between these different market segments so as to maximize revenue from each of them taking into account variations in fares elasticity. Thus a range of prices would be offered to different segments of the market, for example children and adults, peak and off-peak passengers, regular and non-regular users, long and short-distance passengers, etc.

In addition to supply and demand considerations, a third factor having an important influence on pricing policy in the bus industry ever since the 1930 Road Traffic Act has been the belief that bus operators have some kind of a social service obligation. Although the precise role of the bus operator has rarely been defined in practice, the feeling has always been that bus operators should have regard to *equity* in both pricing policy and provision of service. Indeed this idea lay behind the 1930 Act, and was one of the considerations which the Traffic Commissioners took into account when considering fares applications. The effect of introducing equity or 'fairness' into pricing policy is probably to reduce the amount of price discrimination compared with a purely commercial pricing policy.

A fourth factor having a bearing on pricing policy in practice is the way in which travel is charged for. If fares are collected actually on the vehicle (the most common practice in this country) then the fare structure must necessarily be relatively simple. Collection of fares off the vehicle by some form of prepayment system will enable a more complex structure to be applied. This distinction between on-bus and pre-paid fares is the most obvious way of categorizing the various fares systems in use in the bus industry.

4.4.1 On-bus fare systems

4.4.1.1 Graduated fares

The most common pricing structure used by bus operators (at one time almost the only type of structure), is the system of graduated fares paid on the bus. Fares increase with distance travelled, but at a decreasing rate, so that the fare *per kilometre travelled* decreases with distance. This kind of structure is usually based on a network of *fare stages*, every third or fourth bus stop being designated a fare stage and the fare charged for any particular journey being based on the number of stages travelled. Two features which should be noted about this type of system are:

(a) A passenger boarding between stages is charged the appropriate fare from the *preceding* stage, while a passenger alighting between stages is charged the fare to the *following* stage.
(b) Through fares are not normally available, i.e. a journey which requires two buses is charged for separately on each bus, so that the fare for the total journey is higher than it would be if the journey could be made on one bus.

How does a graduated fare structure fit in with the criteria for pricing policy described above? In the first place, the fact that the fare per kilometre decreases with distance travelled means that the structure can be interpreted as comprising a fixed charge per journey plus a rate per kilometre. This is in line with the basic requirement for a cost-related pricing policy. Examination of individual cases, however, shows that the fixed element is often higher than it should be when related to costs, while the variable element is correspondingly lower (see Figure 4.6). Secondly,

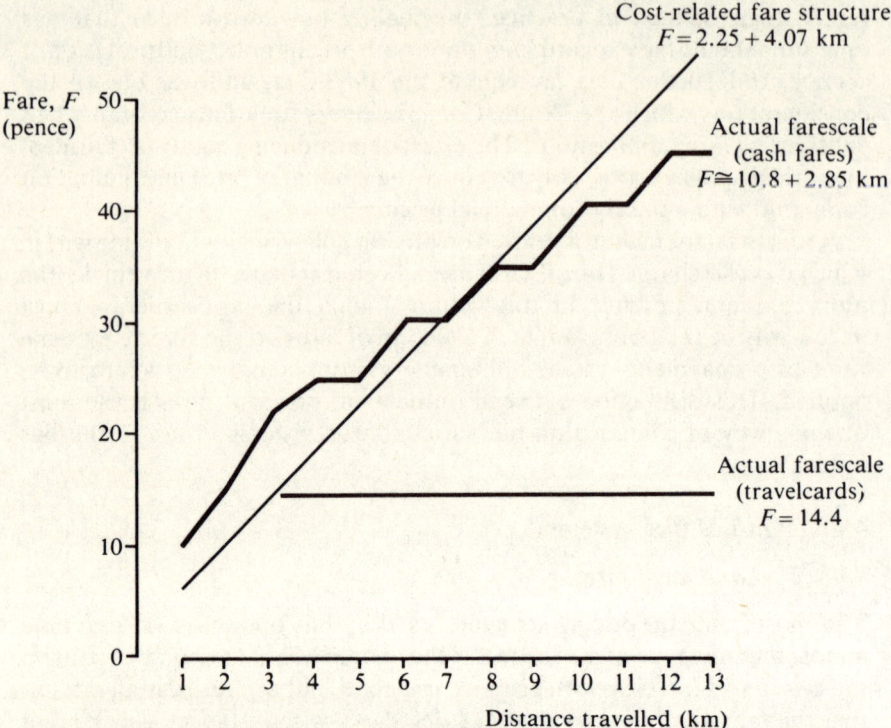

Figure 4.6 Fares in West Midlands, 1980. Both cost-related and actual fare structures are designed to raise the same amount of revenue, but no account has been taken of different fares elasticities for different journey lengths.

the fact that passengers travelling different distances are charged different fares can be interpreted as a form of price discrimination, so the structure bears some relation to the demand curve: it seems intuitively reasonable that passengers travelling longer distances are willing to pay higher fares than those travelling short distances. Paying more for travelling further also tends to be seen as an equitable policy.

It should be pointed out that in practice a bus operator contemplating a fares increase does not take explicit account of the factors we have mentioned. In designing a scale of fares the following considerations are important.

(a) *Yield* The foremost requirement is to design a fare scale which will yield the desired amount of revenue. The bus operator must bear in mind the distribution of passengers according to distance travelled. This distribution is typically fairly skewed towards the short-distance end of the market (see Figure 4.7), so that the fares charged at the

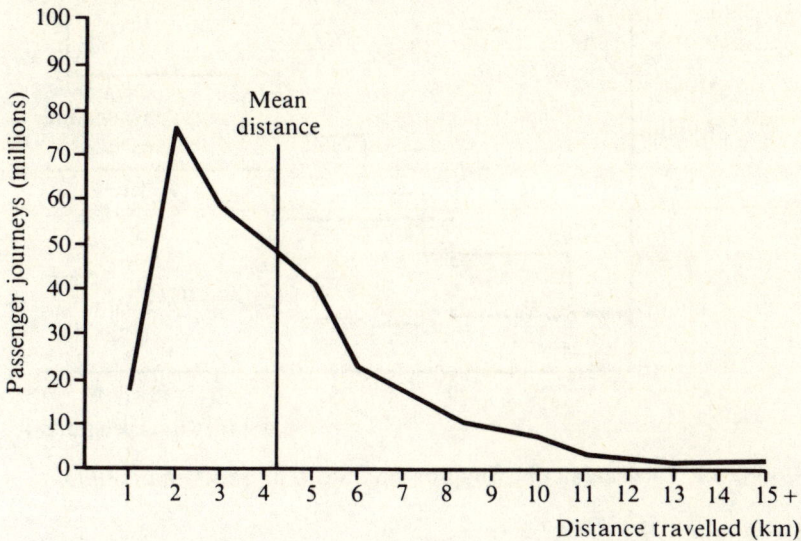

Figure 4.7 Distribution of journey lengths in West Midlands, 1980 (cash fare-payers only).

lower end of the scale are more important, in terms of their effect on yield, than the fares for longer distances.

(b) *Practicality*   The type of ticket-issuing machinery used by the bus operator governs the number of different fares which can be charged in practice. Although modern ticket machines can usually cope with fares of any value, a number of older machines are still in use, even by the largest operators. Furthermore, even where modern ticket machines are used, the need for speedy ticket issue is often paramount, especially in urban areas where the operator has to deal with large volumes of people travelling short distances, and this tends to restrict the number of fare values which can reasonably be used.

(c) *Coinage*   Bus operators like to charge fares which need as few coins as possible, and in the U.K. there is a tendency for bus operators to charge fares in multiples of 5 p. This has the double advantage of assisting the passenger by speeding up boarding rates on one-man-operated buses, and reducing the number of coins which the operator has to deal with. (To see the importance of this, imagine a large bus operator taking £100,000 each day from 500,000 passengers paying 10p, 200,000 passengers paying 15p, and 100,000 passengers paying 20p. If his passengers always use the minimum number of coins he will have to handle 1.1 million coins each day. If the three fares were 11p, 14p and 17p, the number of coins would increase to 1.9 million per day.

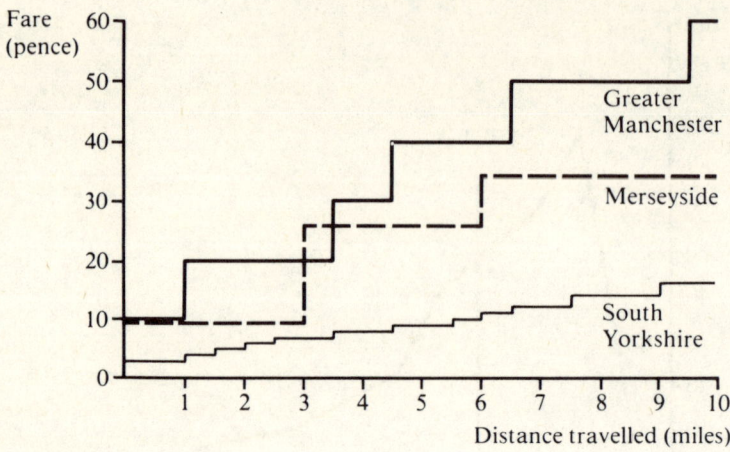

Figure 4.8 Farescales of three bus operators in September, 1980.

This could have a substantial impact on the operator's cash-handling procedures).

(d) *Equitable increase*   There is a tendency when fares are increased to ensure that passengers travelling different distances are treated 'fairly'. If short-distance passengers were subjected to relatively large fares increases at the last fares increase, then the operator will often compensate for this at the next fares increase by charging relatively more to long-distance passengers.

4.4.1.2   *Fine and coarse fare scales*

During the 1960s and 1970s the introduction of one-man operation led many operators to implement fare scales containing fewer fare values, but this move was not universal and in fact there is great variety in the 'coarseness' of different fare scales. Figure 4.8 shows three examples of fare scales actually in force in September 1980. Disregarding the fact that there are differences in the general level of fares between the operators (due to differences in subsidy levels), there are quite striking differences in the number of fares available. The South Yorkshire scale is an example of the finely graduated scale which was once common to all British operators, with thirteen different fares being charged for journeys up to ten miles in length, depending on distance travelled. In Merseyside only three fares are charged for the same range of distances, while Greater Manchester is somewhere in between with six fares. The reason for this variety seems to be that the advantages of coarser fares are not clear cut. Although a simplified scale can help to speed up boarding rates on one-man-operated vehicles, there are other ways of achieving this (e.g. use of pre-paid tickets, push-button ticket machines, no change-giving). Moreover, there are definite disadvantages from coarsening the scale: we noted earlier that one of the problems of graduated fare systems is that passengers whose journeys involve a change of bus have to pay a higher fare, for the distance travelled, than passengers using a single bus. This problem tends to be exacerbated with coarser fare scales. Secondly, a coarse fare scale is less flexible so that the range of fare options open to the operator is more limited.

4.4.1.3   Flat fares
The ultimate in coarse fare scales is to charge a single fare for any journey, no matter how far. Flat fares are sometimes found outside the U.K. (e.g. Athens, Hong Kong) but there are no examples of their use in this country, at least for ordinary fares paid on the bus. The recent introduction of 'travelcards' in many metropolitan areas (see p. 95) is however a form of flat fare.

4.4.1.4   Zonal fares
In some simplified fares systems, notably on the Continent, the network is divided into a series of overlapping zones rather than fare stages. The fare paid depends on the number of zones through which the passenger travels, and the overlaps between zones enable the operator to overcome one of the problems of graduated fare systems, i.e. the fact that a passenger travelling to the stop just past the fare stage is charged the fare to the following stage. When fares are coarsened the 'jumps' between fares tend to be quite large, so the advantages of a zonal fare structure become important. Having said that, the practical problems of drawing up a fair and sensible network of zones often defeat the objectives of introducing zonal fares in the first place, and in practice a zonal fare system may be regarded as no more than a special kind of coarse fare scale.

4.4.1.5   Time differentials
There are two reasons why we might expect bus operators to charge higher fares at peak periods. In the first place, the marginal costs of bus service provision are higher at peak compared with off-peak periods (see Chapter 3), so differential fares will prevent resources being wasted. Secondly, demand elasticities are lower at peak periods (see Chapter 2), so reductions in off-peak fares to compensate for increases at peak periods will tend to produce a net gain in patronage. Despite these arguments in favour of differential fares, the almost universal practice is for common fares at all times of day. It is sometimes argued in urban areas that peak surcharges will tend to encourage passengers to transfer to private cars, thereby adding to road congestion, and that in the absence of marginal

social cost pricing on the roads it is right to reduce bus fares, but although this might be a valid argument for subsidizing peak period bus operations, it is no justification for the common practice of using profitable off-peak services to subsidize unprofitable peak services. A second argument often used by operators against differential fares is that they cause operational problems at the changeover times between peak and off-peak. It should be noted, however, that this has not prevented many operators from imposing limitations on the use of pensioners' concessionary passes at peak periods.

4.4.1.6   Route differentials

The arguments in favour of differential pricing according to time of day are in principle equally valid when applied to individual bus routes. Fare differentials between routes are, however, even less common than fare differentials between time periods. A rather special example is found in Hong Kong, where a different flat fare applies on each route. The arguments against route differentials are more justified especially where graduated fares are used. The imposition of different fare scales on different routes would give rise to administrative problems, it would not be easily understood by the passenger, and it would give rise to anomalies on roads served by more than one route. Furthermore, cost differences between routes are often simply a reflection of differences in the 'peakiness' of the schedule, and would therefore tend to be taken account of by peak and off-peak fare differentials applied across the board.

4.4.2   Pre-paid Tickets

The growth of one-man-operation and the increasing problems of collecting fares on the bus led to widespread use of systems in which travel is paid for in advance and off the vehicle. In principle any kind of ticket could be purchased in this way — in some continental undertakings, for example, it is possible to buy single tickets from automatic machines located in shops and the street — but usually one of the main features of a pre-paid ticketing system is that it enables the sale of bulk travel at a discount.

There are a number of advantages to be gained from prepayment:

1 It enables speedier boarding on one-man-operated vehicles, leading to reductions in operating costs and time savings for the passenger.
2 It reduces the volume of change-giving required on the bus.
3 Cash paid in advance enables additional interest to be earned.
4 It induces a commitment to travel and may encourage journeys which would not otherwise have been made.

Three types of pre-paid ticket are common in this country: season tickets, multi-journey tickets, and travelcards.

4.4.2.1 Season Tickets
Season tickets are purchased for travel over a period of time (e.g. one month) for journeys between specified points. The price paid depends on the ordinary fare for the journey in question, but with a discount. Season tickets are administratively cumbersome and are mostly used where there are large numbers of people regularly making a similar journey, e.g. schoolchildren.

4.4.2.2 Multi-journey tickets
These are strips of card which can be used for a specified number of journeys, the card being 'cancelled' each time a bus is boarded. They are more flexible than season tickets because they are not confined to journeys between specified points and because there is no period of time after which they are invalid — they may therefore be attractive to occasional as well as regular users. A disadvantage is that they require special cancelling machines to be installed on the bus if the advantage of faster boarding is to be achieved. Operators who have used multi-journey tickets have often found them a difficult concept to market to the public.

4.4.2.3 Travelcards
The formation of the Passenger Transport Executives in the late 1960's/early 1970's, with their specific duty to integrate the public transport systems in their areas, acted as a spur to the development of system-wide passes. These passes, marketed under various names (Saver Seven in Manchester, Metro Card in West Yorkshire, Travelcard in West Midlands) may be given the general name of 'travelcards'. Unlike point-to-point season tickets, travelcards are valid for any journey undertaken within a defined area (which may be a whole county or a subdivision of it); unlike multi-journey tickets, they do not require special equipment on the bus, and they have proved to be a very attractive marketing concept. Figure 4.9 illustrates the growth in sales of the West Midlands travelcard since its introduction in 1972.

Travelcards are usually offered at a price which represents a generous discount to long-distance passengers and to passengers whose regular journeys involve a change of bus — in this respect travelcards act as a form of through ticket. They are usually valid for either one week or one month. Most PTEs offer travelcards which allow unlimited rail, as well as bus travel.

To the economist, travelcards present an apparent paradox. Most passengers who use them travel at peak periods, so that peak fares are effectively *lower* than off-peak fares. But we saw earlier that, looked at both from the supply side and the demand side, the economist would expect peak fares to be *higher* than off-peak fares. As demonstrated by

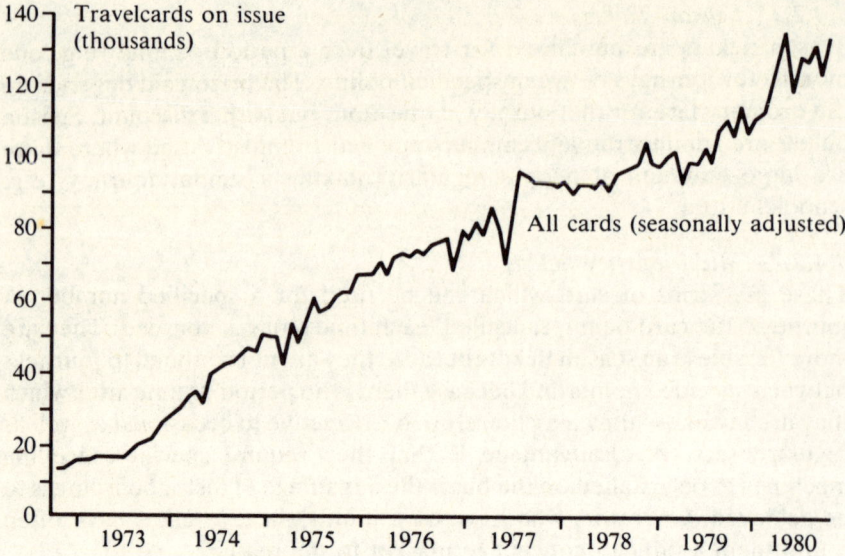

Figure 4.9 WMPTE Travelcard sales.

Tyson[9] and White[10] the paradox can be resolved both in terms of the wider social benefits associated with travelcards and on commercial grounds.

Tyson estimated the costs and benefits to different sections of the community associated with Saver Sevens in Manchester. There were substantial gains to Saver Seven users and other bus users owing to the price discount and reductions in boarding times. Losses were incurred in other sectors of the economy and by the PTE but were not sufficient to outweigh the benefits associated with the tickets, largely because *all* bus users gained and the PTE had reduced operating costs. (See Chapter 6 for a discussion of social cost benefit analysis.)

White examined the impact of the West Midlands travelcard and noted that its users were significantly less price-responsive than ordinary fare-paying passengers. Travelcards also resulted in savings in operating costs owing to faster boarding rates. White calculated that, although the PTE incurred losses during the first few years of operation, the traffic-retention effect plus the cost saving resulted in net gains when the system was implemented over a number of years.

4.5   Pricing for the use of road space

A farm worker driving to work at six a.m. will probably find the roads uncongested and the chances of him delaying other motorists are fairly slight. A motorist leaving the office in an urban area at five p.m., however, almost certainly will find congested conditions, will add to this congestion and, therefore, will impose delay on other road users. It has been estimated that an additional two mile journey in London imposes costs on other road users worth about 25 pence and nearly 50 pence in more congested conditions[11]. These comprise time and operating costs and about one-third fall on public transport users and operators.

Earlier in the chapter we outlined a prescription for optimum resource allocation — marginal social cost pricing. So if we undertake a rail journey the price we pay should, depending on the exact circumstances, closely reflect the *marginal* cost of our journey in terms of rolling stock and staff provision and that of the track and other infrastructure. If our journey imposes social costs such as noise or air pollution the price should reflect that too. When most of us decide to make a car journey we probably do not consider its true marginal costs. We usually take into account only our fuel and time costs and there must be few of us who consider the delay we impose on other road users. If we were obliged to pay the true marginal costs of our car journey, including those of road provision, and our social costs, in terms of the delay we cause other road users, then perhaps we may not make quite so many journeys. This is the basis of the economists' solution to road congestion. We can discuss it more formally with the aid of Figure 4.10.

DD is the demand curve for road space along a particular stretch of road. As the number of vehicles on the road increases beyond a certain level *OE* (determined by the capacity of the road), the average speed will fall and as a result average costs will rise. Demand will settle at OG where the marginal private cost and demand curves intersect and the average cost will be *OB*.

If it were possible to adopt a marginal social cost pricing approach the price will be *OC* and flow, or demand, *OF*. Beyond that flow every additional road user costs other road users (measured by the marginal social cost curve) more than the benefit he himself obtains from using that road (benefit as measured by the demand curve). Moving from flow *OG* to flow *OF* reduces costs by *FKLG* and benefits by only *FKJG*. So if we were able to adopt a marginal social cost pricing policy for the allocation of road space rather than the present system of charging we would save resources equivalent to *KLJ*. Price would be set equal to marginal social cost *OC* and flow would be reduced by *FG* by imposing a charge of *KH* pence. There will still be some congestion in that the road user will impose delays on others. However, economic theory tells us that resources are allocated efficiently as the marginal social cost the user imposes equals the benefit he obtains.

This is the formal economic analysis of the way in which the use of road space might be efficiently allocated by pricing. We do have to pay for the

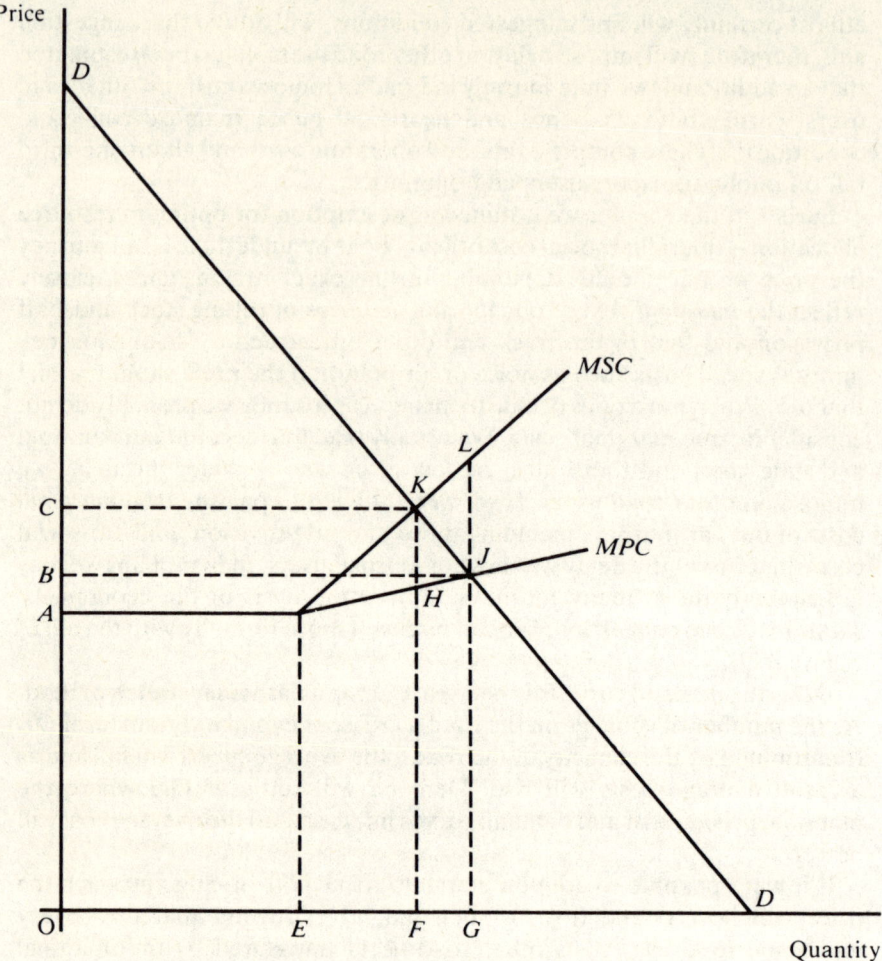

Figure 4.10 Road pricing theory.

use of road space but the way in which we do it is not designed specifically for restraint purposes. We will examine the present system below to see how effective it is as a restraint mechanism. We will also look at the variety of measures proposed to deal with road congestion and judge them against a set of criteria we feel they should meet[12]. These are as follows:

1. Efficiency

(a) To be able to restrain any traffic causing congestion and excluding those who are efficient users of road space or undertaking essential journeys;

(b) To be able to bear on the perceived cost of each journey;

(c) To be flexible in terms of time, area and severity;

(d) To maximize net economic benefits;

2. Practicality

(e) To be simple and cheap to introduce;

(f) To be simple and cheap to administer, and enforce;

3. Fairness

(g) Should not be regressive (i.e. should not impose a greater burden on the poorer road users);

(h) Should minimize the diversion of traffic to unsuitable roads.

4.5.1 The existing method of charging for road space

As we have said the existing method of charging in most countries is not specifically designed for restraint purposes rather it is a means of raising Government revenue. Vehicle owners pay a fixed charge for an excise licence and the price they pay for fuel includes a Government levy. There is often a purchase tax for new cars too. This pricing structure does not accord very closely with the theoretical ideal for two main reasons. Firstly, charges bear only an approximate relationship to the costs vehicles impose in terms of the provision, maintenance and operation of roads. The method by which the Department of Transport allocates such 'track costs' is best described in the form of a chart as in Figure 4.11[13]. Note that community costs such as those for accidents, noise and air pollution are not included. The degree to which excise and fuel tax paid by different vehicle types in Great Britain varies with the costs allocated to them can be seen in Table 4.3.

This topic concerns many people in relation to the environmental consequences of the heavier lorries. The Consultation Document showed that the ratio of revenue to costs of goods vehicles over 30 cwt unladen in 1975/76 in Great Britain was 0.8:1 and 0.7:1 if community costs were included. The ratios for the heavier goods vehicles were even less. For example, that for a rigid 4-axle 30 ton gvw vehicle was 0.6:1 not including community costs. A more recent analysis shows 'underpayers' in the goods vehicle class as shown in Table 4.4. The recent Armitage Inquiry into the effect of the lorry on people and the environment estimated that 4-axle 32.5 ton vehicles in the U.K. would need to pay an extra £800 each year to pay their allocated track costs[14], and government policy is now to increase rates in line with these recommendations.

The second weakness in the present charging system for restraint purposes is that although the fuel tax does increase with vehicle kilometres

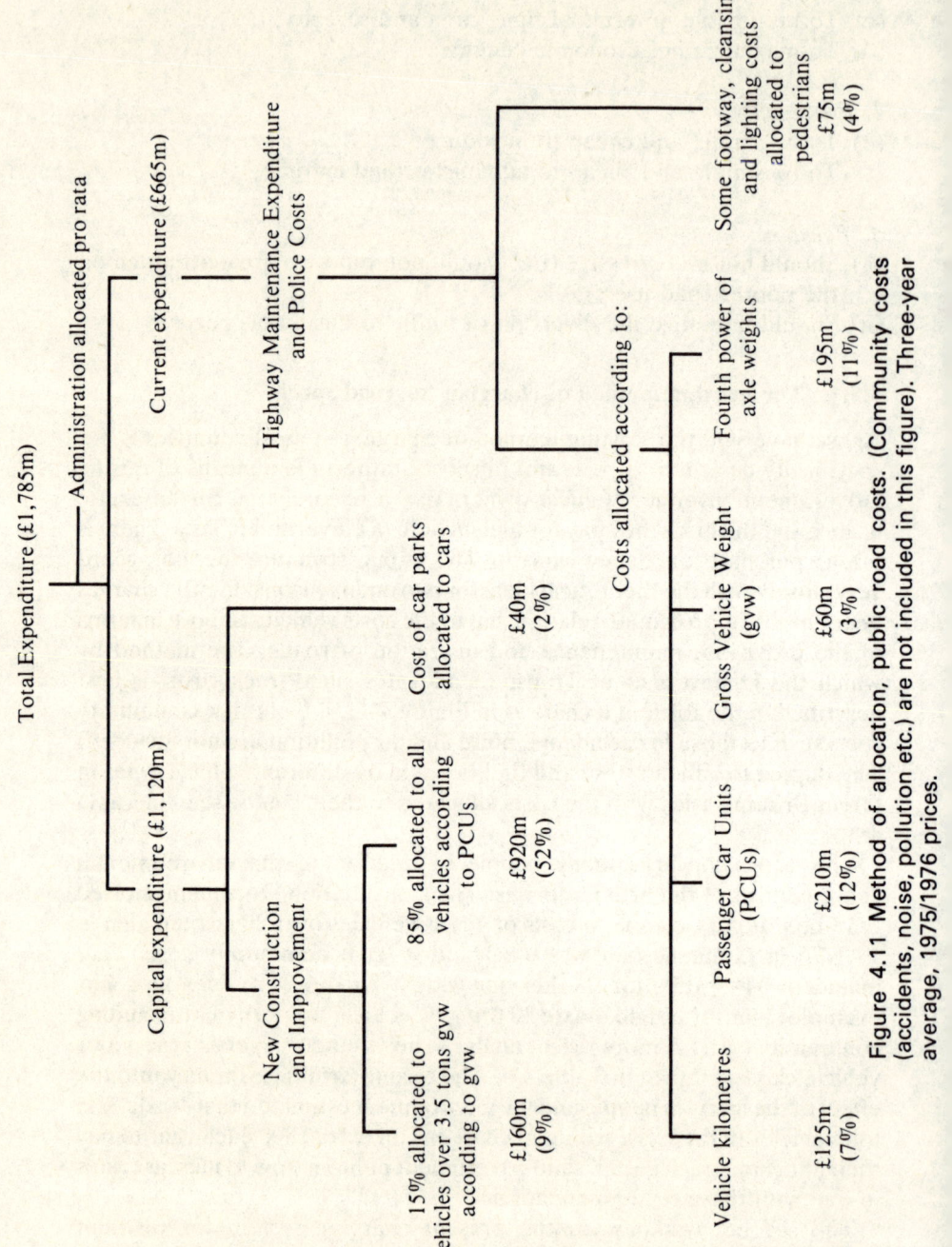

Figure 4.11 Method of allocation, public road costs. (Community costs (accidents, noise, pollution etc.) are not included in this figure). Three-year average, 1975/1976 prices.

it does not increase sufficiently with congestion to have a significant restraint effect. The national medium-term traffic level elasticities with respect to petrol price are about -0.33 and in London it has been estimated that a 1% reduction in road speeds increases operating costs by between 0.2% and 0.3%[11].

Table 4.3 Taxation revenue and public road cost ratios 1975/76, Great Britain

Vehicle category	Vehicle nos 000's	Revenue to cost ratios
Cars and taxis		
non-business	13,760	2.0:1
business		1.5:1
Buses and coaches	75	0.8:1
Light vans (under 30 cwt unladen)	1,085	1.9:1
Goods vehicles (over 30 cwt unladen)	635	0.8:1
All vehicles	15,555	1.5:1

N.B. excluding car tax

Source: *Transport Policy — A Consultation Document* (HMSO: London 1976)

Table 4.4 Underpayment of track costs

Vehicle size (tons)	No. of vehicles	Underpayment per vehicle £	Total £
32	85,400	793	67,722,000
31	500	628	314,000
30	13,700	416	5,699,200
29	100	116	11,600
3 axle 24	25,800	104	2,683,000
3 axle 23	400	115	46,000

Source: J. Wardroper, *Juggernaut* (Temple Smith: London, 1981)

If we do regard the existing system of charging as a means of restraining traffic then compared with several of the others it has the advantage of being tried and tested and is relatively simple to administer.

The various proposed traffic restraint measures fall into the main categories of (a) pricing methods — road pricing, supplementary licencing and cordon pricing (b) physical control and (c) parking control (which includes both physical and pricing methods).

4.5.2   Restraint measures using pricing

5.5.2.1   Road pricing
This has yet to be tried anywhere but is the nearest to the theoretical ideal outlined above. One method would require each of us to have a meter in our car which would be triggered by a cable in the road as we enter a restricted area. The system is designed so that the rate at which the meter reading changes can be varied with the level of congestion by geographical area and time period. At regular intervals we would take our vehicle to a meter reading station for payment. Another method is to have a centralized recording machine which adds to your account as signals (which identify your vehicle) are received when you pass over cables in the road. Your account is sent at regular intervals listing your unit consumption as the telephone company does.

So with either method a unit would have to be installed in the vehicle. Two obvious problems are the cost of introduction and possible fraud and there is the question of how to deal with visitors to an urban area or, if the system is to be nationwide, with those from abroad. There is also the delicate problem of having your movements monitored!

JUDGEMENT

1. Efficiency
(a) *Selectivity*   It would be a simple matter to exclude certain vehicle types and journey purposes (However, deciding what constitutes a journey purpose which merits exemption might be difficult. Medical personnel and emergency services would be obvious exemptions. Some might argue that those going about their business such as salesmen needing cars to carry samples and having to travel in peak times should be exempted. Economic theory would find recourse in the pricing mechanism and suggests that the importance of the journey would be reflected in 'willingness to pay'. So with the obvious exceptions the only decision maker in this context is the consumer not the transport planner.
(b) *Perceived cost*   This system has the obvious advantage, if the meter/unit has a visual display, of indicating to the driver the true marginal cost of each trip.
(c) *Flexibility*   It is also the most flexible. It can vary the charge by area and time of day to a fine degree.
(d) *Maximizing benefits*   It has been suggested[12] that road pricing will not be the best method for maximizing benefits because of the expense and difficulty in setting optimum prices.

2. Practicality
(e) The costs of introducing the system in the U.K. were put at £1,000 million in 1964 in administration and control of fraud would present problems.

3. Fairness
(f) There is a big question mark against road pricing on equity grounds as most pricing methods will discriminate against poorer consumers but given the relationship between car use and income it can be argued with some confidence that such a system would be progressive rather than regressive[15].
(g) There is the possibility that traffic will divert to unsuitable roads, where the increase in noise and air pollution levels will be more significant.

4.5.2.2   Cordon pricing
A cordon will be drawn around the restricted area and toll booths would be constructed where radial roads intersect. As you enter the inner area a charge is imposed. This has not yet been tried in an urban area although, of course, there are many examples of tolls at bridges, tunnels and on truck roads.

JUDGEMENT

1. Efficiency
(a) *Selectivity*   It would be possible to discriminate in favour of high occupancy cars. However, once the motorist is inside the restricted area he can travel and cause as much congestion as he wishes at no extra charge.
(b) *Perceived cost*   The cost of entering the area is explicit but for the reason described above the perceived cost does not bear on each journey within the restricted area.
(c) *Flexibility*   Although the cordon area is fixed, variation with time of day would be possible.
(d) *Maximizing benefit*   This method would compare quite favourably with the others in terms of maximizing benefits.

2. Practicality
(e) If suitable sites for toll booth location with adequate space for queuing vehicles can be found then this system is probably one of the easiest methods to introduce. You might try drawing a cordon on a street map of a city known to you to enclose the congested area. Decide how many crossing points would be needed and try to determine their exact location. You might find this no simple task. Administration and enforcement should present no major problems.

3. Fairness

(f) The same arguments may be applied with cordon pricing as with road pricing.

(g) There may well be diversion to unsuitable roads as motorists attempt to by-pass the restricted area.

4.5.2.3 Supplementary Licencing

This system was introduced in Singapore in 1975. The restricted zone covered about 500 ha and had 22 entry points. To use the restricted area a supplementary licence costing approximately $1.7 U.S. in 1978 had to be obtained and displayed in the vehicle. The scheme was designed to operate from 07.30 h to 10.15 h. Park and ride schemes were introduced to compliment the scheme. The before and after study[16] shows that the number of cars entering the restricted zone between 07.30 h and 10.15 h fell by 73%. There was evidence that the peak period was reduced in intensity by motorists driving to work earlier. The volume of cars entering the zone in the half hour prior to 07.30 h increased by 23%. The Singapore authorities appear satisfied with the results of the experiment and it is obvious that its success is due mainly to good planning and management. The public were well educated in the mechanism and aims of the scheme and the planners were prepared to take a pragmatic approach, monitoring performance and making necessary changes.

JUDGEMENT

1. Efficiency

(a) *Selectivity*   The system is selective in that all congested roads can be covered but those travelling in non-congested directions would be penalized too.

(b) *Perceived cost*   If the licences are given on a weekly, or even a daily, basis then the perceived cost of each journey is not apparent.

(c) *Flexibility*   The time of operation can be varied but varying charges with time would be difficult.

(d) *Maximizing benefits*   The Singapore study referred to above estimated a rate of return of 15%. This was based on the assumed value of time of between 25 and 30% of the average wage rate. The calculation included the capital cost of fringe car parks, shuttle bus facilities, signs and ticket booths, and was based on net travel time savings only. Licence revenues exceeded operating costs (including policing) by $6 million per annum, which amounted to an annual cost return to the Government of more than 90% of the total capital cost.

2. Practicality

(e) It has been successfully introduced in Singapore but there was the advantage of a clearly defined Central Business District. Cities with a land-use distribution like Hong Kong might find it more difficult!

3. Fairness

(f) The same argument regarding the possible regressiveness of such a pricing system apply. It would depend to some extent on how revenues are distributed.

(g) The Singapore experience is that diversion to roads outside the restricted zone did occur.

4.5.2.4 Physical restraint

This covers a rather large number of measures which are designed to delay or divert vehicles enabling entry to the congested area to be controlled. These might include the reduction of road capacity by, for example, introducing bus lanes or by creating controlled access points with Area Traffic Control schemes. The Nottingham zone and Collar Scheme is an oft quoted experiment but many towns and cities use area-wide co-ordinated traffic light systems.

JUDGEMENT

1. Efficiency

(a) *Selectivity*   Such measures may not be very selective unless priority vehicles can be exempted. High occupancy cars might be allowed to use bus lanes but in an area-wide control scheme it may be difficult to make such provision. Policing a general rule 'No right turn except buses, high occupancy vehicles and doctors' might present problems for example! Certainly in the Nottingham experiment it was difficult to prevent motorists 'jumping' the lights at junctions designed to restrict access to main radial routes.

(b) *Perceived cost*   The delays incurred by motorists would bear directly on the perceived cost of each journey but they would need to be very high to change the modal split between private and public transport significantly.

(c) *Flexibility*   By restricting the hours of operation and changing traffic light settings the system could be quite flexible, particularly if the system is responsive to the actual traffic flow at any one time.

(d) *Maximizing benefits*   Because these measures work on time delays they are wasting resources and unless there is a significant change in modal choice welfare will not be increased very much. It should be said, however, that individual bus lanes normally show very good rates of return.

2. Practicality

(e) As with cordon restraint the ease of introduction depends very much on the suitability of the road system. However, bus lanes are fairly cheap to lay down, once designed, and Traffic Control systems are fairly common now. As we have already noted, enforcement was a problem with the Nottingham experiment and policing bus lanes is not easy but administration is fairly straightforward.

3. Fairness
(f) As no pricing mechanism is used there is no discrimination against the poorer road user and if the value of time is related to income then the system is to a degree progressive.
(g) Unless schemes are carefully designed there is the possibility of traffic diverting to unsuitable roads.

4.5.2.5   Parking controls
Parking controls have been the most common measure of restraint and comprise both the restriction of parking spaces and charging to deter certain types of traffic.

JUDGEMENT

1. Efficiency
(a) *Selectivity*   Parking controls are inefficient in that they cannot restrict those causing congestion but passing through the area, or using private parking spaces. In Leeds and Bradford it was found that about half the traffic on the approach roads in the morning peak were destined for the centres and of those about half had private parking spaces[12]. So only about a quarter of all the relevant traffic would be affected by a parking restraint policy. Also, in practice the long-term parker is penalized even if he uses the road system outside peak hours. Furthermore, congestion may be caused by motorists driving round looking for a space.
(b) *Perceived cost*   The parking charge will bear on the perceived cost of each journey and would discriminate in favour of high occupancy vehicles if the charge is shared.
(c) *Flexibility*   It is possible for parking provision and charging to vary with time of day and area but in practice it seldom does.
(d) *Maximizing benefits*   Operating costs are low and if parking provision is restricted resources will be saved. If a proportion of motorists can be persuaded to arrive and depart outside peak hours then congestion and time delays will be reduced. On the other hand time spent driving round looking, and queuing, for spaces may increase and this will represent a resource cost.

2. Practicality
(e) The system is already tried and tested and is relatively easy to

introduce. There may be conflicts of interests where one body (say, a County Council) wishes to restrain traffic and another wishes to encourage traffic for commercial purposes but, of course, this would apply with all the measures. Administration is relatively simple but enforcement faces problems particularly with on-street parking.

3. Fairness

(f) If the system is based purely on the rationing of spaces then parking controls are progressive. If pricing were introduced the chances are that this would be regressive.

(g) The diversion to unsuitable roads is unlikely.

4.6 Conclusions

This chapter deals with a very important part of transport economics. Pricing is a major tool for allocating our scarce resources, and the way in which pricing policy is pursued can determine the success or failure of individual enterprises. We have seen that economic theory gives a general prescription for pricing efficiently and we noted the problems in adopting it. The importance of market structure on pricing policy was recognized. If we relate this relationship to the MCP principle it is reasonable to conclude that few transport organizations price as the theory recommends. Even in the road haulage sector (where there is evidence of perfect competition and we would expect optimum price/output relationships) prices accepted by individual firms in times of recession do not make for stable long-term equilibrium. The kinds of decision which transport operators have to make when formulating pricing policies are often dominated by practical considerations which have no part in economic theory, and we illustrated this by reference to pricing in the bus industry. We have seen too that pricing theory has so far had little impact on how we allocate road space. At a time when national politics tends to be dominated by economic considerations, it is interesting to reflect that there are some parts of economic theory which have not been fully absorbed into practical policy-making.

Examination questions

1 In economic theory the Hotelling-Lerner pricing rule for public enterprises states that, in order to maximize net social benefits, the level of output should be that at which price is set equal to marginal cost. Set out the reasoning on which this theoretical prescription is based and comment on the practical problems that arise in applying this principle to the services of publicly owned transport undertakings.

2 Discuss the economic considerations which can influence the charges governments levy on road users.

3 'The strict economic approach to pricing would be to ensure that the user pays at least the full marginal resource costs of his transport; then there would be (in theory) no misallocation of resources.' (*Transport Policy. A Consultation Document*, (HMSO: London, 1976) Volume I). Discuss.

4 What are the advantages and disadvantages of transport undertakings charging for their services in accordance with 'what the traffic will bear'?

5 'In an ideal world there might be no need for government intervention in transport policy. A perfectly functioning market could be left to determine the quantity, quality and price of transport services according to consumer preference and subject to resource constraints. The government's role in the transport sector would be confined to that of a producer and a consumer.' (P. C. Stubbs, W. J. Tyson and M. Q. Dalvi, *Transport Economics*). Comment on this statement.

6 'There is a strong argument for lorry taxation to be more systematically related than it is now to the best estimates that can be made of the resource costs which lorries impose.' (*Transport Policy. A Consultation Document*, (HMSO: London, 1976) Volume I). Discuss.

7 'In situations which are quite common in urban areas the real costs imposed by car use may be greater than the perceived costs faced by the motorist.' (*Transport Policy. A Consultation Document*, (HMSO: London 1976) Volume 2). Explain this statement and indicate its policy implications.

8 Under what circumstances will a policy of pricing at marginal cost result in the undertaking failing to cover total costs by total receipts? How might a transport undertaking, operating under these circumstances, balance its financial accounts while pursuing a policy which accords with the economic principle of 'marginal-cost pricing'?

9 Argue the case for and against adoption of the marginal-cost pricing principle by state-owned transport undertakings.

10 Outline the economic theory on which it is argued that public undertakings should price their services at marginal cost. Discuss the practical problems that are met in the application of this theoretical prescription to the services of transport undertakings.

5

Subsidies in Transport

5.1   Introduction

In this chapter we shall consider the various forms of subsidy applicable to transport. Therefore, we shall consider cross-subsidization between routes or activities and the effects of hidden subsidies. We shall consider the justification for subsidizing public passenger transport and make international comparisons of subsidy levels. Finally, we shall consider the need for subsidy to ensure the provision of minimum levels of mobility in rural areas.

5.2   Cross-subsidization and contributory revenue

Cross-subsidization exists where one activity does not meet its full costs and is supported by another more profitable activity. This cross-subsidization can exist at many levels, a bus service at certain times of day or on certain days of the week may be cross-subsidized by profitable operation from other times or days on the same route. Identification of the extent of cross subsidy will depend upon the nature of the cost allocation used. Whether the 'peak period' cross-subsidizes the off-peak or vice versa partly depends upon whether the prime purpose of the service is seen as providing an all day service or matching peak demand. This issue was considered in the Bradford Bus Study[1] thus:

> 'The distribution of vehicle costs between the days of the week depends upon what the main purpose of bus operation is assumed to be. If it is to provide a basic service throughout the week (a 'basic service approach'), then it is appropriate to apportion vehicle costs according to the utilization of buses throughout the week.'

Thus the form of cross-subsidization will depend upon the costing philosophy adopted. At a more aggregate level there may be cross-subsidization of certain lightly trafficked routes by busier routes, particularly if these have a uniform, rather than peaked, demand. Traditionally, this approach was adopted by British bus services in the period after the introduction of route licensing in the 1930 Road Traffic Act. In return for *de facto* area monopolies, operators were expected to operate socially desirable but unremunerative routes and cross-subsidize these from profitable routes elsewhere. Although the post-war decline in patronage and profitability has curtailed the practice, it is still used as a justification for restricting competition on stage carriage services. Cross-subsidization and jointness of costs were used, successfully, by Cumberland Motor Services when objecting to competition on Whitehaven town services from a private operator, on the basis that if the viability of town operation was reduced rural operation would have to be curtailed.

Cross-subsidization has also been a practice adopted by the railways, although again the identification of subsidies is complicated by the jointness of costs. However in the 1960s, the Beeching report[2] identified that one third of the route mileage carried only one per cent of the passenger traffic and that one third of the stations produced, in total, less than one per cent of passenger receipts. It was therefore considered under the commercial remit of Beeching that substantial parts of the network were being cross-subsidized and that this could not be justified on commercial terms. Accordingly, a substantial programme of closures of rural and cross country lines took place in the mid 1960s.

This suggests that cross-subsidization is in commercial terms (as opposed to social consideration) a bad thing. However, consideration must be given to the avoidability of costs and to contributory revenue. Suppose a junction station has a marginally profitable main line and a loss-making branch line. The two lines share the facilities of the station such as booking office, signal box etc. and the costs of these are apportioned accordingly. If the branch line is closed it will still be necessary to man the booking office and signal box so these costs will not be 'avoided'. Therefore they will be transferred to the mainline service whose financial performance therefore appears to decline. In addition, passengers may have used the branch line to catch mainline services. Whilst some may still travel to the junction to board this service, others may switch to another mode or cease to travel (indeed results show this is often the case[3]). Therefore revenue, which has contributed to the mainline service because of the existence of the branch line, is lost and again the financial position of the mainline service deteriorates. If the mainline service is now loss-making it in turn might be a candidate for closure, but this would affect the viability of other services with which it shares facilities, such as a terminal station, and contributes revenue. However cross-subsidization *could* be justified if the loss incurred was outweighed by contributory revenue and contribution to shared costs. Thus cross-subsidization is not necessarily incompatible with a 'commercial' or profit-making remit.

5.3 Hidden subsidies

Before considering a formal case for deliberate subsidies, we should note that subsidies can be hidden or unintended. These can occur between groups of users of the same facility and are distinguished from cross-subsidization because they are unintended or covert. The problem that they present is one of misallocation of resources. If an activity is priced below its true cost, then the result may be that the activity is 'over-demanded' (see Chapter 4). In transport terms this could mean that modal split is distorted or, alternatively, if transport as a whole is underpriced then patterns of land use may be excessively transport-intensive.

There are two cases to examine therefore, the first being cross-subsidization within a mode and whether this in turn affects modal split. The second is the consequence of underpricing of a mode as a whole, which can occur if the externalities created by that mode remain uncompensated (see Chapter 4).

In the case of shared costs (see Chapter 4) it is considered that heavy lorries bear too little of the costs of the road network in relation to their usage and damage to the road surface (their track costs). Thus, road transport is underpriced compared to the true cost of the resources used. In consequence, the demand for road freight transport is higher because of the lower price and so freight may be diverted from other modes, such as rail. Doubtless the railways will point to 'unfair' competition and various solutions will be suggested to correct the imbalance. If for whatever reason, perhaps the strength of the road lobby, charging lorries their full track costs is unacceptable, then a subsidy to rail may be used to correct the imbalance in modal costs. Indeed grants are available under section 8 of the 1974 Railway Act to provide sidings, loading equipment and rolling stock to assist the transfer of freight from road to rail. It should be noted however that according to Lipsey and Lancasters' theory of the second best, there is no reason to assume that such a solution is better than leaving the imbalance uncorrected since both solutions are sub-optimum.

The argument can be further developed when consideration is given to the externalities associated with road transport, although road transport is not alone in producing these. In the nineteenth century railways were opposed on grounds that we would now categorize as visual intrusion and the presentation of a hazard in terms of fire and pollution. Air transport also causes substantial uncompensated externalities (see for example Buchanan's 'No way to the airport'[4]). If externalities associated with road transport such as noise, vibration damage to buildings, visual intrusion etc., are uncompensated then road transport is underpriced. Many of the externalities are difficult to price. As an example, research[5] suggests that traffic levels influence peoples' sense of neighbourhood and community. People on heavily trafficked streets are less likely to know their neighbours, have tighter boundaries and have a less positive attitude towards their neighbourhood. How can you value or compensate this externality? Yet unless some attempt is made to correct the imbalance of modal costs caused by uncompensated externalities then modal choice will be distorted.

If it proves impractical to make road users pay their full costs, both private (internal) and social (external), to correct this distortion then an alternative is to subsidize alternative modes or activities in an attempt to correct modal split.

5.4   A justification for subsidies

What then justifies subsidies to transport or to particular aspects of transport operation? There are three general reasons, the first being the role of transport in development as discussed in Chapter 1. Transport can be seen as being the vital infrastructure required to promote industrial growth. It is therefore not necessary for transport to be profitable as such. The various arguments for and against transport's role in development are discussed in Chapter 1 but it should be noted that developing countries do see a role for transport without a specifically commercial remit.

The second reason is to correct modal imbalance caused by one mode not meeting its true costs. This argument can be applied in circumstances where true internal costs are not being met, as in the case of road haulage in Britain, or when true social costs are not being met, which is arguably the case for road transport as a whole (for detailed discussion on these two issues readers are recommended to read the works of Wardroper[6], Tyme[7] and Adams[8]). If we take the case of private car use in peak periods as an example: private cars in these circumstances can cause congestion. As a result the private motorist imposes costs, in terms of additional journey time, on other road users including bus passengers. The private car user is not required to compensate other road users for the costs he imposes on them or society as a whole for the general impact of noise, pollution, visual intrusion and accidents. He also probably feels that whatever the ideal solution from society's point of view a unilateral decision to abandon use of his car will make little impact on the problem as a whole. The increase in bus journey times has three effects. The first is to raise the generalized cost of making a bus journey which, you will recall, is the summation of the fare plus appropriately valued walking, waiting and in-vehicle time. Bus travel is therefore relatively more expensive at the margin, so some passengers will transfer from bus to other modes, possibly walk for some short journeys, or use car or motorcycle for longer journeys. (Also unless demand for bus transport is completely inelastic then some passengers will also cease to travel). Thus the first effect is modal transfer.

The second effect is that slower running times for buses result in less efficient use of vehicles and crews. More resources are required to provide the same capacity. Congestion also results in a decline in service reliability (which in turn may further increase generalized cost) which may require additional supervisors, spare vehicles etc., to correct. Thus the second effect is an increase in operating costs.

The third effect is that loss of patronage as a result of increased journey times reduces revenue whilst attempts to maintain a reliable service increase costs. Therefore the financial position of the bus operator deteriorates. This is the beginning of the fares increase/service cut/passenger loss spiral, for, without subsidy, the bus operator has only two choices to correct the financial imbalance. It can either attempt to reduce costs by cutting services (which in turn is likely to increase waiting times, increase generalized cost and therefore cause passenger and revenue loss) or raise fares, which given some price elasticity of demand will result in passenger loss. This cycle or spiral has been a feature of British bus operation for several decades. The consequences have been a steady modal shift from public to private transport, a decline in the route structure and frequency of public transport operation and an increase in the social costs associated with private transport. Not all of this is due to the congestion effects which were taken as an example but rather to the change in relative modal costs.

If society takes the view that the social costs of this change in modal split are unacceptable, then it can either attempt to internalize for the motorist some of the social costs incurred perhaps by some form of road pricing which takes into account congestion (see Chapter 4). Whilst this is technically feasible, governments have shown themselves unwilling to accept the political consequences. The alternative then is to alter the relative costs of the modes by reducing that of public transport. This can be achieved by improving service frequencies (hence reducing waiting time) improving journey times (by bus priority measures) and by reducing fares (which although increasing patronage rarely results in an improvement in revenue). All these measures require financial support for the bus operator. One area where these policies have been pursued is the Metropolitan County of South Yorkshire which has frozen bus fares since 1975 and improved services.

The third argument consists of a range of social considerations which can be grouped under the heading of equity. Whatever the level of car ownership there are groups who are unable to be car drivers; the young, the elderly, various groups of disabled people, people unable to afford a car. Even car drivers within car owning households do not necessarily enjoy ready access to a car. As Adams[8] states 'estimates of the percentage of the population ever likely to qualify as car drivers even given the improbable assumption of universal affluence suggests that there will always be a minimum of 40 per cent who can never have full participating rights in a car-owning democracy . . . If we reject the assumption of universal affluence as unrealistic and concede that in the foreseeable future there are also going to be very many people too poor to buy cars then it appears unlikely that those with full participating rights will ever be in a majority'.

Thus a majority of people may be denied mobility, or at least comparable mobility to car drivers, unless public transport is available. These people may not be able to pay the full costs of the public transport they require, particularly as increasing car ownership increases the cost burden on remaining public transport passengers. However inability to pay does not necessarily prove absence of need. Economists use the idea of 'revealed preference' by observing conduct and presuming that people act rationally, and with perfect knowledge (see p. 71). It is therefore presumed that if a person is unwilling to pay a fare of £1 then the journey is not worth £1 of 'utility' to that person. This presumes however that the person has £1! A penniless man dying of thirst in the Sahara desert may not be able to pay £1 for a bottle of water but that does not prove that the water has less than £1's worth of utility to him!

5.5 Subsidies in practice — rail

Subsidies in Britain tend to be paid on a modal basis with money for bus revenue support channelled through local government whilst railway support is paid directly by central government to British Rail, except for payments to support rail operation in Metropolitan counties. Subsidy practice has often developed pragmatically probably because of a general absence of national transport planning. Thus, rail subsidies started with deficit financing. The railways, in a run-down state after 1939—1945 war years were taken into public ownership in 1948 along with long distance road haulage, road passenger transport, London Transport, inland waterways and docks. The overall body, the British Transport Commission (BTC) was given the task of ensuring the provision of 'efficient, adequate, economical and property integrated transport'. This implied that transport as a whole should break even, although some modes/activities could cross-subsidize others. Much of the nationalization of the 1947 Act was undone by the 1953 Transport Act but the railways remained in state ownership. They were in poor physical shape and were not earning sufficient revenue to finance investment. A major investment scheme, the 1955 Modernization Plan, was launched at a cost of £1,240 million to provide new investment and improve productivity. The railway's financial performance was however declining, initially by achieving an operating surplus but failing to cover central charges and then in 1956 incurring an operating deficit. As a temporary measure the Transport (Railway Finances) Act 1957 allowed deferrment of interest charges on the accumulating deficit and on the Modernization Plan investment. It was clear that the railways were not viable but the chosen solution was not a recognition of the role of subsidy but a further capital reconstruction under the 1962 Transport Act with provision for limited deficit financing until the railways could break even. A new British Railways Board (BRB) Chairman, Dr Richard Beeching, was given the task of achieving this under what he saw as a purely commercial remit. Accordingly, the Beeching Plan[2] mentioned previously was introduced which it was anticipated would eliminate much of the deficit by 1970. In practice this was not achieved and deficits of £130 million — £150 million per year were incurred during the late 1960s. A Labour Government introduced the 1968 Transport Act which included a further capital reconstruction for the railways, which reduced debt charges and was intended to provide a basis for financial self-sufficiency without further recourse to deficit financing. A major policy change though was the recognition of the distinction between commercial services and socially desirable services. Specific grants on a line by line basis were to be paid and the initial list, covering 222 services at a cost of £61 million, including the bulk of the non-intercity network.

Thus the 1968 Transport Act brought a change from deficit financing to specific subsidy of individual lines. This was further developed by the 1974 Railways Act which introduced the Public Service Obligation (PSO) grant. This was a grant to permit British Rail to operate the existing network, of some 9,000 route miles, at the existing level of service. It was therefore replacing individual service subsidies by a block grant or contract for what has been characterized as the 'Social railway'. The 1974 Act also introduced grants, termed Section 8 grants, towards the installation and equipping of rail freight facilities to encourage modal transfer from road haulage. The PSO then is the main form of rail operating subsidy together with finance for urban rail operation in Metropolitan counties provided under Section 20 of the 1968 Transport Act. The overall subsidies for British Rail are shown in Table 5.1.

It should be noted that the real, as opposed to money, value of the PSO has declined since its inception and in 1982 is some 20% less than in 1975 for a broadly similar network and service level.

Table 5.1

British Rail Subsidies 1982	£ million
P.S.O.	804
Special Replacement Allowance	88 est.
Section 20 Payments	80 est.
	972

5.6   Subsidy practice — buses

In comparing subsidy for bus services and public transport in urban areas we must be aware of institutional differences between countries both in the structure of central/local government and in the ownership of transport operators. The British system is outlined in Chapter 8 and its implications for subsidy described here. Other countries may have more complex local government incorporating a regional tier and subsidy may be provided by both regional and local tiers. Ownership of operators may also vary and although bodies like the British Passenger Transport Executives exist their function may be restricted to co-ordination, planning and the allocation of subsidy without actually owning or operating public transport themselves.

In England bus revenue support in the non-metropolitan, or 'shire' counties is financed through the TPP/TSG system described in Chapter 7. Payments are made to the National Bus Company (NBC) operators in each county and possibly to independent (private) operators and to municipal operators controlled by District Councils. With the exception of schools transport shire counties do not operate in their own right, although it is now possible to carry ordinary passengers on schools' buses. Not all municipal operators have been in receipt of subsidy from shire counties but instead have received specific payments from district councils for facilities such as elderly persons concessionary fares. There may also be an element of cross-subsidization through shared use of workshop and administration facilities with other council activities.

In the Metropolitan Counties, which have Passenger Transport Executives, funds are again provided through the TPP/TSG system and from rate income. The Passenger Transport Executives are bus operators themselves and in the case of Glasgow and Tyne and Wear also operate railways. Subsidies are provided to bus operators, generally NBC although there are some private operators of stage carriage services within PTE areas. Rail subsidies are provided separately through the Section 20 system.

Subsidies in Metropolitan Counties fall into two categories; specific subsidies and general revenue support. Specific subsidies are paid for such items as elderly persons' concessionary fares schemes, whilst the overall network and fare level is subsidized through general revenue support. Subsidy levels have both increased and diverged in Britain in recent years. As a rule of thumb British bus operators have received 90% of their revenue from passengers and 10% in the form of subsidies. In 1981, subsidy payments accounted for 8% of NBC stage carriage revenue. However, differing fares policies between metropolitan authorities have caused wide divergence around this figure. South Yorkshire (which includes Barnsley, Doncaster, Sheffield and Rotherham) has operated a fares freeze since September 1975 with the ultimate objective of providing 'free transport' without direct user charges. Other metropolitan authorities have also had fare policies which have held fare increases below the prevailing level of cost inflation and thus necessitated subsidy. The ability to do this was questioned in the courts by the challenge to the GLC's 1981 'Fares Fair' 25% fares reduction which was ruled to be inconsistent with London Transport's statutory obligations. However, the legislation involved—the 1969 Transport (London) Act—is separate from the 1968 Transport Act provisions governing the conduct of the PTE's which therefore escaped similar challenge.

The general performance of the PTE's is set out in Table 5.2 and it will be noted that, where comparative figures are available, subsidy proportions have increased sharply. Many British operators receive 25% of their income in the form of subsidy whilst South Yorkshire's operation covers only a third of its operating costs from passenger receipts. Comparable figures for overseas operators show that the majority raise only one half of their income from passenger receipts with the rest coming from central or local government sources. In consequence, fares seem modest by British standards; a monthly season ticket in Paris covering all inner city bus and rail travel costs less than £6 in 1981. Subsidy levels are, in consequence, higher. RATP in Paris receives some £350 million in 1980 from central government, local government and a commuters tax levied on employers, whilst L.T. received £150 million.

So far we have considered subsidy in the urban context, aiming to influence modal split although also recognizing the needs of the non-motoring public. The prospect for these is indeed grim if some of the predictions of increasing car usage combined with the reduction or complete withdrawal of public transport come to pass.

5.7   The rural transport problem

5.7.1   Defining a rural area

There is no simple definition of a rural area nor do rural areas necessarily share a similar range of characteristics. Features we might expect are low

Table 5.2   Farebox ratios of major European urban transport undertakings

	Income from passengers as a proportion of operating costs (%)	
	1971	1979
Glasgow	97	76
Greater Manchester	97	75
Merseyside	108	59
London	106	75
South Yorkshire	N.A.	35
Tyne and Wear	N.A.	68
West Midlands	N.A.	76
West Yorkshire	N.A.	75
Barcelona	101	38
Berlin	55	39
Brussels	56	30
Dublin	108	58
Frankfurt	54	50
Hamburg	81	67
Helsinki	52	49
Lyon	94	59
Milan	N.A.	29
Munich	87	52
Paris	65	44
Rotterdam	47	28
Stockholm	62	43
Stuttgart	72	50
Zurich	88	65

Operating costs exclude expenditure on capital and on depreciation and renewals.
N.A.=Not Available
Source: J. E. Allen *Public Transport Who Pays* Nottingham University Conference paper

population density (see Table 5.3) a relatively high proportion of the workforce in agriculture and related industries and a high proportion of people travelling a significant distance to work and school. Some rural villages may be in decline as job opportunities are reduced by the mechanization of agriculture and the collapse of other local industry such as mining. Other rural areas adjoining urban areas may be expanding with a new role as dormitory areas, yet others may have an influx of second home owners. Thus there is a diversity of rural types but one feature that these areas do share is the relatively high cost of providing services, including transport.

Table 5.3   Relative population densities: England

Region/metropolitan counties	Population density (Number Km^2)
Northern	201
Tyne and Wear MC	2,158
Yorkshire and Humberside	316
West Yorkshire MC	1,014
South Yorkshire MC	836
East Midlands	240
East Anglia	146
South East	618
Greater London	4,378
Outer Metropolitan Area	587
Outer South East	277
South West	180
West Midlands	396
West Midlands MC	3,016
Nort West	889
Merseyside MC	2,385
Greater Manchester MC	2,070

Source: *Social Trends, 1980* (HMSO: London, 1981).

5.7.2   Rural transport provision

Rural transport provision can be subdivided into private (car, motorcycle) and public (stage carriage bus, schools and contract buses and railways). Table 5.4 shows that rural areas have relatively high levels of car ownership and this is often cited as 'proof' that there is no need for public transport provision.

Thus rural regions such as East Anglia and the South West have a significantly smaller proportion of households with no car (34% and 35% respectively compared with the national average of 43%) and quite high rates of two car ownership (15% and 14% respectively).

That high levels of car ownership exists is not in itself proof that such levels are desired or can be readily afforded. Some families endure considerable hardship in order to be able to own a car because it provides the only means of transport to work and this may be described as enforced or unwanted car ownership.

Public transport in rural areas is in serious decline. The railway closures of the 'Beeching era' in the 1960s, deprived many areas of railway services. Whilst the 1974 Railways Act stabilized the railway network and provided finance for rural lines through the Public Service Obligation (PSO) its real value has declined and vital renewals and maintenance have been deferred. Unless additional funds are provided further closures of rural lines are

Table 5.4 Households with regular use of car(s) by economic planning region: December 1978

	No Car %	One Car only %	Two or more cars %
North	50	41	9
Yorkshire and Humberside	49	41	9
East Midlands	40	47	13
East Anglia	34	51	15
South East			
(excluding Greater London)	33	49	18
Greater London	46	42	11
South West	35	51	14
West Midlands	41	46	13
North West	48	41	11
Wales (mid-1979)	38	49	13
Scotland	52	39	9
Great Britain (Average)	43	44	13

Any discrepancy between the sum of the constituent parts and the total is due to rounding.
Source: *Transport Statistics Great Britain, 1970–1980* (HMSO: London, 1981).

likely. Bus services are also in decline. The National Bus Company (NBC), a major operator of rural services, cut its vehicle fleet by 25% from 21,830 vehicles in 1970 to 15,981 in 1980, whilst stage carriage mileage operated was cut by 8% between 1980 and 1981. Some replacement services are provided for certain journey purposes. Contract vehicles may be used for school and certain work journeys and the easing of licencing restrictions may permit these to carry fare-paying passengers as well. The network of post buses is expanding, but the timing of such services is geared to the requirements of mail collection and delivery, thus making them suitable for only certain journey purposes such as shopping, whilst excluding others such as the journey to work and hospital visiting. In some areas various forms of community efforts such as lift sharing schemes, volunteer-driven minibuses and shared taxis seek to provide minimum mobility.

One explanation of the rapid decline of rural public transport lies in low subsidy levels. Table 5.5 shows some comparisons of accepted expenditure on transport. (See also p. 175).

It will be noted that the metropolitan counties spend a significantly higher proportion of their transport expenditure on public transport support. Clearly, there are a variety of reasons for this contrast including

Table 5.5   Transport supplementary grant 1981/82 accepted expenditure

County	Public transport revenue support £ m	%	Highway maintenance other current and capital expediture £ m	%	Total £ m
Greater Manchester	24.488	44.3	30.806	55.7	55.294
West Yorkshire	17.030	33.6	33.658	66.4	50.688
West Midlands	10.800	21.8	38.796	78.2	49.596
Cornwall	1.160	9.8	10.696	90.2	11.856
Cumbria	1.500	14.3	9.002	86.7	10.502
North Yorkshire	0.900	5.2	16.314	94.8	17.214
Oxfordshire	0.174	2.2	7.565	97.8	7.739

Source: *Transport Statistics 1970–1980* (HMSO: London, 1981)

which party is in power and the relative size of road networks. However, the figures do suggest that support for public transport in non-metropolitan county rural areas is at best 'modest'.

5.8   Why subsidize rural services?

But why should rural public transport be subsidized at all? The first answer concerns the finances and public transport operation, whilst the second concerns social considerations. A first justification is that a combination of factors including increases in car ownership together with changes in shopping and leisure patterns have resulted in a decline in public transport patronage in rural areas and hence in revenue. Given limited scope for generating new business the operator must consider either increasing revenue (through higher fares) or reducing costs (by increasing efficiency or reducing services). Low patronage means that the level of fares increases needed would be intolerable for existing passengers. Scope for improved efficiency may be restricted since one-man operation is already the norm in rural areas and smaller vehicles may offer only marginal cost savings (since staff costs remain similar), whilst lacking the capacity to cater for peaks of demand. The solution is often to reduce services, thus headways are extended until a route may become merely a handful of journeys in turn gradually whittled down until the service ceases altogether. The alternative to this spiral of increasing fares, declining patronage and reduced services may be revenue support.

The second justification depends upon the concepts of accessibility and mobility combined with the contentious issue of equity. The terms mobility and accessibility are often confused as Moseley[9] notes. A simple distinction is that people need access to workplaces, schools, hospitals, shops and recreational opportunities. Such access may be easily achieved if these facilities are located nearby and in urban areas, we may take this degree of accessibility for granted. However, in rural areas population is more dispersed whilst facilities may be concentrated in towns, thus restricting access unless people have mobility. The ability to move is not wanted for its own sake but because it improves the accessibility of basic facilities. Some people such as Adams[8] are wary of too much mobility fearing that it will lead to global uniformity whilst others fear that improving mobility will destroy the essential qualities of attractive areas. This is not a new debate. In 1844, Wordsworth on hearing of the proposal to build a railway from Kendal to Ambleside wrote 'Is there no nook of English ground secure from rash assault[10]', since he feared that the Lake District would be overrun by day trippers from urban Lancashire. These arguments may seem somewhat esoteric to the rural elderly faced with the necessity of making long journeys with little or no public transport available. People lacking mobility are described by Moseley[9] as experiencing mobility deprivation and this may have both social and economic consequences. For example, if a bus service to the nearest town used for shopping trips and access to entertainment is discontinued then, in the absence of access to private transport, shopping may have to be done in the village shop (if there still is one!) which is likely to be more expensive and has restricted choice, a financial impact. School children may be deprived of access to out of school activities and youth club, a difficult to value but, nonetheless real, social consequence. Thus, in the absence of public transport the young, the elderly, the poor, and the disabled may be subject to mobility deprivation and therefore it can be argued that it is 'equitable' in our society to provide some basic level of mobility through public transport and to subsidize it where revenue falls below costs. No such minimum level currently exists and in consequence people do suffer real hardship.

5.9   Measuring the effects of reducing rural services

An example of the effects of a loss of mobility can be found in the Transport and Road Research Laboratory report on reductions in rural bus services[11]. This study considered the impact of the withdrawal or reduction of bus services in three study areas within North Lincolnshire/South Humberside, Northamptonshire and Shropshire, through before and after studies of travel patterns. It found that 'those journeys conventionally considered essential—work, school and medical—were almost without exception still made. Those journeys which were not made were very largely social trips such as visiting friends or relatives; in Shropshire these accounted for over 60% of all last trips. Shopping trips no longer made accounted for over 30% and, at an individual level, were usually lost by virtue of less frequent shopping trips being made rather than such journeys not being made at all'. This suggests then that inconvenience rather than hardship is the general result but what is the value of the lost journey? Quoting the study again 'unless an unrealistically high price is placed on such journeys the net savings achieved by the operating companies will outweigh the aggregate increase in personal costs borne by the former bus passengers'. How can we determine what is a 'realistic' price through to place on the lost journeys? One method might be that of revealed preference described on p. 71; suppose that the journey could still be made by taxi at a fare of £5 but it is still not made. This might suggest that £5 is preferred to the journey and hence the journey is worth less than £5, although the journey was worth the bus fare. However, a difficulty is that this presumes the ability to pay since £5 is a substantial sum for a pensioner. Ability to pay should not be confused with need. Another problem exists where service changes benefit some but at the expense of others. Thus the study notes for two Lincolnshire Services 'those affected for the worse were in the minority and the levels of use of the revised services showed that any fall in use by these respondents was more than offset by an increase in use by other people'. But this ignores the difficulties of making interpersonal comparisons of utility. Suppose the loser is an elderly person sacrificing the only opportunity to visit other members of their family whilst the two gainers are people now able to use the bus to visit a public house for the evening rather than walk. Numerically two gainers outweigh one loser but can we presume that the journeys are of equal value?

The report concluded that financial savings to the operator outweighed the costs to former bus passengers but what of the distributional issues involved? Using a compensation test (see Chapter 6) the gainers (initially the bus company, but ultimately rate payers, and tax payers through avoidance at subsidy) could compensate the losers (the former bus passengers) and still gain so the service changes seem worthwhile. It should be noted that this 'compensation test' does not actually require that compensation be paid. However, suppose the losers are pensioners on low incomes, whilst the gainers are the relatively more affluent tax payers, the effect then is a redistribution from poor to rich, a regressive change so does this alter the desirability of the service changes?

5.10 Possible solutions

What then are the solutions to the problems of rural accessibility? Are the problems transport problems amenable to a transport solution or are there non-transport solutions? Moseley[18] identifies two sets of solutions:

1 To render rural residents more mobile, or to provide mobile services (shops, libraries, surgeries).
2 To use land-use planning policy to persuade people to live closer to centres of service provision,
   or to maintain fixed outlets for rural services.

Mackay and Laing's study of Scotland[12] notes that 'In recent years most suppliers and providers (of service) have taken the former course [improving transport connections] and thus we have seen the closure of local schools and the transport of children to schools outwith the area. The same is true for most health, social and government services'. Yet whilst the solution adapted has been transport-intensive the resources devoted to transport have declined. Mackay and Laing concluded that ' . . . the widespread dissatisfaction with public transport in remote areas, coupled with complaints about high petrol prices, suggests that the alternative policy — local supply on an occasional basis — may be more preferable in current circumstances. This would entail a major change in the policies of suppliers and providers but our interpretation of the results of the CORA [Consumers in the Rural Areas] study is that this is what local people would prefer.

This might imply that subsidy should be redirected. In rural Norway subsidies are paid to shops instead of to transport. However, this approach may only solve certain accessibility problems and still leave a stark contrast between those with and those without private transport, necessitating public transport subsidy to guarantee minimum mobility.

5.11 Conclusion

This chapter has sought to consider the justification for subsidies in transport and to comment on subsidy levels. Two general justifications for subsidy have been advanced to alter modal split in urban areas and to provide minimum mobility for all in rural areas. The recognition of these has been long coming in Britain. As the railways example showed we have moved pragmatically from deficit financing, through specific service subsidy, to a recognition of network support. However, transport operators are often set conflicting aims to be both financially viable and maintain services even in times of declining revenue support. Indeed subsidy is sometimes seen as inherently wrong and financed targets are set paramount, irrespective of the consequences. This suggests that the case for subsidy is still not understood, although hopefully the reader no longer experiences this difficulty!

Examination questions

1 It has often been argued that, as a means of financing unremunerative public transport services, direct subsidies from government sources are to be preferred to the practice of internal cross-subsidization. Why?
2 As instruments of transport management in urban areas, assess the relative merits of:
   (a) traffic restraint
   (b) subsidization of public transport and
   (c) road pricing.
3 'In the case of rural transport the growth of private transport may be responsible for the drastic fall in public transport services, but curtailing private transport is not the best way of restoring them.' (C. A. Nash, Public versus Private Transport, Macmillan, 1976). Discuss.
4 In reviewing the financial problems of public passenger transport, the British Government has argued that 'generalized or undiscriminating subsidies are economically insufficient and socially wasteful'. (*Transport Policy. A Consultation Document* (HMSO: London, 1976) Volume I). Discuss critically.
5 For what reasons do some economists prefer direct subsidies from government sources to the practice of cross-subsidization, as a means of financing unremunerative public transport services?
6 Argue the economic case for and against the subsidization by government authorities of public passenger transport services.
7 The British Government has stated that 'to cross-subsidize loss-making services amounts to taxing remunerative services provided by the same undertaking, and is as objectionable as subsidizing from general taxation services which have no social justification'. (*The Economic and Financial Objectives of Nationalized Industries*, White Paper Cmnd. 3437 1967). Discuss, with particular reference to the finance of unremunerative public passenger services.
8 British Rail operates a number of unremunerative services, the retention of which is deemed to be desirable for 'social' reasons. For such services, the central Government makes a direct grant, to cover the deficit between cost and revenue. Discuss the problems involved in determining the amount of grant required in respect of services over a particular route.
9 To what extent might a policy of supplying public transport free of charge help in reducing the scale of the 'urban transport problem'?

6

Investment

6.1 Introduction

The need to replace obsolete equipment, or the possibility of expanding the business, involve important decisions in any firm. As most investments require relatively large amounts of money to be spent now on equipment which will last for a number of years and on which a positive profit will only be realized after a period of time, it is necessary to have methods of comparing the returns in the future with the money to be spent now. In transport, as in other industries, these investment criteria are important to the efficiency and profitability of firms. This chapter will therefore be concerned to answer questions such as:

1 If a haulage firm sees an opportunity to expand its market, how should it decide whether additional lorries should be purchased?
2 If the firm's maintenance facilities are becoming obsolete, how does it decide when to replace them — would it be worth postponing replacement for another year?

The particular importance of 'investment' as a subject in transport derives, however, from the existence of large-scale expenditures for which conventional financial criteria are inappropriate, for example road-building. The chapter will also be concerned therefore with methods which have been developed to answer questions such as:

1 How does the Department of Transport decide whether it is worth building a by-pass around a country town?
2 If there are two by-passes proposed in different parts of the country, and financial restrictions mean that only one can be built, how does the Department choose between them?
3 How can the costs and benefits of closing unremunerative rail lines be assessed?

Investment criteria are therefore used:

1 To decide whether to replace obsolete plant and machinery,
2 To decide whether to expand and purchase new equipment,
3 To choose between projects,
4 To optimize the timing of investment.

This chapter begins with a brief consideration of two investment criteria which are still sometimes used, despite their disadvantages. These are the Average Rate of Return method and the Pay Back Method. The main reason for including these methods is that their drawbacks serve to indicate some of the desirable features of an investment criterion. We then turn to the technique known as Discounted Cash Flow, which is the preferred method of appraising projects with financial returns. The remainder of the chapter is concerned with a description of the method developed for public sector projects for which financial criteria are inappropriate, i.e. Cost Benefit Analysis.

6.2   Average rate of return

The average gross return on an investment can be calculated simply as the sum of the net benefits of the project, divided by the project's life to get an average benefit value per year, and expressed as a percentage of the initial capital expenditure. For example, Table 6.1 shows the net returns in each year which the CARRIO general haulage company expects to achieve if it

Table 6.1   Carrio General Haulage Company returns from purchase of new lorry

Year	Return £000
1	10
2	10
3	9
4	8
5	7
6	6
7	6
8	6
9	6
10	12
Gross return	80
Initial capital cost	50
Net return (80−50)	30

buys a new lorry at a cost of £50,000. The returns consist of increased income for the firm as a result of expanding the business, less tax and depreciation, plus the lorry's scrap value of £6,000. It is assumed that the lorry's useful life to the firm will be ten years. The gross return on the investment is £80,000, and the average return per year is 80,000/10 or £8,000, and the *average rate of return* is 8,000/50,000×100=16%. If the firm had to choose between buying a new lorry, and say, renewing its maintenance facilities so as to reduce costs and become more competitive, it would choose that project with the larger average rate of return.

An alternative way of measuring the average rate of return is to calculate the average *net* return on an investment. In the example, the total net return is the gross returns less the initial investment, i.e. £80,000−£50,000=£30,000. The average net return is therefore £3,000 per year, and the *average net rate of return*, calculated in this way, is 3,000/50,000×100=6%. Other ways of calculating the average rate of return will produce different rates although, if applied consistently, they will each produce the same ranking when comparing different projects. However, all methods of calculating the average rate of return suffer from two disadvantages.

(a) They take no account of *when* returns occur.
(b) They do not distinguish between projects with differing lives.

Table 6.2   Alternative investments

Year	Return £000			Cumulative returns		
	Project A	Project B	Project C	Project A	Project B	Project C
1	10	20	10	10	20	10
2	10	20	10	20	40	20
3	9	5	10	29	45	30
4	8	5	10	37	<u>50</u>	40
5	7	5	10	44	55	<u>50</u>
6	6	5	5	<u>50</u>	60	55
7	6	5	5	56	65	60
8	6	5	5	62	70	65
9	6	5	5	68	75	70
10	12	5	5	80	80	75
11	—	—	3			78
12	—	—	2			80
	80	80	80			

Pay Back Period with capital cost £50,000   6 yrs   4 yrs   5 yrs.

To see the force of these disadvantages, Table 6.2 compares the lorry example of Table 6.1 with two alternative projects. All three projects have a total return of £80,000 and would give identical rates of return using each of the above formulae. But Project B produces twice as great a return in the first two years compared with Project A — shouldn't this be taken into account? And Project C produces the same total return but only after 12 years, compared with 10 years for Projects A and B — shouldn't this also be taken into account?

6.3 Pay back period

The pay back period is another means by which investments are traditionally compared. The pay back period can be defined as the number of years which are expected to elapse before the cumulative sum of net returns equals the initial capital expenditure. In Table 6.2 the pay back periods are seen to be

Project A — 6 years,
Project B — 4 years,
Project C — 5 years.

Using this criterion, Project B would be selected as the most 'worthy' investment. The advantage of this method compared with the average rate of return is that it pays some attention to the timing of returns — in the example quoted, the returns in the first two years of Project B's life are taken into account. The main problem with this method, however, is that it pays no regard to returns which may result *after* the pay-back period.

6.4 Discounted cash flow

We have seen that neither average rates of return nor pay back methods take fully into account the *timing* of costs and returns from a project. What we need is a method of investment appraisal which takes account of our preference for early returns but which also recognizes the value of returns in the future, i.e. it takes account of the *pattern* of cash flows. This requirement is satisfied by discounted cash flow (D.C.F.) techniques.

The pattern of cash flows associated with a particular project can be represented in diagrammatic form as in Figure 6.1. The year when the project comes into operation — the 'base year' for the project — is designated as Year 0. Year −1 and Year 0 are each characterized by negative cash flows as a result of the outflow of capital necessary to fund the project. In Years 1 to 4 the project produces profits for the company giving positive cash flows of equal amounts in each year; in Year 5 a similar level of profit is earned, but cash flow is higher because the equipment is sold to make way for further new investment.

6.4.1 The present value concept

Having determined the pattern of cash flows throughout the life of a project, the object of D.C.F. is to express all the cash flows on a comparable basis by relating them all to a common base year. This is done by expressing *future* cash flows (Years 1—5) in terms of their *present values* in Year 0. Because we prefer cash sooner rather than later, this means that cash flows occurring in the future are given less and less weight when expressed in present value terms. Similarly, cash flows prior to the base year are given relatively more weight. Figure 6.2 illustrates the way in which the pattern of cash flows is translated into a Present Value.

We have seen that returns occurring in the future are given less weight in the calculation of present value than returns occurring now. In practice this is achieved by the use of *discount factors*. To understand how these work, it is helpful to compare them with the interest rate principle. If you deposit £100 in a building society savings account at a rate of interest of 10%, then after one year your savings will have grown to £110 $\{100+[(10/100)\times100]\}$ after two years to £121 $\{110+[(10/100)\times110]\}$, and so on. The future value of your savings in any year can be calculated using the compound interest formula

$$\text{Future value}=\text{Present value} \times (1+i)^n$$
where $i=$ the rate of interest,
$\quad\quad n=$ the number of years.

If we reverse this formula to find out how present value can be calculated

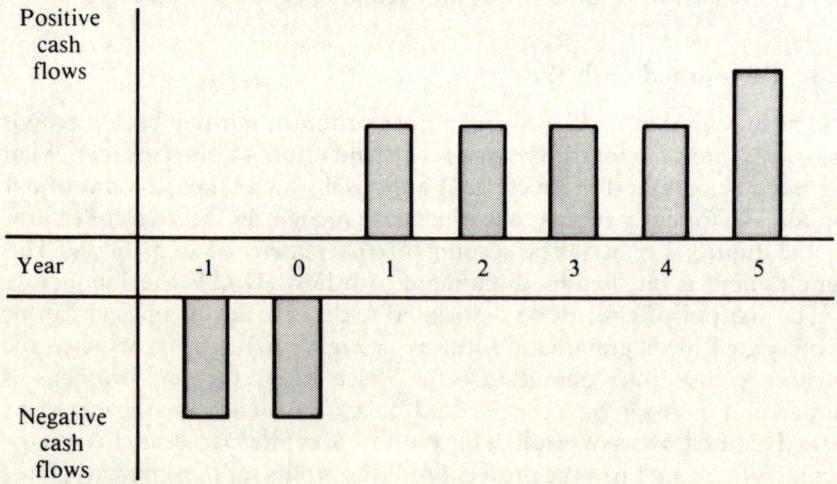

Figure 6.1 Annual cash flows.

from any particular future value, we get

$$\text{Present value} = \text{Future value}/(1+i)^n$$

This is precisely the formula we use in D.C.F. analysis, except that the rate of interest is called a discount rate, to reflect the fact that we are deflating future values instead of inflating present values. The discount rate that is used in practice will be the minimum acceptable rate of return, which will vary depending on the type of project. The choice of discount rate is discussed later in this chapter.

6.4.2 Decision criteria under D.C.F.

When it comes to appraising investment projects using D.C.F. principles, there are a number of methods which can be applied. We will deal with the three most common methods, namely:

(a) Net present value

(b) Benefit—cost ratios

(c) Internal rate of return

A description of the three methods is followed by an example of their use.

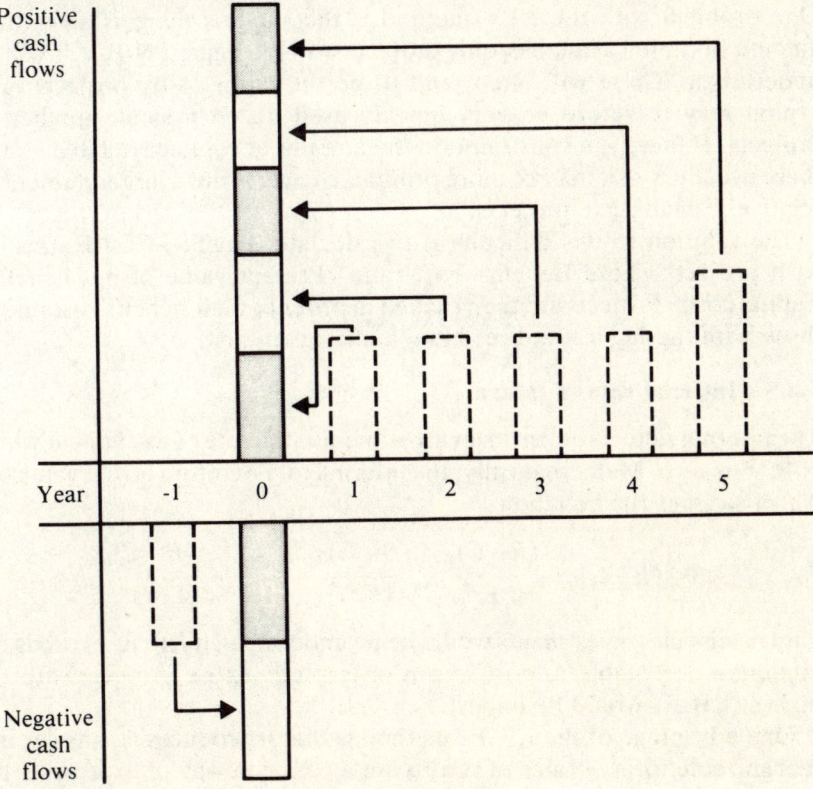

Figure 6.2 Present value of annual cash flows.

6.4.3   Net present value (N.P.V.)

Using the net present value rule, projects will be undertaken if the present value of the benefits exceeds the present value of the costs, i.e. when the net present value is positive. N.P.V. is calculated by discounting the positive and negative cash flows in each year of the project, using the appropriate discount rate, and summing them. Mathematically,

$$\text{N.P.V.} = (B-C)_0 + \frac{(B-C)_1}{1+d} + \frac{(B-C)_2}{(1+d)^2} + \cdots + \frac{(B-C)_n}{(1+d)^n}$$

where B refers to benefits or positive cash flows,

$\quad$ C refers to costs or negative cash flows, and includes the capital costs of the project,

$\quad$ subscripts $0, 1 \ldots n$ refer to years,

$\quad$ d is the discount rate.

6.4.4   Benefit—cost ratios

One problem with the NPV method is that, unless there is an infinite amount of capital available, only projects with the highest N.P.V.'s will be undertaken. These will often tend to be the more costly projects, and capital may therefore be very quickly used up on a small number of projects. If there is a constraint on the amount of capital available — and there usually is — it may be more profitable to carry out a larger number of relatively small-scale projects.

The solution to this difficulty is to calculate Benefit—Cost Ratios for each project, where Benefit—cost ratio=Present value of net benefits/ Capital costs. Projects are then ranked in order of their benefit-cost ratios, those with the highest indices being undertaken first.

6.4.5   Internal rate of return

The internal rate of return on an investment is the rate of discount at which N.P.V. is zero. Mathematically, the internal rate of return is that value of r which satisfies the equation

$$0 = (B-C)_0 + \frac{(B-C)_1}{1+r} + \frac{(B-C)_2}{(1+r)^2} + \cdots + \frac{(B-C)_n}{(1+r)^n}$$

Under this rule, investments would be be undertaken if I.R.R. exceeds the minimum acceptable rate of return on capital. Those projects with the highest I.R.R. would be undertaken first.

One advantage of the I.R.R. method is that it produces an answer in a recognizable form — rates of return are a common way of expressing the worth of doing something. The method also produces an answer which immediately allows projects to be compared—whereas the N.P.V. method may also require benefit—cost ratios to be calculated. However, the method has a number of disadvantages, not the least of which is the tedious trial-and-error process necessary to find the appropriate rate of return. A more fundamental objection is that situations may arise where a project has no unique I.R.R. — mathematically this is because the I.R.R. is the solution to a polynomial equation, which may have more than one root. In practice, this problem is only likely to arise where a stream of negative cash flows is followed by a stream of positive cash flows which is then followed by a further stream of negative cash flows.

We have noted the advantages and disadvantages of the different D.C.F. methods. All of them are commonly found in practice, although the theoretical preference is for the N.P.V. method. A simple example of D.C.F. calculations is shown in Table 6.3. Imagine a transport investment costing £110,000 to implement in the base year, and yielding annual benefits of £20,000 for the subsequent ten years. With a discount rate of 10%, is the project worth considering? Column 4 in the table shows the present values in the base year of the annual cash flows: the net present value is positive and estimated at £12,900, so the project is worth including in the investment programme. In a situation of capital-rationing, where the return on capital invested is important, the benefit-cost ratio would show a rate of return of 11.7%. The internal rate of return on the investment is approximately 12.5%, as shown by the calculations in column 5 which show a N.P.V. close to zero at a 12.5% rate of discount.

6.5 The discount rate

One important way in which D.C.F. methods differ from cruder investment appraisal techniques such as the average rate of return and pay back method is the use of a discount rate to reflect our preference for present rather than future consumption. We now consider how the discount rate can be calculated.

The importance of the discount rate should not be underestimated. The higher the discount rate, the lower the level of investment; the lower the discount rate, the greater the importance given to future benefits arising from a project.

At this point we need to introduce a distinction between projects in the private sector and those in the public sector. In the private sector we are concerned with the way in which investment affects the profitability of the enterprise, and the discount rate will reflect this consideration. In the public sector we are usually less concerned with *financial* costs and benefits, and more with the *social* costs and benefits of an investment. When the latter are being considered, not only does this require a more complex

Table 6.3 Examples of D.C.F. calculations

Year	Benefits (positive cash flows) £000	Costs (negative cash flows) £000	Present value in year 0 (10% Discount Rate) £000	Present value in year 0 (12.5% Discount Rate) £000
0		−110	−110	−110
1	20		18.2	17.8
2	20		16.5	15.8
3	20		15.0	14.0
4	20		13.7	12.5
5	20		12.4	11.1
6	20		11.3	9.9
7	20		10.3	8.8
8	20		9.3	7.8
9	20		8.5	6.9
10	20		7.7	6.2
	200	−110	12.9	0.8

Net present value=£12,900
Benefit-cost ratio=12.9/110=11.7%
Internal rate of return=12.5%

analysis (as we shall see later in the chapter), it also suggests a different discount rate.

The discount rate to a private firm, such as a coach operator or a road haulier, will reflect the cost of capital to the business. This really means the cost of long-term funds as reflected in the interest it pays on long-term loans, interest paid on dividends to shareholders etc. It is normal for these interest rates to provide only the lower limit for the choice of discount rate. The rate will often be set higher to allow for uncertainty associated with returns from a particular investment (although this is a questionable method of allowing for uncertainty, as discussed later), or because funds are needed on projects where it is difficult to measure a rate of return e.g. investment in vehicle radio equipment.

When we turn to the public sector, the obvious approach at first sight would be to set the discount rate on the same principles, i.e. to reflect the cost of capital to the government. This would mean using the rate of interest on long-term government securities. There is a problem however in using *any* market rate of interest for investment decisions in the public sector. Rates of interest may be changed by the government for all kinds of reasons connected with economic management — e.g. to counter balance of payments difficulties — and there is no reason to suppose that the rates reflect in any way society's preference for present rather than future consumption.

An alternative approach would be to use a *social time preference rate* (S.T.P.R.) for discounting, reflecting the government's judgement of society's preference for present consumption. Here it is relevant to ask a question which we have carefully avoided up to now — how can we be sure that society has a positive rate of time preference at the margin? There are a number of arguments which could be put forward for a positive rate, but not all of them are valid.

1 *Inflation means that £1 next year is worth less than £1 now.* This is true, but it is no argument for a positive discount rate. Investment appraisal is concerned with real cash flows, that is after correcting for inflation.
2 *Risk of uncertainty.* Returns in the future become less and less certain for a number of reasons. Again this is true, but it is not a good argument for a positive discount rate. Use of a discount rate to reflect uncertainty would imply that uncertainty increases smoothly with time, whereas in fact it is not difficult to imagine situations in which returns in some early years could be less certain than later returns.
3 *Death is inevitable.* From an individual's point of view there can be no question that present consumption is preferable to future consumption, simply because the individual cannot be certain how long he is going to survive. It is not clear whether this argument should apply to society, however, on the grounds that the welfare of future generations should be taken into account.
4 *Diminishing marginal utility of consumption.* If we can assume that total real consumption per head will rise over time (which it will if there is economic growth) it follows that the same increase in consumption per head will gradually yield less and less utility. This is the main argument for a positive social time preference rate.

It is all very well to argue that society has a positive S.T.P.R., but can it be calculated? To do this we would need to know how utility varies with consumption, and how consumption per head is likely to grow in the future. And should we add something to reflect the 'inevitability of death' argument? The ways in which this might be done are beyond the scope of this book, but it can be said that no one has solved the calculation problem.

A third possible approach to the problem of defining a discount rate in the public sector is to calculate a *social opportunity cost* (S.O.C.) rate of interest. This would reflect the value to society of the use to which the resources employed in the project would otherwise be put. Proponents of the S.O.C. approach usually argue that the most appropriate assumption to make is that public sector investment is displacing private sector investment, so that the discount rate should equal the rate of return on private investment.

There are problems with the S.O.C. approach. In the first place, the appropriate rate might be difficult to calculate. Private investments will produce a variety of different rates of return in practice, and it would be difficult to calculate an average rate. Secondly, market rates of return do not necessarily reflect social values—private investments may produce benefits or disbenefits to society which are not reflected in financial calculations. Thirdly, why should private investment be taken as the alternative use to which resources can be put? Public investment may displace private consumption, or government current expenditure.

The fact that the S.O.C. rate takes no account of society's rate of time preference (as implied by the S.T.P.R.) has led some economists to suggest that the correct social discount rate should take both approaches into account, to produce a 'synthetic' rate. This is reasonable if we view the S.T.P.R. as reflecting the fact that public investment means foregone consumption, and the S.O.C. foregone private investment. The problem of calculating the rate remains, however.

6.6   Cost benefit analysis

The techniques which we have described so far in this chapter are appropriate to decisions regarding investment in projects where the returns are purely financial. They are therefore useful to transport operators facing decisions about whether to purchase new vehicles, depot facilities etc. However, in the previous section on the discount rate we introduced the idea that public sector investments might require a different kind of treatment, because there may be *social* costs and benefits associated with a project which are not reflected in the financial returns. This is particularly the case with large-scale investments in road-building, new railway lines, airports etc. Cost benefit analysis (C.B.A.) was developed to deal with such cases.

There are some similarities between cost benefit analysis and the discounted cash flow methods that we described earlier. In both financial and cost-benefit appraisals, decisions are made on the basis of N.P.V. or I.R.R. criteria, although different discount rates may be used. Both C.B.A. and D.C.F. use money as the yardstick for decision-making. Where C.B.A. differs from D.C.F. is in the types of costs and benefits included in the analysis, and in the valuation of costs and benefits.

6.6.1   Which costs and benefits?

Whereas a financial appraisal is generally concerned with the effects of a project on the investing agency itself, C.B.A. aims to include all social costs and benefits associated with the project. For example, a private company contemplating building a new railway line would be solely interested in the effect on the company's profits, and would include in their project appraisal only those items having a bearing on this, such as estimated revenue, operating costs and so on. C.B.A. on the other hand would include such items as the time savings to passengers using the railway line in preference to their present means of transport, or the benefits from reduced road congestion as a result of road users transferring to rail. The differences between the social effects of a project, and those which are purely private, are known as external effects.

There are two kinds of external effect, known as 'technological' and 'pecuniary'. It is sometimes argued that pecuniary externalities should be excluded, when undertaking a cost-benefit analysis. A technological externality occurs when an investment affects the production function of a producer other than the investing agency, or the utility fuction of a consumer. Thus, a new motorway built on agricultural land will adversely affect farmers' production functions, but will increase the utility of road users who benefit from reduced congestion. Both factors should be included in C.B.A.

A pecuniary externality occurs when a production function or utility function of a third party is changed owing to changes in the level of demand. For instance, a petrol station situated near to a new motorway will find its trade increased. This is not due to any change in the technical relationship between inputs and outputs, but merely reflects changes in demand generated by users of the motorway. As the benefits to motorway users will already have been counted in the cost-benefit analysis, it would be double-counting to include benefits to the garage proprietors. In fact in most cases it is easy to see that pecuniary externalities are merely transfers from one group to another: in our example, the extra trade experienced by garages near the motorway will be mirrored by reduced trade for garages further away.

Although in strict economic terms pecuniary effects are not relevant in C.B.A., it can be important to take them into account if the distributional consequences of the investment are of interest.

6.6.2 Valuation of costs and benefits

In C.B.A., two types of problem arise when placing values on costs and benefits.

1 Some costs and benefits may be directly measurable in financial terms, but their market prices may not reflect social values.
2 Some costs and benefits may not have market prices.

In both cases we use what are known as *shadow prices* to value the costs and benefits.

6.6.2.1   *Shadow pricing of market items*

We saw in Chapter 4 that consumer surplus will be maximized if prices are set equal to marginal social cost. It follows that if we are trying to measure the social costs and benefits of an investment, the appropriate valuation is at marginal social cost. If market prices do not reflect marginal social costs then they need to be adjusted. There are two reasons why market prices may not reflect marginal social costs.

1 Market prices may not equal marginal private costs.
2 Marginal private costs may not equal marginal social costs.

The second problem occurs when there are significant externalities, and we saw in the previous section that these must be taken into account in cost benefit analysis. The first divergence may occur for a number of reasons, but in practice it is not possible to make all the adjustments which would be necessary to satisfy economic theory, because the price structure is so distorted that this becomes an impossible task. All we can do is to make the more obvious adjustments to market prices. Two fairly common cases where adjustments are needed are for indirect taxes and unemployment.

Market prices will usually contain some element of indirect taxation —for example petrol prices include Value Added Tax and excise duty. Whereas financial appraisals are generally calculated after tax, C.B.A. uses before-tax returns, because taxes are merely a transfer payment between one section of the community and another. The rationale for this can be seen if we assume that petrol consumption is reduced because of a new motorway which reduces the distance between two towns. The reduced consumption of resources is a clear benefit in C.B.A., but in valuing the benefit it would be illogical to include that element of the petrol price which represents tax, because the government has to raise the revenue from another source.

Wage costs are usually a major element in C.B.A., whether as part of the capital costs of constructing the project in question, or whether as part of the costs of operating the facility once it has been built. But if there is an economic recession, and the people employed on the project would otherwise be unemployed, then the true cost to society of their labour is virtually zero.

6.6.2.2   *Intangibles*

The placing of monetary values on social effects for which there is no market was perhaps the most innovatory aspect of C.B.A. when it was first introduced into transport planning. It has also given rise to considerable controversy. The original hope of some economists was that C.B.A. would one day be capable of embracing *all* costs and benefits in a single monetary measure showing the 'economic worth' of a project. We describe below some of the attempts which have been made to value three kinds of 'intangible' costs and benefits common to transport, namely time savings, accidents, and environmental effects.

The valuation of time savings   Travel is considered to be a disutility and the basis of the valuation of time is that time spent doing it has an opportunity cost. We make a distinction between travelling in *working time*, when the value of work is the opportunity cost and travelling in *non-working time* when leisure activity is foregone. Travelling to and from work is considered to be in non-working time because it is your leisure activity which is given up not your time spent working.

The problem for the economist is the determination of time values. The obvious place to start is the labour market. The *marginal productivity theory of factor awards* suggests that the wage rate will give the value of time in working time. This theory argues that the employer will continue to employ labour as long as it is worth his continuing to do so. The cost of the last man employed (which is normally the going wage rate for all the employees) will represent his *marginal value product* i.e. the additional value he contributes as a result of his labour. The wage rate (plus overheads like national insurance contributions and cost of uniforms) therefore represents the opportunity cost, and therefore the value of that employee's working time.

The Government publishes value of time figures for working time for a variety of categories although it recognizes regional differences may require some modification for specific projects. Working time values for 'modal' groups (i.e. car driver, car passenger, rail passenger, bus passenger, underground passenger and 'all workers') are based on mileage-weighted incomes derived from National Travel Survey data. They also include the latest information relating to Employers National Insurance and Pension Contributions. Values for bus drivers, bus conductors and goods vehicle drivers are based on Department of Employment earnings surveys. Although working values of time based on wage rates are generally used for forecasting and evaluation purposes there are some objections raised to this method of estimation. Firstly, the wage rate may not reflect the true opportunity cost of the resources used as wage rates are strongly influenced by, for example, a sense of equity or pressure for the maintenance of inappropriate wage differentials. Secondly, there is the assumption that individuals are indifferent between work and travel. If there is a greater disutility attached to travelling then perhaps the value of time savings should be increased. Thirdly, there is also the assumption that travelling time is wasted, which in many cases is not true. Time savings for the executive working on the train or aircraft may be of negligible importance in some instances.

We might turn to the labour market for the valuation of *non-working time*. We could say that if someone gives up income to enjoy leisure activity then his wage rate (less overheads) must reflect his value of non-working time. However, most people (with the obvious exception of the self-employed) have to work a set minimum number of hours per week and so they are unable to adjust their working hours to ensure the marginal value of leisure equals the marginal rate of income. Another reason why the wage rate is unsuitable in this context is that for most of us working involves some effort and, therefore, involves a degree of disutility. The wage rate exceeds the value of leisure time foregone to reflect this disutility. Finally, for some of us travelling may not be a disutility. Many rail commuters, forced to drive to work during industrial action, found they had to find extra time to read their papers. Time savings to a commuting bridge school may be of a very low value!

So if we cannot use wage rates to estimate the value of nonworking time we must turn to the traveller himself to see if we can determine from his travel behaviour how he values his time. We used the example in Chapter 2 of route choice — the more expensive shorter route across the bridge or the slower but cheaper journey around the estuary — to value a traveller's time. The most successful method, however, has been the examination of commuters' choice of mode where they trade-off a quicker more expensive mode against a slower but cheaper one. Sophisticated statistical techniques have been used in the study of modal choice to produce values of time[1,2,3] and results suggest that non-working values are somewhere between 15% and 50% of the average wage rate and that walking and waiting time were valued at between two and three times in-vehicle time. The Department of Transport distinguishes between behavioural and resource values of non-working time and the difference is the effective average rate of indirect taxation in the economy. The resource value is approximately 85% of the behavioural value.

The importance of obtaining as accurate values of time as possible cannot be overestimated because such a large part of the benefits of most transport projects comprises time savings. It was estimated that about 64% of the first year gross benefits of the M1 in the UK constituted time savings. In many cases, a small change in the time value used in the appraisal could determine whether or not a project is acceptable. For this reason and because there are many problems involved in determining time values it is often advisable to take a range of values to determine how sensitive results are to them.

Notwithstanding the difficulties of estimation there are some fundamental problems to be recognized. For example, we do not really understand how time values vary with journey distance, comfort or how they change over time. In addition, we have not decided whether there is a minimum level of time savings below which there is no value. Is an hour saved by one person the same as one minute saved by sixty persons? This is very important because many projects such as by-passes and bus priority measures give small time savings which when summed over all travellers represent large benefits.

Accident costs   An important benefit which usually attaches to road schemes is a reduction in the number of accidents. Accidents can be divided into those which cause fatal injuries, those which cause serious injuries but no fatalities, and those where injuries are only slight. As might be expected, a different value is usually placed on each type of accident. Perhaps because we are in a sense trying to place a value on life itself, the valuation of accident savings has given rise to controversy.

How do we go about placing a value on accident savings? We can distinguish three types of cost associated with accidents.

1 Direct financial costs to the various people involved, i.e. police, medical costs, legal costs, repair of vehicles.
2 Loss of output of those killed or injured.
3 'Pain, grief and suffering' resulting from death or injury.

The first type of cost is quite straightforward to estimate. Data on the costs of all the various organizations involved is readily available and it is simply a matter of estimating what proportion of their time, staff resources, etc. is taken up by road accidents.

Loss of output of those killed or injured can be estimated by taking their expected loss of earnings in each year up to the expected date of retirement or death, and calculating the present value of these amounts. It is sometimes argued that the individual's expected future consumption should be subtracted from his earnings, but this would ignore the benefits derived by the individual from staying alive!

It is the third type of cost which has given rise to argument. How can we place a value on people's pain, grief and suffering as a result of being killed or seriously injured? A number of approaches have been suggested.

(a) The most extreme argument is that the value of life is infinite and that to place a finite value on it is impossible. But this ignores the fact that people do appear to place a finite value on life by taking risks, e.g. mountain climbing, not wearing seat belts, or even by travelling at all!
(b) At the other extreme, the Department of Transport used to use what they called a 'notional minimum' allowance based on the idea that the minimum value which society would be willing to pay to avoid an accident could be measured by the present value of future consumption of an average non-productive member of society. There

seems little merit in this other than to suggest a minimum value of life.

(c) Some people have suggested that the amount people spend on life assurance is an indication of the value of their lives to them. This is usually criticized on the grounds that buying life assurance does not actually reduce the risk of death, it merely provides some monetary compensation to relatives.

(d) The most logical approach which has been suggested is to attempt to find situations where we can genuinely measure peoples' willingness to pay for reductions in the risk of having an accident. (This is similar to the most common way of measuring the value of time, where we observe peoples' choices when faced with a trade-off situation). For example, we can observe the choices people make when faced with crossing a road directly or using a longer route via a subway. If we know the probability of having an accident while crossing the road and the value of time, it is possible to infer what value people place on accident avoidance.

Environmental costs   Transport investments affect the environment in a number of ways, for example noise, vibration, air pollution, visual intrusion, and severance. These effects have proved to be the most difficult to bring into the C.B.A. framwork; so difficult, in fact, that few economists now argue that it is appropriate to value environmental effects in monetary terms. It is nevertheless instructive to examine the most comprehensive attempt made to place monetary values on the environment, namely the evaluation of aircraft noise by the Roskill Commission on the Third London Airport[4].

It is relatively easy to measure noise levels and to construct noise contours around an airport, which show how the noise level changes at different distances from the airport. The Roskill Commission used the Noise and Number Index (N.N.I.), which takes into account the number of aircraft and the average noise level. N.N.I. contours were predicted for each of the airport sites which the Commission were considering.

The Commission argued that noise could affect peoples' homes in three ways:

1 The value of their property may depreciate.
2 People who move away to escape the noise may lose consumer surplus, i.e. the difference between the market price of their house and the price at which they would be willing to give it up in the absence of noise.
3 People who do not move away may suffer because of the noise nuisance.

Values were placed on these three categories by the use of questionnaire techniques. Estate agents around Heathrow and Gatwick airports were asked to estimate how property values depreciated in areas subject to different degrees of noise nuisance. Households were surveyed to determine what price people would be prepared to accept for their house if it were required for a large development. An earlier attitude survey was used to relate each N.N.I. contour to a noise nuisance score, and these scores were valued at the property depreciation values for the appropriate N.N.I. contour.

The population living within each noise contour was divided into those who would move away from the area (because their valuation of noise nuisance was greater than their loss of consumer surplus plus property depreciation) and those who would remain (valuing noise nuisance less than consumer surplus plus depreciation). The total noise costs could then be estimated for each site. In doing this the 35 N.N.I. contour was taken as a cut-off point, and people living outside this contour were ignored.

Despite the apparent sophistication of these methods, they were criticized for a number of reasons. For example, Mishan[5] makes the following points:

1 Householders' consumer surplus was estimated from answers to the question, "Suppose your house was wanted to form part of a large development scheme and the developer offered to buy it from you, what price would be just high enough to compensate you for leaving this house and moving to another area?" The question does not indicate how far the householder might have to move, and Mishan argues that the answers to the question are therefore likely to underestimate the loss of consumer surplus as a result of having to move away from an area subject to aircraft noise.
2 The results obtained from the above question suggested that 8% of respondents would not be prepared to move at any price. It would therefore seem logical to value their consumer surplus at a very high price indeed — in theory the value would be infinite. The Commission adopted the arbitrary value of twice the market price as the amount which these people would need to compensate them. This is clearly open to criticism — why not take ten times the market price, or a hundred times?
3 People remaining in the area affected by aircraft noise are assumed to suffer, at the most, the expected depreciation in their house value. Mishan argues that property values cannot be taken as proxies for noise nuisance, because if noise increases everywhere over time, then differences in noise will diminish. Property values will not then reflect the original depreciation induced by noise.
4 The arbitrary exclusion of people living outside the 35 N.N.I. contour is contrary to the standard practice elsewhere in C.B.A. (e.g. time savings) of including all costs and benefits, no matter how small.

The Roskill Commission of Inquiry was something of a turning point for cost benefit analysis. It was by far the most ambitious project ever undertaken using C.B.A., and when the Commission's recommendations were rejected, this was taken by many to be a criticism of the analytical techniques themselves. In hindsight, it is possible to view this period as a watershed in the development of investment appraisal techniques in the public sector. It is now generally accepted that economic and environmental appraisals cannot use the same yardstick of monetary values. We go on later to give two examples of modern cost-benefit analysis and the way in which they relate to the overall appraisal of the investment project being undertaken. Before that, however, there are two aspects of C.B.A. which we have not yet dealt with, namely the treatment of risk and uncertainty, and the effects of investments on the distribution of income.

6.6.3 Risk and uncertainty

There are obvious problems involved in predicting future costs and benefit, and it is important, particularly when comparing one project with another, to take account of how accurate the results of the cost benefit analyses are likely to be. Problems of estimation may arise because sufficiently good data is not available, or because of the possibility of technological change, or because consumer tastes may change. How can we deal with these uncertainties?

We do not propose to cover this subject in detail. There is a fair amount of technical literature on the subject, but we will only summarize one or two methods for dealing with the problem.

In the literature a distinction is drawn between risk and uncertainty. 'Risk' is defined as a situation where future outcomes, although not known with certainty, can at least be assigned probabilities. 'Uncertainty' is defined as a situation where it is not possible to define the probability of any particular result occurring.

One way of coping with risk and uncertainty would be to add a premium to the discount rate. This might be a satisfactory approach if all the costs and benefits of a project were subject to risk, and if riskiness increased in a smooth fashion over time. Normally, however, this is not the case, and some costs and benefits will be more certain than others. We therefore need to devise a method which treats each item of costs and benefits individually.

In general, the best way of dealing with risk and uncertainty is to undertake a 'sensitivity analysis' by taking different values for those costs and benefits which are least certain, and seeing what effect this has on the overall C.B.A. result for the project in question. The only problem with this approach is that, if there are a large number of risks and uncertainties, the number of calculations required will multiply dramatically, and the results may prove confusing to decision-makers. It could be argued, however, that such confusion is the proper reflection of the risk and uncertainty inherent in the project, and that if as a result projects whose outcomes are more clearcut are the ones that are undertaken, then this is perfectly reasonable.

6.6.4 Distributional questions

In this chapter we have not explicitly mentioned the fact that C.B.A. has its roots in the theory of Welfare Economics, a specific branch of economics devoted to the pursuit of 'socially optimal' policies. We need to make some reference to welfare economics in order to deal with the question of the distributional effects of transport projects, and the way they are dealt with in C.B.A.

Welfare theory derives from an Italian economist called Pareto. Applying his criteria to cost benefit analysis would suggest that a project is strictly only worthwhile if at least one member of society gains from it and nobody loses from it. This is clearly a very restrictive statement — it would be very difficult to think of a transport investment from which no one suffered some disbenefit. The criteria for deciding whether an investment is worthwhile (so far as welfare theory is concerned) was therefore modified by the so-called 'Kaldor—Hicks compensation principle', named after the two economists who suggested it. This principle states that an investment is worthwhile if the gainers could compensate the losers, and still be better off than they were before. In other words, if gains outweigh losses, the project is worthwhile. Note that the principle does *not* say that compensation should actually be paid. This raises the problem that income will be redistributed as a result of most investment projects — a simple example is road construction, which tends to benefit those who can afford cars considerably more than those without cars, although the latter have to contribute (through taxation) to the capital costs.

How are distributional questions handled in cost benefit analysis? The most common approach is in fact to ignore them! Two arguments are advanced to justify this. One argument is to say that redistributive effects are not usually significant. But even if this is true for individual projects, it does not mean that the cumulative effects of a number of investments will be insignificant. A second argument asserts that to consider distributional questions requires 'value judgements', and that this is not the province of economics. But this ignores the fact that value judgements are implicit in many economic principles — e.g. consumer sovereignty — and if consumers are concerned about income distribution then why should their feelings be neglected?

It seems therefore that some account should be taken of the distributional effects of investments. This could be achieved by applying weights to individual gains and losses to reflect society's preferences for distributional changes, but it would be difficult to do in practice owing to the problems of determining the appropriate weights. Another approach is to assume that society does not want 'the rich to get richer and the poor to get poorer', and to scale down the benefits to the former in comparison with the latter — this kind of thinking underlies the Department of Transport's use of an 'equity value of time' in their own investment appraisals, where the same value of non-working time is attributed to all individuals despite the evidence that time values are related to income.

Both the approaches mentioned in the previous paragraph involve the cost-benefit analyst making some kind of adjustment to his calculations in order to reflect distributional preferences of society. A further way of dealing with the problem of distributional effects is to ignore them when carrying out the calculations of the cost-benefit analysis, but to categorize costs and benefits in such a way as to summarize the net effect of the project on different types of people. The decision-maker can then, if he wishes, place his own weights on the net benefits of these different groups. The advantages of this kind of approach are:

(a) It lends itself to the inclusion of costs and benefits other than those which can be expressed in monetary terms — this is because the analyst is forced to look at each group of people affected by the scheme in turn and to list their costs and benefits.

(b) It makes the distributional effects of a project explicit. One thing to note in applying this method is that *all* externalities, including pecuniary ones, should really be included, otherwise the distributional effects of the project will be incompletely stated.

6.7   Practical examples of investment appraisals using cost benefit analysis

6.7.1   Inter-urban trunk road schemes

Most inter-urban trunk road schemes in this country are evaluated with the assistance of the Department of Transport's COBA computer program. COBA was developed in the early 1970's to satisfy the need for a standard method of evaluating the many proposals for road-building put forward by local authorities and other organizations. It is in many respects a simplified form of cost benefit analysis in that it concentrates solely on benefits which it is relatively easy to value, i.e. those obtained by existing road users. Although it is used to evaluate about 75% of all trunk road schemes, it is not suitable for major schemes such as motorways, nor for most urban road schemes — the reasons for this will be described later.

COBA calculates the net present value of a road proposal over a 30-year period—a length of time which has come to be regarded as a standard period for cost benefit analysis of transport projects. Annual costs and benefits are discounted using a test discount rate specified by the government—originally 10%, it has since been revised to 7%. COBA takes account of the following costs and benefits:

1 Construction costs,
2 Road maintenance costs,
3 Delays to traffic during construction,
4 Time savings to road users,
5 Road accidents,
6 Vehicle operating costs.

How then does the Department of Transport go about evaluating the effect on road users of a road proposal using the COBA system? The basic inputs to the process are the traffic flows on the existing road network, and traffic speeds on the existing and improved networks. Existing traffic flows are available from surveys. Future traffic flows are predicted on the basis of national traffic forecasts, which are related to car ownership levels, economic growth, and fuel prices. COBA takes account of uncertainty in these forecasts by using high and low forecasts for economic growth and fuel price changes, and produces a range of N.P.V.'s reflecting these different forecasts.

Traffic flow data are divided into types of vehicle—cars, buses, HGVs etc.—and each type of vehicle is expressed in terms of the amount of road-space which it requires in relation to a 'passenger-car unit' (pcu), for example a bus is taken to be equivalent to 3 pcus. Traffic speeds are related to the flow of traffic (in terms of pcus) using observed relationships which compare the speed-flow characteristics of different types of road—e.g. a given traffic flow is able to attain a faster speed on a dual carriageway compared with a single carriageway road. Typical speed-flow curves used by COBA are shown in Figure 6.3.

In calculating the time savings that will result from the road proposal, COBA includes *all* time saved (whether 10 seconds or 10 minutes), and takes into account not only the time saved by the traffic using the new road (e.g. a village by-pass) but also the time saved by traffic continuing to use the old road. It deals separately with time saved on the links between junctions and traffic delays at the junctions themselves. The values of time incorporated into the program reflect different mixes of vehicle types and trip purposes, for instance lorry drivers are assigned a higher value of time than people driving to work.

The effect of the road proposal on accidents is evaluated by using accident rates for different types of road and standard accident cost

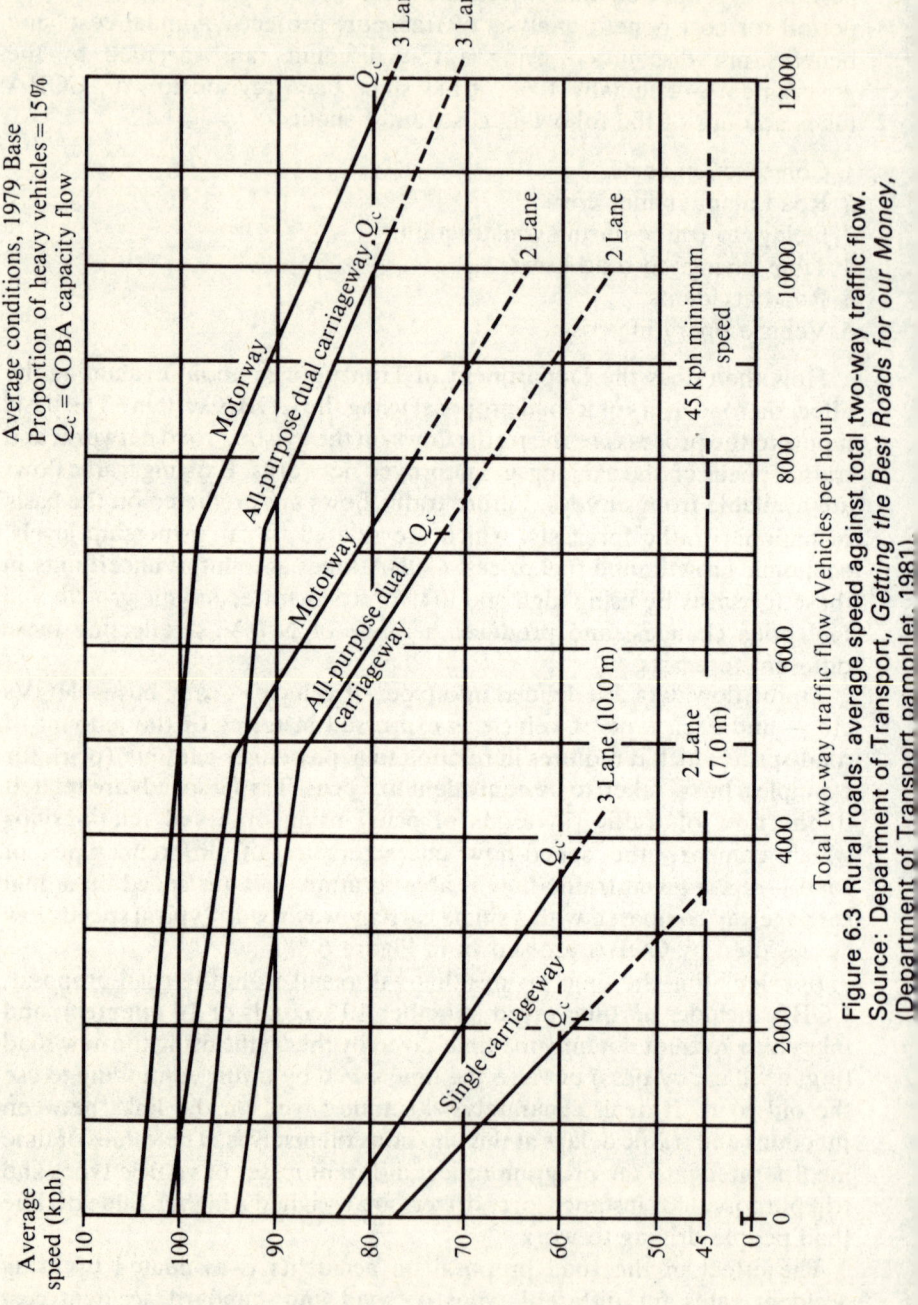

Figure 6.3 Rural roads: average speed against total two-way traffic flow.
Source: Department of Transport, *Getting the Best Roads for our Money,*
(Department of Transport pamphlet, 1981).

valuations. Accident rates on the existing and improved road networks can be calculated from statistics which show how accidents vary on roads of different widths, with single or dual carriageways etc. The value of accident savings takes account of the three elements described earlier in the chapter, i.e. the financial cost to hospitals, the police etc., the loss of output resulting from death or injury, and an allowance for pain, grief and suffering.

The third effect on road users which COBA takes into account is one which has not so far been mentioned in this chapter, namely the change in vehicle operating costs as a result of the road proposal. In COBA these costs comprise the costs of fuel, oil, tyres, vehicle maintenance and depreciation. An important point which should be stressed is that it is not the costs actually incurred by road users—often known as behavioural costs—which are included in an economic evaluation, but the cost of the resources employed. Resource costs in practice are calculated as behavioural costs less indirect taxation. The change in costs associated with a road proposal will depend partly on the change in distance travelled, and partly on the change in speed. Very often the cost change will be negative—this is usually the case with a by-pass, for example, where vehicle mileage will tend to increase leading to increases in all vehicle operating costs, even though the increased speeds may reduce fuel consumption.

The COBA system is used in a number of ways in the development of road proposals. For example, it may be used:

(a) To assess the need for improving a route,
(b) To compare alternative solutions to the problem, e.g. different junction types and road widths,
(c) To determine the priority given to an individual scheme,
(d) To assess the optimal timing of a scheme.

We noted earlier that COBA is not designed to cope with all types of road proposal. This is because it does not allow for the possibility of completely new trips being generated by a road improvement, nor for the possibility of people switching from other modes of transport. The omission of these two factors would be a serious problem in major interurban schemes like motorways, and in most urban trunk road schemes. In these situations it is necessary to employ transport modelling techniques (described in Chapter 8) to predict the effects of the proposed scheme over the whole network.

It is important to note that COBA is only one element of the appraisal process for inter-urban road schemes. It is also necessary to evaluate the effects of proposals on the environment. Following the recommendations of the Leitch Committee[6] these factors are considered in non-monetary terms within an appraisal 'framework' which sets out all the effects of a scheme and its alternatives on the various people concerned, i.e. road user, non-road users such as property owners, those concerned with the intrinsic value of the area, and others. The appendix to this chapter sets out the example framework included in the Leitch report.

6.7.2 Urban rail investments

The benefits of transport schemes outside urban areas, as reflected for example in COBA, accrue almost entirely to those who use the facility provided. When we move into urban areas, however, we often find that benefits to *non-users* are more important than benefits to users. This can be illustrated by reference to urban rail investment.

Table 6.4 shows the results of a cost benefit analysis carried out by Foster of two suburban railway lines in Greater Manchester[7]. These were existing railway lines on which services would be withdrawn if the only considerations were commercial. The figures in the table are based not just on retaining the services but include the effects of improving the rail service and providing bus feeder services. The figures show the present value of each item from 1973 to 1997, discounted at 10% per annum back to 1973.

The costs and benefits are calculated on the basis of what would happen if services were withdrawn instead of improved. Of the six factors quantified, only one relates to the disbenefits to former rail users — this is the effect of rail users transferring to slower bus services. By far the largest factor contributing to the positive N.P.V. is the disbenefit to existing road users as a result of increased road congestion caused by rail users transferring to car.

Table 6.4 Costs and benefits of withdrawing rail services in Manchester, 1973–1997

	Present value £m
Disbenefits to road users through additional congestion	14.8
Disbenefits to former rail users transferring to bus	0.7
Changes in road accident costs	0.3
Resource costs of replacement bus services	1.3
Resource costs of replacement car journeys	1.9
Avoidable costs of rail services	−6.0
N.P.V. of improved service	+13.0

CBA is but one element of the appraisal framework, similarly, the appraisal of urban rail investments should not simply rely on an analysis of those elements which can be quantified in terms of money. For example, the Glasgow Rail Impact Study[8] has assessed the impact of a series of suburban rail and underground improvements on various groups of people. The cost benefit analysis is only one of the topics analyzed in the study, the full list being shown in Table 6.5. This broad framework reflects the view that CBA is not sufficient by itself to provide a means of taking decisions about rail investment, although it is still one of the major elements in the appraisal process.

Table 6.5   Glasgow rail impact study—list of topics for analysis

Overview
   Topic 1   Cost and benefits

Characteristics of the area
   Topic 2   Study area characteristics
   Topic 3   Station catchment areas

Travel patterns
   Topic 4   Travel trends
   Topic 5   Patterns of rail travel

Travel for specific purposes
   Topic 6   Work
   Topic 7   Shopping
   Topic 8   Education
   Topic 9   Leisure and recreation
   Topic 10 Health services

Travel within the central area
   Topic 11 Travel within the central area

Competition between and co-ordination of modes
   Topic 12 Competition between rail and bus
   Topic 13 Competition between underground and bus
   Topic 14 Competition between public and private
              transport
   Topic 15 Co-ordination of modes

Transport and social policy
   Topic 16 Travel by the disadvantaged
   Topic 17 Transport and social policy

Effect of transport on activities, land use and environment
   Topic 18 Impact on Activities
   Topic 19 Land use
   Topic 20 Environmental change
   Topic 21 Market forces

Examination questions

1 'A value is put on accidents saved because traffic accidents give rise to several identifiable costs.' (*Report of the Advisory Committee on Trunk Road Assessment* (The Leitch Report), Department of Transport: HMSO: London, 1977). Identify the costs referred to and examine the methods by which they may be evaluated in monetary terms.

2 Show how the net present value (N.P.V.) and internal rate of return (I.R.R.) criteria can be applied in the appraisal of transport investment projects.

3 Outline the fundamental methodology employed in a social cost benefit analysis of public expenditure. Examine the main problems involved in undertaking cost-benefit analyses of public expenditure on transport facilities.

4 What is the purpose of discounted cash flow (D.C.F.) analysis in investment appraisal? Show how D.C.F. techniques can be used in the transport sector.

5 In cost-benefit analyses, it is often necessary for monetary values to be placed on costs and benefits associated with a commodity or factor for which there is no market price. Discuss the problems involved in making these evaluations and comment on methods used for the evaluation of savings in travelling time.

6 Outline the methodologies employed in economic appraisals of transport investment projects. In what ways does a 'financial' appraisal differ from a 'social cost-benefit' appraisal?

7 In cost-benefit analysis, why is a distinction often made between savings in working time and savings in non-working time? What methods can be used for the evaluation of these savings?

8 Transport projects often generate different kinds of external effects. Identify the kind of effects which should enter an assessment of the magnitude of net benefit accruing from a public investment project. Discuss the difficulties encountered in the evaluation of this kind of external effect.

9 Outline the fundamental methodology involved in undertaking a cost-benefit analysis of public investment in a transport facility. Examine the difficulties of evaluating costs and benefits associated with commodities or factors for which there is no market price, and comment on some of the methods proposed for the evaluation of *one* of the following:
   (a) Savings in travelling time,
   (b) Reductions in the number and severity of road accidents,
   (c) Adverse effects on the environment caused by the noise of traffic.

10 How can estimates be made of values of travelling time?

Appendix 6.1 Framework for appraisal of trunk road schemes proposed by the Leitch Committee

Example of the framework for the assessment of trunk road schemes—Westfordly By-pass

Group	Interest	Units	Scheme alternatives			
			Red	Green	Blue	'Do nothing'
1.0 Road users directly affected						
1.1 All road users	Reduction in casualties: fatal	Number	3	4	2	—[1]
	serious	Number	15	20	11	—
	slight	Number	30	26	15	—
	Value of accident savings £m (N.P.V.)		0.8	0.59	0.59	—
	Comfort and convenience	Rank	2	1	4	3
	Attractiveness of view from road	Rank	3	4	1	2
1.2 Car drivers/passengers (working time)	Time savings	£m (N.P.V.)	1.94	1.7	1.7	—
	Vehicle operating costs	£m (N.P.V.)	−0.21	−0.14	+0.13	—
1.3 Car drivers/passengers (to and from work and leisure time)	Time savings	£m (N.P.V.)	1.83	1.66	1.67	—
	Vehicle operating costs	£m (N.P.V.)	−0.21	−0.08	+0.19	—
1.4 Heavy goods vehicle operators	Time savings	£m (N.P.V.)	0.91	0.43	0.09	—
	Vehicle operating costs	£m (N.P.V.)	−0.08	−0.03	+0.01	—
1.5 Light goods vehicle operators	Time savings	£m (N.P.V.)	1.0	0.93	0.88	—
	Vehicle operating costs	£m (N.P.V.)	−0.08	−0.03	+0.06	—
1.6 Bus operators and users	Time savings	£m (N.P.V.)	0.59	0.58	0.58	—
	Vehicle operating costs	£m (N.P.V.)	−0.02	−0.07	+0.07	—

Group	Interest	Units	Scheme alternatives			
			Red	Green	Blue	'Do nothing'
1.7 Pedestrians	Time savings	£m (N.P.V.)	1.03	0.41	0.5	—
	Amenity	Rank	4	1	2	3
2.0 Non-road users directly affected						
2.1 Owners/occupiers of residential property	Demolition	Number of properties demolished	—	—	—	—
	Noise increase	Number of properties subject to increases of:				
		$+10$–20 dB(A)L$_{10}$	96	64	9	—
		$+5$–10 dB(A)L$_{10}$	180	116	102	—
	Noise decrease	Number of properties subject to decrease of:				
		>5 dB(A)L$_{10}$	1,450	1,682	1,276	—
	Visual intrusion	Number of properties subject to:				
		severe	30	12	3	—
		significant	183	139	9	—
		slight	399	351	17	—
	Disruption during construction	Rank	4	2	3	1
2.2 Owners/occupiers of shops and business	Demolition	Number of properties demolished	—	—	—	—
	Noise increase	Number of properties subject to $+5$dB(A)L$_{10}$	1	1	—	—
	Noise decrease	Number of properties subject to -5 dB(A)L$_{10}$	70	96	85	—

Group	Interest	Units	Red	Green	Blue	'Do nothing'
					Scheme alternatives	
	Visual intrusion	Number of properties subject to:				
		severe	—	—	—	—
		significant	1	1	—	—
		slight	—	—	—	1
	Disruption during construction	Rank	3	4	2	1
2.3 Owners/occupiers of industrial and commercial property	Demolition	Number of properties demolished	—	—	—	—
	Noise increase	Number of properties subject to +5 dB(A)L$_{10}$	—	—	—	—
	Noise decrease	Number of properties subject to −5 dB(A)L$_{10}$	1	—	—	—
	Visual intrusion	Number of properties subject to:				
		severe	—	—	—	—
		significant	1	—	—	—
		slight	1	—	—	1
	Disruption during construction	Rank	4	2	3	1
2.4 Occupiers/users of public buildings: (a) Schools	Demolition	Number of properties demolished	—	—	—	—
	Noise increase	Number of pupils subject to +<5 dB(A)L$_{10}$	150	—	—	—
	Noise decrease	Number of pupils subject to −>5 dB(A)L$_{10}$	97	97	52	—

Group	Interest	Units	Scheme alternatives			
			Red	Green	Blue	'Do nothing'
(b) Churches	Visual intrusion	Number of pupils affected	150	—	—	—
	Disruption during construction	Rank	4	2	3	1
	Demolition	Number of properties demolished	—	—	—	—
	Noise increase	Number of properties subject to $+<5$ dB(A)L$_{10}$	—	—	—	—
	Noise decrease	Number of properties subject to $->5$ dB(A)L$_{10}$	1	1	—	—
	Visual intrusion	Number of properties affected	1	1	—	—
	Disruption during construction	Rank	3	4	2	1
2.5 Users of public open space	Landtake	Hectares taken	—	—	—	—
	Noise increase	Number of people subject to $+<5$ dB(A)L$_{10}$	350	—	—	—
	Noise decrease	Number of people subject to $->5$ dB(A)L$_{10}$	—	50	185	—
	Visual intrusion	Number of people affected	350	—	—	—
	Disruption during construction	Rank	4	3	2	1
2.6 Farmers	Landtake	Hectares taken:				
		Grade II	18	26	24	—
		Grade III	—	—	17	—

Group	Interest	Units	Scheme alternatives			
			Red	Green	Blue	'Do nothing'
	Severance	Number of farms affected	3	3	8	—
	Noise increase	Number of farms subject to +<5 dB(A)L_{10}	—	1	3	—
	Noise decrease	Number of farms subject to ->5 dB(A)L_{10}	1	—	—	—
	Visual intrusion	Number of farms affected	—	1	3	—
	Disruption during construction	Rank	2	3	4	1

3.0 Those concerned with intrinsic value of area

| 3.1 Landscape/townscape value | General assessment | Rank | 2 | 1 | 3 | 4 |

Items specific to the scheme:
National Parks
Areas of Outstanding Natural beauty
Heritage Coasts
Country Parks
National Trust land
Conservation Areas
Other items
} Description of effect

Group	Interest	Units	Scheme alternatives			
			Red	Green	Blue	'Do nothing'
3.2 Value of historic buildings	Ancient Monuments					
	Listed Building:					
	Grade 1					
	Grade 2	Description of effect	Part of castle moat to be used as carriageway			
	Other structure of character					
3.3 Ecological value	General assessment	Rank	3	1	4	2
	Sites of Special Scientific Interest	Description of effect				
	Nature Reserves					
3.4 Archaeological and historic value	General assessment	Rank	1	3	4	2
	Interest of specific sites	Description of effect				
4.0 Those indirectly affected						
4.1 Effect on resources	Sterilization of mineral deposits	Description of effect				
4.2 Land use planning effects	Job opportunities					
	Number of jobs gained	Number of jobs gained	—	—	—	—
	Number of jobs lost	Number of jobs lost	3	—	—	—
	View of county council	Rank	1	3	2	4
	View of district councils	Rank	2	1	4	3
	View of parish councils	Rank	2	1	4	3
	View of statutory objectors	Rank	1	3	2	4

Group	Interest	Units	Scheme alternatives			
			Red	Green	Blue	'Do nothing'
4.3 Other transport operators and users	Rail	} Description of effect				
	Air					
	Waterways					
4.4 Other factors specific to the scheme		Description of effect				
5.0 Financial authority						
	Construction cost	£m (N.P.V.)	6.2	4.9	4.1	—
	Land cost	£m (N.P.V.)	1.0	1.0	1.0	—
	Compensation cost	£m (N.P.V.)	0.5	—	—	—
	Maintenance cost	£ (N.P.V.)	28,400	28,500	43,500	—
	Total cost	£m (N.P.V.)	7.7284	5.9285	5.1435	—
	Total gross benefits	£m (N.P.V.)	7.5	5.95	6.83	—
	Difference between discounted cost and sum of discounted benefits quantified in monetary terms	£m (N.P.V.)	−0.2284	0.0215	1.6865	—

1. — indicates no effect for the scheme option.

7

The Role of Government

7.1 Introduction

Early economists marvelled at the workings of their economy. They observed that most commodities were produced by large numbers of small businesses and bought by even larger numbers of customers yet, year in year out, barring natural disasters, there never seemed to be large surpluses or shortages. They saw also that most people able and willing to find a job succeeded, so neither was there any great unemployment problem. This was achieved with almost negligible government interference; in other words the economy was controlled by *free market forces*. Many economists today believe in the efficiency of the *market economy* and wish to see the role of government in the economy reduced. In this chapter we will examine why the government may need or want to become involved. We will then consider the ways in which the State may influence the working of the transport sector and examine the role of both central and local government.

7.2 The market mechanism

The interaction of supply and demand in a particular market was described in Chapter 3. This market mechanism which can be witnessed within and between many commodities, dictates the prices of commodities and the quantities demanded and supplied and its responsiveness depends on the elasticities of supply and demand.

Adam Smith in *The Wealth of Nations* in 1776 spoke of the 'invisible hand' of the price mechanism which allocated resources to the most profitable field and did so in an *optimum* manner. The definition of an optimum allocation of resources was made rigorous by Pareto who stated that optimization was achieved when 'it was not possible to re-arrange resource allocation so as to make anyone better off without making someone else worse off as a consequence'.

This is essentially an 'efficiency' measure i.e. for any given income distribution, set of tastes and technological development there will be an allocation, or distribution, of resources which will provide maximum satisfaction for society. Many economists have believed in the past, and many still do, that if the economy is left to its own devices, that is, government does not interfere, the activities of a multitude of producers and consumers acting in their own interests will ensure that society as a whole will benefit to the maximum too. This is sometimes termed the *laissez-faire* doctrine.

Relating this view to the transport sector we have already seen that elasticities are low and, therefore, responsiveness to market forces in the short term is slow. However, in the long term the location of economic activities and the efficiency of the economy will be affected by prices in the transport sector. These prices must, therefore, reflect the true costs. Those who believe in the efficiency of the market mechanism would suggest that the most efficient firms will survive, competition would ensure prices reflect costs and varying costs between firms of different sizes will ensure all markets will be satisfied.

In practice, of course, we see at least some measure of government involvement in all economies, even in those like Hong Kong and the United States with strong laissez-faire traditions. We will now attempt to determine why this should be so in the transport sector. The reasons range from the purely economic, to those where the government is dissatisfied with the outcome of the market mechanism and finally to those of a more immediately practical nature.

7.3 Reasons for government involvement

7.3.1 Fundamental problems with the market mechanism

There are perhaps four areas where the market mechanism has a fundamental flaw. The first we have met before in previous chapters, and it relates to the *external effects*. In order to remedy the resulting misallocation of resources the government may wish to use a tax or subsidy. Secondly, for the market mechanism to work properly the purchase of a commodity by one customer must preclude anyone else from consuming it. If the commodity was, for example, the defence of a country it would be unlikely that one person would purchase such protection and allow everyone else to benefit at no cost. Examples in transport include such facilities as maritime navigation aids and street lighting. These are called *public goods* and are provided by the Government. Thirdly, in Chapter 4 we suggested that road congestion is caused partly because motorists are unaware of the true costs of their journeys. This *inadequacy in perception* is again a serious threat to the efficient working of the market economy and road congestion is merely one example of the resulting misallocation of resources. Finally, there is the problem of *indivisibilities*. Some investments in transport are so large that the private sector would be unlikely to make the necessary decisions without Government initiative. Examples in the U.K. include the Tyne and Wear Metro, the Channel Tunnel and the Third London Airport. Even in Hong Kong, one of the most extreme market economies, Government encouragement was required for the building of the Mass Transit Railway and the large Kwai Chung Container Terminal. The above four factors are all reasons why the market economy may not achieve the optimum allocation of resources. These are all intrinsic to the mechanism which would require some Government involvement regardless of its political views on the desirability of free market forces.

7.3.2   The government and market forces

We have seen in Chapter 4 that firms in monopolistic situations can exploit their market position resulting in a serious misallocation of resources. The government may feel it should protect the consumer from such exploitation. There are many examples of government involvement *to prevent the growth of monopoly* and most developed countries have established anti-trust machinery. In the U.K., the Monopolies Commission was asked to investigate the operation of British Rail's south-east commuter network, and the 1980 Transport Act aimed to encourage more competition in the bus industry. This kind of action has been considered necessary by governments because the market economy has failed to prevent firms growing to such a position of dominance that they can control the market instead of remaining at its mercy as the textbook description of perfect competition suggests it should (see Chapter 4).

We have also seen in the past, governments attempting to prevent wasteful or cut-throat competition between operators. In the United Kingdom in the 1920s there was excessive competition between public transport operators in the major cities, particularly in London. The problems caused were outlined by Sir Henry May in evidence to the Royal Commission on Transport in 1928, the situation:

'was rapidly becoming chaotic, as some twenty new omnibuses were being placed on the streets each week. This intensive competition between the various road services led to further abuses such as "chasing" and "racing" in order to secure passengers . . . while as a result of the unnecessary and wasteful competition, there was every prospect that some of the tramway systems would have to cease operation. Further, there was no incentive to develop new services in outlying areas, where there was a growing need for travelling facilities, because there was no guarantee against excessive competition when these services promised to become remunerative.'

Such intense competition is a characteristic of industries where the capital costs are low (i.e. there are low *'barriers to entry'*) and so the road haulage and coaching markets exhibit such features. The main problem is that, with smaller profits, operators are tempted to cut costs which may well lower safety standards. In addition, it is argued, there will be a waste of resources as too much traffic chasing too little demand results in spare capacity. It should be said, however, that this particular view is not taken by all economists. Notable exceptions are Ponsonby[1] and Hibbs[2] who argue very persuasively that not only will there be no waste of resources but that services will be improved if the government allowed free competition in the bus industry.

In some cases, governments may wish to interfere with the market economy because they feel that the structure of a particular industry is such that *economies of scale* are not being exploited. We have already seen that the Passenger Transport Executives were established in the U.K. partly for this reason but we have also seen that the extent of economies of scale in transport is rather limited and the structure of many of our nationalized transport industries bears witness to this.

We can conclude that governments may be dissatisfied with the structure created by market forces in a number of ways and the transport sector contains examples of all of them. On a number of occasions, the government has wished to create a monopoly in order that it can control the industry better, and on other occasions it has attempted to enhance competition by encouraging the growth of smaller firms. At other times it has felt that there has been too much competition.

The final area in this section involves government concern with *income distribution*. The economies most orientated towards *'laissez-faire'* tend to have the greatest ranges of wealth. A government may feel that a more equitable distribution is desirable. So, in addition to an efficiency optimum, it may superimpose an *'equity' optimum* by, for example, taxing the rich and giving benefits to the poor. In transport, a subsidy for bus transport might be a good example as a greater proportion of the poor travel by bus. The point is more debatable for rail transport. Government figures suggest that subsidizing the railways benefits the better off to a greater extent than the poorer sections of the community and some argue that the way road provision is financed represents a subsidy to the private sector.

7.3.3   More practical considerations

Transport by its very nature is a dangerous activity. We have argued that cut-throat competition might lead to a lowering of safety standards. The Government might then wish to change the way transport is operated to ensure that *minimum safety standards* are met to protect operators, users and third parties, and they will lay down basic rules of behaviour. Ships cannot drop anchor where they please in the harbour; aircraft have to follow air corridors; we drive on one side of the road and we are required to obey speed limits. Laws, therefore, are introduced and enforced in the interests of safety. Similar rules exist for environmental reasons such as those for controlling noise and exhaust fumes. The aim of all these rules is to control the quality of operations rather than their quantity.

The nature of an economy changes over time. New industries are developed and other older ones become less important and decline. Very often the demise of the older industries brings with it *social and industrial relations* problems. We have seen this at times with coal mining, the docks, and steel manufacture. It may also be observed in many railway operations. In these instances it is very difficult for governments not to become involved in such practical issues.

There are also *international aspects*. The poorest nation appears to have its state airline for the prestige it brings, but more important transport involves national governments in the international economy. There must obviously be minimum standards of operating efficiency and safety in international airline operation and most Governments belong to the International Civil Aviation Organization. Similarly, the International Maritime Organization is responsible for establishing international conventions in maritime transport which require the signature and support of individual governments.

Strategic military factors also play a part. State railways are often considered an essential part of a nation's defence system and may be maintained partly for this reason. In some countries, road networks have been developed for military purposes. Sweden, for example, has designed roads to be used by military aircraft. Airlines and shipping fleets have obvious uses in moving troops and equipment as seen when the U.K. task force was sent to the South Atlantic in 1982.

We have considered a range of factors which encourage governments to become involved in the transport sector and not to leave it to market forces. No government is likely to leave transport unregulated for environmental and safety reasons and, clearly, there are pure economic reasons why they must become involved. However, as we have seen, other factors will inevitably result from political persuasion, social attitudes and for reasons of national prestige.

7.4 Means of government influence

How might a Government exert its influence over a particular sector of the economy? In the transport sector, a whole range of measures have been used and the ones which we shall examine are state ownership, and control by means of licensing, financial provision and planning.

7.4.1 State ownership

Operations are usually nationalized because they are considered essential to the nation's interest and because, if they were not state-owned, they could not survive or because the government wants to ensure they follow what they consider to be the correct policy. In some cases, as with the U.K. road haulage industry in the 1940s, the Government attempts to influence the modal split of traffic and the structure of the industry makes this a difficult task.

The most extreme form of nationalization would be to make the operation part of the government. The Post Office in the U.K. was in this position for many years and in Hong Kong the Kowloon—Canton Railway was likewise a government department. In most cases in the U.K., however, state ownership takes the form of the creation of a corporate body with an independent executive board. The chairman of the board is chosen by the Minister and it is to Parliament via the Minister, that he reports. Other board members are normally chosen by the chairman with the approval of the Minister. The nationalized transport industries in the U.K., at the time of writing, are the British Railways Board, the British Waterways Board, the National Bus Company and the Scottish Bus Group and British Airways. The National Freight Corporation and Associated British Ports have recently been transferred to the private sector and the present Government hopes to transfer the NBC and BA as part of its 'privatization' programme.

7.4.2 The relationship between a nationalized industry and the central government

The relationship between a nationalized industry and the government is a complicated and difficult one. Essentially, the government lays down policy and the executive board is responsible for day-to-day management. However, there is a great deal of overlap. Often, governments have used nationalized industries as instruments for macro-economic adjustments with, for example, pay and price freezes and changes in investment plans. Yet most large operations need to plan far into the future; most corporate plans certainly look further ahead than the life of a particular parliament and problems may occur if a change of government brings with it a change of policy. Many a chairman has complained of the inconsistency in government policy and of ministers interfering in the executive function of the Board. C. D. Foster[3] believes, however, that the nationalized industries in the U.K. have a great deal more freedom of movement than is often realized. He suggests, for example, that the power of selection of Board chairmen and members is ineffective as posts do not become vacant often enough and there is strong pressure to appoint people for their general qualities not for their political persuasion. In addition, public enterprises are created by statutes which are deliberately vague in their wording, therefore giving the Boards wide powers of interpretation over which ministers have very little control. In theory, financial control is a powerful instrument but, in practice, Foster suggests the vague nature of the relevant rules again has limited the effectiveness of the Treasury's control over expenditure.

A report in 1976 by the National Economic Development Office discussed whether government should stand back from the nationalized industries and operate an 'arms-length' relationship or whether it should be more closely involved. Its conclusions are worth quoting in some detail:

'It seems to us that the thinking behind the wholly arm's length approach is based on a false analogy with the private sector. The financial structures and disciplines in the public and private sectors are very different — not least because the ultimate sanction of liquidation is in practice absent in the major nationalized industries. Moreover, their importance as employers, suppliers and customers, and the economic and social implications of their actions make it right as well as inevitable that government should take a close interest in their strategies. The issues of public policy involved are so large and politically sensitive that it is not realistic to suppose that they would ever be left for long to management alone to determine, subject only to periodic checks on their financial performance.'[4]

Accordingly it recommended a change in the structure. It proposed that each nationalized industry should be run by a Policy Council responsible for strategy and a Corporation Board carrying out day-to-day activities. The Council would establish corporate objectives and the strategies to achieve them; establish performance criteria; endorse corporate plans and monitor performance. Although agreeing with NEDO's view on its strategic role the Government felt such an institutional restructuring was not necessary and it set out a series of proposals including those concerning the powers of ministers to issue specific as well as general directives.[5]

Public ownership can also take place at a local level. We have already seen in Chapter 3 that, in the bus industry, many operators are controlled by local authorities. Rather than reporting to Parliament and the Minister the executives will report to their transportation committees comprising locally elected councillors. Municipal docks and airports are controlled in a similar manner. We will examine the role of local government in more detail below.

Just how effective state ownership is as a measure of control is a difficult question to answer. Certainly, we have seen British Airways purchase inappropriate aircraft following government pressure and it is likely that road and rail networks would be a lot smaller without government subsidy. However, these are the result of the government holding the purse strings rather than the assets. In other words Government policy can be achieved by financial control in many instances and this could occur even if the operation was in the private sector. Many private bus operators maintain loss-making but socially necessary services with the aid of state financial assistance. Perhaps these other forms of control would be just as effective. The next method we will consider is that of licensing.

7.4.3 Licensing control

To be allowed to drive a car or a motor cycle we need a driving licence and an excise licence for the vehicle. In most developed countries anyone wishing to run a transport business needs an *operator's licence* as well. All these licences have requirements attached to them which the applicant must meet and often some form of examination is required. This then is a potentially powerful form of control. If you wished to operate a road haulage business in the U.K. you would be asked to show to the Licensing Authorities before you were given an operator's licence that you are:

(a) of good repute,
(b) financially sound,
(c) professionally competent,
(d) able to provide environmentally suitable operating premises.

The Licensing Authority is mainly concerned that you are able to operate competently, safely and with as little inconvenience to the general public as possible. Prior to 1968 in the U.K., however, you were also required to show that there was sufficient work for you to do. There is a fundamental difference here. Following the Transport Act 1968 the road haulage industry has been subject only to *quality* licensing. Provided you meet the minimum requirements regarding your safety, finance, competence and environmental suitability you would automatically receive a licence. Before this, however, the government exerted influence on *the market* by asking you to show that there was sufficient traffic and that no existing operator could carry it. This is known as *quantity* licensing and it still operates in part of the bus industry and in airline operation. The Civil Aviation Authority is responsible for granting licences not only for personnel, aircraft and airlines but also for routes. It aims to ensure that routes are properly serviced and at the same time to avoid over-capacity.

The Transport Act 1980 resulted in a relaxation of the licensing requirements in the bus industry. Operators must have drivers and vehicles licensed and an operator's licence is required but a Road Service Licence specifying the route to be taken is no longer necessary for Excursion and Tour and Express services. This then was a change from quantity to quality licensing. In stage-carriage services, however, some form of quantity control remains. The onus is now on existing operators to show a new operation is against the public interest but an appeal on the grounds of *abstraction* (the taking away of traffic) and the subsequent inability to cross-subsidize (see Chapter 5) is likely to be successful.

So government interference in the market mechanism by licensing control is very much in evidence in parts of the bus industry and in airline operation. In Europe, particularly in Germany and France, quantity control in road haulage is used to protect the heavily subsidized railways (see Chapter 9). Maritime transport is probably the least controlled by licensing partly because it was in existence before Governments began licensing procedures and partly because the potential danger to the safety of the public is not as great as with domestic transport or airline operation. Nevertheless, although there is no operator's licence as such, each ship requires a certificate of registry, a loadline certificate and, amongst others, certificates for safety equipment and safety radio telegraphy and rodent level inspection, Lloyds hull and machinery inspections and an oil pollution prevention certificate. The Department of Trade also requires an owner to have a certificate of responsibility which satisfies the British Government that he could honour his debts were claims to be made against him, for instance in a massive pollution claim.

All licensing is, of course, an infringement on the working of free market forces in that barriers to entry into markets are raised, but it is hard to disagree with the imposition of those quality controls described above. Licensing is only effective, of course, if it is properly enforced. In many countries this is not so, mainly due to the shortage of enforcement staff and it is obvious that if there is a general reluctance to conform to licensing requirements there is not a great deal the overstretched authorities can do. The important question for economists, however, is whether quantity licensing can be justified in the face of arguments in favour of allowing market forces to operate freely.

Table 7.1 Government expenditure on transport

	£ million cash 1981—82	Estimated 1984—85
Central government finance		
Department of Transport		
Motorways and trunk roads	639	770
Subsidies to transport industries	919	1,050
Ports	109	110
Other transport services	60	70
Driver and vehicle licensing	73	90
Department of Environment		
British Waterways Board	28	35[1]
Other transport services	22	10
Department of Trade		
Shipping	31	30
Civil aviation	19	15[1]
Scottish Office		
Roads and transport	131	148[1]
Welsh Office		
Roads and transport	114	143[1]
	2,145	2,471
Local government finance		
Capital		
Roads, new construction and improvment	338	⎫
Car parks	15	850
Public transport investment	250	⎬
Local authority airports	31	35
Scottish Office	148	168[1]
Welsh Office	49	· 61
	831	1,114
Current		
Roads maintenance	692	⎫
Car parks	−18	
Road safety etc.	13	1,540
Local authority administration	230	⎭
Passenger transport subsidies		
British Rail	47	
Bus, underground and ferry service	377	
Concessionary fares	157	
Scottish Office	215	244[1]
Welsh Office	93	116[1]
	1,806	1,900
Total	4,782	5,485

[1] (In the absence of more detailed figures these have been broken down on the basis of the same proportions as in 1981—82)

Source: *The Government's Expenditure Plans 1981—2 to 1984—5,* (HMSO: London).

7.4.4 Financial and planning control

Financial and Planning control by Government are considered together because in practice the two are very closely related. Put bluntly if plans do not follow Government guidelines financial help might well be withheld. This chapter has as its theme the extent to which market forces are interfered with by the state. We are concerned in this section with the financial and planning relationships between U.K. operators and the state, and between central and local government. This latter relationship is important as recent history indicates that conflict between the two levels often occurs because different views prevail over the extent to which the state should be involved, and, therefore the degree to which market forces should be manipulated.

Table 7.1 gives a breakdown of the U.K. Government's expenditure on transport. You can see it is divided into central and local government expenditure. Central government funds (about 45% of the total) are mainly directed towards motorway and trunk road construction and maintenance and subsidies to transport industries. A much smaller sum is allocated to shipping and civil aviation.

7.4.5 Central government finance

7.4.5.1 Motorways and trunk roads
The Government's stated priorities for spending on trunk roads in England are:

1 Roads which aid economic recovery and development,
2 Roads which bring environmental benefit, and
3 preserving the investment already made.[6]

The Government is also particularly concerned to reduce the traffic hazards to small towns and villages by increasing the number of trunk road by-passes. Obviously, the road programme is a major source of influence on traffic patterns. Roads will compete for funds with other modes, particularly rail, and lowering motoring costs will have a marked effect on passenger and freight modal split.

7.4.5.2 Transport industries
This mainly concerns British Rail and the U.K. Government has certain obligations under European Community Regulations. The government must compensate the British Railways Board for the costs which they incur in carrying out the Public Service Obligation (PSO) imposed upon them by the Government to provide passenger railway services comparable with those provided in 1974, that is, for those loss-making but socially necessary

services. In fact, in the past the Government's subsidies to BRB have exceeded that required for the public service obligation as costs have risen and passenger revenues declined.

Nationalized industry finance for capital projects is arranged through the *National Loans Fund (NLF)*. A nationalized transport industry may borrow from the NLF only for properly agreed purposes where there is a real expectation of it being able to meet the interest and payment commitments and over periods which relate to the book lives of the industry's principal assets. A statutory borrowing limit is imposed (in 1982 it was set at £1,100 million for British Rail) and the industry must ensure this is not exceeded. In addition to the statutory borrowing limit, an industry's borrowing is restricted in any year by the operation of its *external finance limit* (EFL). The EFL is a limit, set in advance by the Government, on the total amount of external finance which an industry can take in a financial year and its elements include grants and leasing as well as borrowing. In the case of BRB the external finance has to cover both the cash required for operating deficits and the cash required for investment.

Other financial provision for transport industries includes that for new bus grants (currently being phased out) whereby grants are given towards the purchase of new buses provided that they are adapted for one person operation. There is also a 'Section 8 Grant' under the Railways Act 1974 towards the costs of providing rail freight handling facilities and wagons in cases where a transfer of traffic to rail will produce worthwhile environmental benefits.

Most of the provision for ports is to encourage the development of modern port facilities and the British Waterways Board receives a grant towards essential maintenance work. In shipping, financial assistance covers expenditure on the Coastguard, the inspection and surveying of ships and equipment, the examination and licensing of seafarers, search and rescue, research and the U.K. subscription to the International Maritime Organization (IMO). Central government funds for civil aviation services include those for capital investment by the Civil Aviation Authority and for the administration of air traffic control.

We have examined central government financial arrangements for transport industries in some detail. The important question in this chapter is how much this involvement restricts the independence of operators to act as they wish in the face of market pressures. If the public service obligation imposed on an operator is clearly defined and paid for by government explicitly there should be few problems. The operator can act commercially in the other services knowing loss-making ones are being taken care of by separate government grants. Problems arise where the distinction between the socially necessary services and commercial services becomes blurred and one has to be financially covered by the other. There is also the problem for the operator where the government provides funds for investment and can, therefore, influence investment decisions. C. D. Foster was astonished, when he joined the Ministry of Transport in the sixties that

> 'no railway investment project had been turned down in spite of (i) the large deficit the railway had run for many years, and (ii) the widespread feeling, shared by many officials, that a very large slice of that railway investment had been dragging BR deeper into the red since the mid-fifties'.[3]

More recently, however, we have seen, as over BR electrification, the government looking at individual schemes much more closely and attaching conditions on productivity before permission is given for investment. This is a clear example of the government using its financial control to exert influence on the executive function. It would argue, perhaps, that it needs to do this to increase efficiency in the absence of market pressures. The bus grants described above were clearly designed to encourage productivity and many companies found operating difficulties with one-person-operation, particularly in city centres and we have already referred to the pressure the government placed on British Airways to purchase certain aircraft.

7.4.6   Local government

Table 7.1 shows that local authorities are responsible for about 55% of government expenditure and they play an equally significant role in planning for transport services. We are concerned with local authority functions in transport and the relationship between local and central government.

Since April 1974 there has been a two-tier structure in local government with 47 County Authorities (termed Non-Metropolitan Counties) and 333 District Councils in England and Wales. In London, there is the Greater London Council with 32 London Boroughs and the City of London. The six main conurbations outside London are governed by Metropolitan County Councils and contained within these areas are 36 Metropolitan Districts. Figure 7.1 outlines their responsibilities.

There is a third tier of lesser significance; Parish councils are responsible for footpaths and bridleways, off-street parking, footway lighting, parks and open spaces, allotments, swimming baths and cemeteries.

There are three main instruments in which local authorities present their plans for transport and by which central government in the U.K. can monitor and influence the transport plans of local authorities. These are (1) Structure Plans, (2) Transport Policies and Programmes (TPPs) and (3)

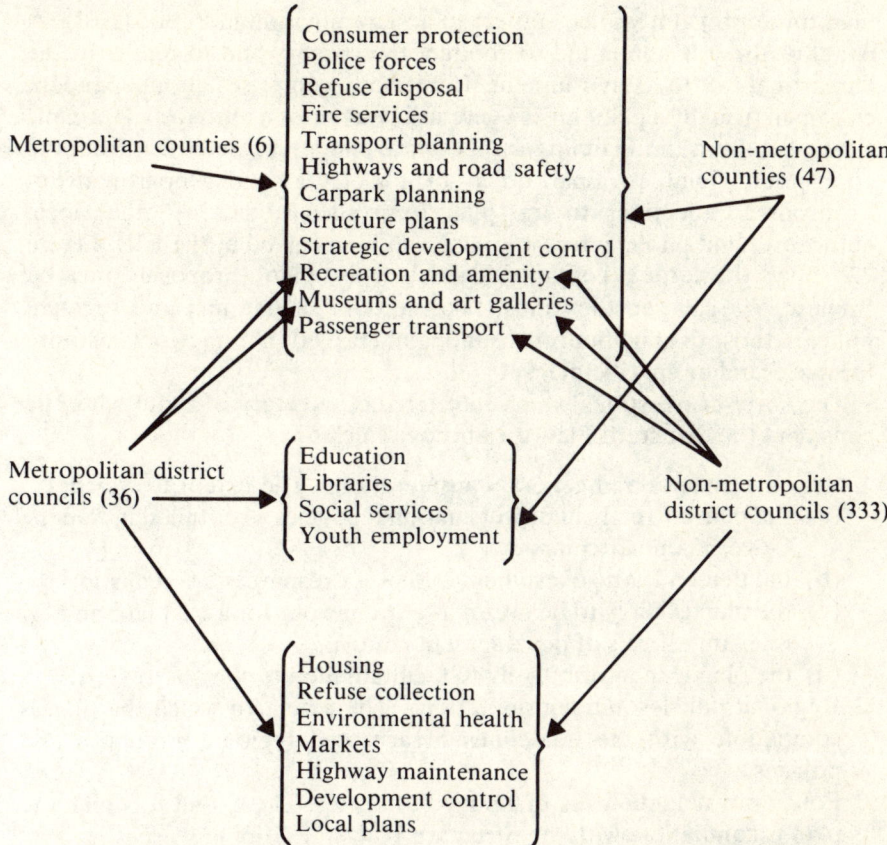

Figure 7.1 Local authority responsibilities in England and Wales (not including Greater London Area).

Public Transport Plans (PTPs). In all three cases, local authorities are obliged to submit their plans for approval to the Secretaries of State for the Environment or Transport. We shall examine each in turn.

7.4.6.1 Structure Plans

The Town and Country Planning Act 1971 obliged county councils to submit for approval to central government a structure plan outlining their strategic policies for the following fifteen years or so. The areas to be covered in addition to transportation included economic development, housing, shopping, commercial and industrial development, leisure, waste disposal and the environment.

Before the Secretary of State for the Environment considers a structure plan for approval it will be subject to an Examination in Public (EIP). A panel of three is appointed to conduct the enquiry and to report to the Department of the Environment. It normally comprises an independent chairman (usually a planning lawyer, an academic or a retired civil servant) a member from the Planning Inspectorate and a representative from the appropriate joint regional office of the DOE and Department of Transport. Objections to the plan from such bodies as other local authorities and public interest groups will be received at the EIP. Figure 7.2 shows the context within which a structure plan's proposals must be framed. We can see they must take account of national and regional policies, those of neighbouring counties and provide a framework for more localized and/or specific plans.

The sorts of questions which interest the Secretary of State when he considers the Structure Plan for approval include:

1 National policies and general considerations. The extent to which:
   (a) the plan correctly interprets national policies as outlined in Papers, Government Circulars etc.,
   (b) the demands on government and other resources are realistic,
   (c) the plan is likely to be useful as a framework for local plans and for relevant aspects of development control,
   (d) the plan is in a form likely to facilitate monitoring and review.
2 Regional policies and considerations. The extent to which the plan is compatible with the guidelines of accepted regional strategies and policies.
3 Policies of neighbouring planning authorities. The extent to which the plan is compatible with the Structure Plans for adjoining areas.
4 Conflicts within and between the policies and general prospects of the plan
   The extent to which:
   (a) the plan contains adequate reasoned justification for the policies and general proposals put forward,
   (b) the policies and proposals put forward in the plan are consistent with each other and related to the issues identified by the authority.
5 Controversy
   The extent to which the plan deals with points which have aroused substantial controversy.[7]

Quite clearly, the procedures developed indicate that central government has the intention to monitor and, if necessary, change proposals by Local Authorities in all aspects of planning. Indeed, one study[8] which examined the structure plan system did provide evidence, as for example with those plans for Berkshire and South Yorkshire, where central government expressed its disapproval and demanded change.

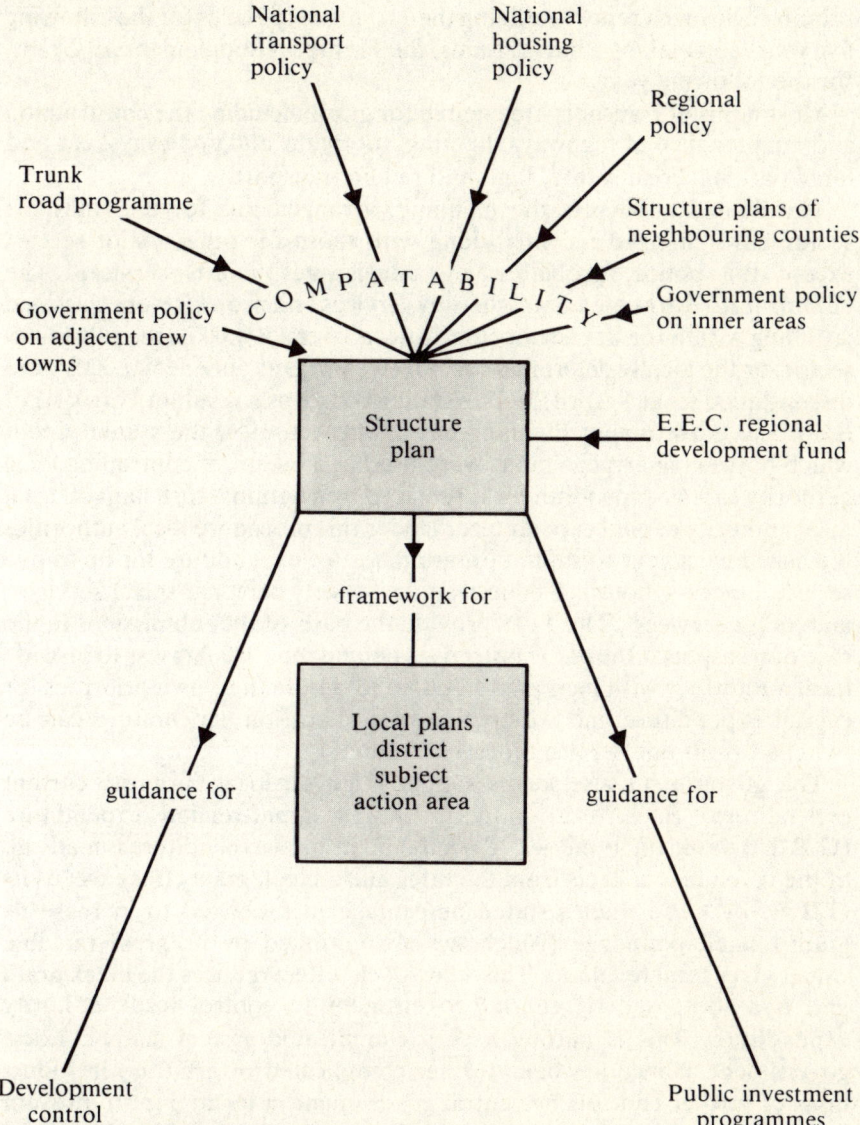

Figure 7.2 The framework for a structure plan.

7.4.6.2 *Transport policies and programmes*

These cover a shorter time period than structure plans and are concerned only with transport matters. The Local Government Act, 1972 made County Councils responsible for the promotion of a co-ordinated system of transport to meet the needs of its area. Accordingly, they were required to submit each year a report outlining their transport policies for the following five years and making a bid for funds, the Transport Supplementary Grant, for the following year.

Most items of transport are eligible for grant including the construction and maintenance of highways, lighting, footpaths and cycleways, car and lorry parking, road safety, land and public transport.

The financial, but not the planning, arrangements for the transport sector have changed recently along with those for other major sectors except the police, probation and magistrates' courts services. The administrative arrangements whereby services and projects were classified as falling within the key sector (for projects over £500,000), the subsidiary sector, or the locally determined sector (for projects under £500,000) were discontinued from 1 April, 1981. From that date as a result of Part VIII of the Local Government Planning and Land Act, 1980 the system under which borrowing arrangements were used as a means of controlling local authority capital expenditure was replaced by a national cash limit on total local authority capital expenditure. Under this procedure local authorities are asked each year to submit programmes for expenditure for up to five service blocks — housing, education, transport, personal social services, and 'other services'. The TPPs provide the basis of the submissions in the case of transport. One of the objectives behind the 1980 Act was to provide local authorities with increased freedom to decide their own priorities for capital expenditure and within the total allocation expenditure can be switched from one service block to another.

The government also keeps a tight reign on local authority current expenditure. Each local authority has a grant-related expenditure (G.R.E.) based on its measured needs and its total expenditure is made up of the revenue it collects from the rates and a block grant. If it exceeds its G.R.E. by more than a stated percentage it is obliged to increase its grant-related poundage (which, when multiplied by its gross rateable value, gives total revenue). This 'claw-back' effect reduces the block grant and is a tool used by central government to control local authority expenditure. This is putting a very complicated system simply. Local government finance has been further complicated by arbitrary introductions of further controls by central government in its attempt to prevent local authorities 'overspending'. This has included 'target' levels of local authority expenditure aimed at cutting spending in real terms. The procedures are being changed quite regularly. Between 1979 and 1982 there were seven different grant systems applied to local government!

It is worth noting that the calculations used by the Department of the Environment to allocate funds can be manipulated to favour particular types of local authority. For example, if factors determining allocated expenditure include 'Number of Agricultural Workers' this will obviously favour the shires at the expense of the urban authorities.

The central government had exerted control with a variety of discretionary and mandatory grants for many years before the 1972 arrangements were introduced, but it was felt there was an inherent bias towards capital projects, particularly road investments. The objectives of the new grant system were to:

(a) Promote the development and execution of comprehensive transport plans by the new county councils and the GLC;
(b) Eliminate bias towards capital or current expenditure or towards particular forms of expenditure;
(c) Distribute central government grant in a way that reflects as far as possible the needs of individual areas;
(d) Reduce the degree of detailed supervision by central government over individual schemes.[9]

So, although the Government was intent on reducing its detailed supervision of individual schemes, it aimed to maintain control over policy and was able to do this because it was responsible for a large part of the finance. The Government issues guidelines to local authorities on the total sums likely to be available and upon which areas of transport finance it will look favourably or otherwise. One area, that of revenue support for bus operators, is a good illustration of the control that central government exerts.[10]

In the circular setting out the arrangements for the first year's submissions,[11] local authorities were encouraged to support bus operations:

'In their early years, TPPs, will be regarded as an opportunity for exploring the practical applications in particular circumstances of policies designed to favour public transport, and to help develop criteria for evaluating revenue support measures.'

However, because the counties began supporting low fares policies from the rates and subsidies were high (£86 million at November 1973 prices) the Government decided revenue support had to be a separate item in the TPP submission and it accepted £102 million for 1975/76 compared with a bid of £110 million (at November 1973 prices). In the following year's circular, local authorities were informed that revenue support for buses and the underground railways was to be reduced by half in real terms within three years. After this, accepted expenditure was much below that demanded and following negotiation (with the exception of South Yorkshire Metropolitan Council) counties agreed to reduce bus revenue support which in effect fell by a third in real terms in the next two years. This battle between local authorities and central government over revenue support for public transport continues. In Department of Transport Circular 3/82 it was stated that the Secretary of State was not prepared to accept proposals for subsidies intended to implement generalized low fares policies. In the case of London, the conflict was taken to the House of Lords which ruled against such low fares policies. It is clear that the wider conflict over the independence of local authorities in transport (and other) matters will continue.

7.4.6.3   Public Transport Plans

These apply only to non-metropolitan counties and were established by the Transport Act, 1978 which gave duties and powers to local authorities and public transport operators for:

(a) The co-ordination and financial assistance of public transport;
(b) The preparation and publication of county transport plans; and
(c) The conclusion of agreements between counties and operators for the financial support of public transport.

There is obviously a great deal of overlap between Public Transport Plans (PTPs) and TPPs and of course they must be compatible, but the PTPs mark a development in three ways:

(a) They treat the subject in more detail and include a wide range of services in addition to conventional ones such as home to school transport, hospital and welfare services, community buses and social car schemes,
(b) They reflect closer and more extensive consultation with the operators, and
(c) They are formally published as the county council's considered policy for public transport.

Each plan must include information on the following:

(a) Need and present position
     Local authorities are required to develop principles upon which they can assess the need and these should be presented in the report.
(b) Objectives, policies and proposals
     The authorities are required to set out their policies and to make clear how compatible they are with the operational and financial resources available.
(c) Financial resources
     These should include revenue, and expected grant income.
(d) Particulars of agreements
     The Government is more concerned with the practical effects of agreements in terms of service levels and income rather than the detail of actual agreements.

(e) Concessionary fares
   These will include concessions for pensioners, the blind and disabled and contributions towards childrens' fares and welfare services.

These three documents, which the local authorities are required to produce, represent levels of central government supervision ranging from the strategic with the structure plans to the extremely detailed operational in the public transport plans. Government is clearly very much involved in the transport sector. Conflicts between central and local government have occurred mainly because there has been a difference of views on the degree to which public transport should be controlled by financial means. Soon after the TPP system was introduced central government believed local authorities, particularly the non-metropolitan counties were not encouraging, and therefore, subsidizing operators enough. Subsequently though, and particularly with a Conservative government, it has been more a question of central government demanding that the public transport sector be increasingly subjected to the vagaries of the market place.

7.4.7 Government organization and the transport sector

Having looked at the way government is involved in transport we will now examine the way it is organized for administration in the U.K. There are a number of governmental departments with responsibilities in transport and, we have seen how local authorities play a major part. We will now deal with central government.

7.4.7.1 *The department of transport*
This is naturally the department most involved in transport and therefore it will be examined in some detail. Its status was restored in 1976 when it was taken from under the umbrella of the Department of the Environment and, recently, its Secretary of State has been given Cabinet Status. Figure 7.3 shows the higher levels of the Department's organization. Reporting to the two ministers is the Permanent Secretary and he is responsible for three main divisions each headed by a Deputy Secretary.

The first is that responsible for the *transport industries* and comprises four directorates. *The freight directorate* is responsible for the control of road haulage and covers the question of heavier lorries, the transport of dangerous goods (including radio-active materials) and licensing and statistics. *The railways directorate* comprises five divisions responsible for investment programmes, performance standards, EEC matters, all the passenger services, parcels, Freightliner and engineering services and the

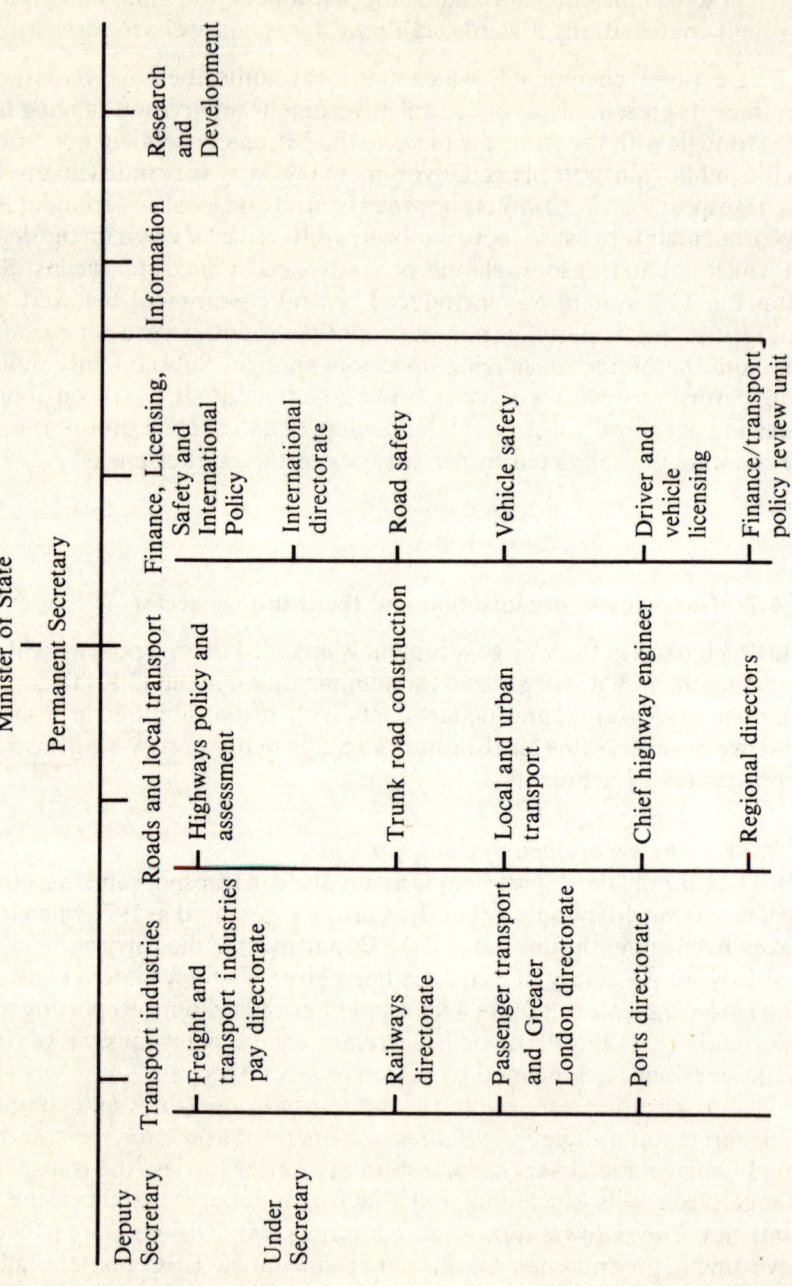

Figure 7.3 The structure of the Department of Transport.

various grants available to British Railways. One division is concerned with the privatization of parts of British Rail and another with line closures and re-openings. There is also the *Railway inspectorate* concerned with safety. The third Directorate is responsible for *Ports*, and the fourth is the *Passenger transport and Greater London Directorate*. It covers NBC, the bus grant, revenue support and concessionary fares. It is also responsible for licensing and therefore deals with the Traffic Commissioners. London requires two sections; one for passenger transport and one for roads and traffic.

The largest division in terms of personnel is that responsible for *Roads and local transport*. The first Directorate is that of *Highways policy and assessment*. This is concerned with trunk road policy and spending control, compensation and public enquiry procedures. It also contains the Assessment policy and methods section which is made up of nine parts and is responsible for producing the COBA and TAM manuals (see Chapter 6) and for traffic forecasting methodology. The second Directorate is *Trunk road construction* and is responsible for getting roads built. It comprises the Administration of road construction, the Road programme management and the Contracts division, together with the Maintenance division. Sitting rather uneasily besides these large road directorates is that for *Local and urban transport* which covers urban traffic policy, traffic management, new urban transport systems and land transport aspects of airports.

The *Chief Highway Engineer's* Directorate performs a non-executive function fulfilling an advisory, supervisory and policy-making role. The titles of its divisions are reasonably self-explicit — Bridges, Engineering technical approvals, Bridges engineering design standards, Engineering intelligence, Traffic engineering (including traffic signals and motorway lighting and National Traffic Census), Traffic control and communications (motorway and urban communication systems) and finally the Highway engineering computer branch. There are also the regional offices with executive functions and responsibility for liaison with local authorities.

The third Division is that for *Finance, licensing, safety and international policy*. *The Road safety directorate*'s responsibilities include legislation, enforcement, police, drinking and driving and seat belts, medical aspects and publicity, education and public relations. It is also concerned with vehicle standards and accident investigation and prevention. Another directorate is responsible for *driver and vehicle licensing. The International Transport Directorate* covers all international agreements and EEC matters and includes the Channel Tunnel Unit. Finally, *Finance* is concerned with the financial aspects of the nationalized industries, licensing, the Channel Tunnel, defence planning and local transport finances. It also has responsibilities in highway finance and deals with the regional office's schemes.

7.4.7.2   Department of Trade

We would expect this department to be involved with transport as the two areas are so closely related and it has responsibilities in tourism, civil aviation, airports, shipping and marine services. The Civil Aviation Act, 1971 gave the Secretary of State powers of direction and appointment in relation to the Civil Aviation Authority so the department has ultimate responsibility for the maintenance of standards in civil aviation operation, air navigation, air safety and the design, development and production of aircraft. It covers, therefore, the licensing of operators, personnel, aircraft and routes. The Secretary of State is also responsible for the appointment of the Chairman and Members of the British Airways Board. Tour operators are also supervized by the department and are required to be licensed. In shipping, the department is responsible for ensuring compliance with regulations concerning safety and welfare at sea under the Merchant Shipping Acts and covers navigation, the coastguard and the investigation of accidents at sea. Pipelines also come under its control. In June 1983 shipping and aviation responsibilities of the Department of Trade were transferred to the Department of Transport.

7.4.7.3   The Department of the Environment

This Department is specifically responsible for the 2,000 miles of inland waterways but its greatest influence lies in the supervision of *land-use planning* which is inextricably tied up with transport planning. We have already seen that County Structure Plans are submitted for approval to the Secretary of State and he also has joint responsibility with his counterpart in the Transport Department for the approval of highway schemes.

7.4.7.4   Other government departments

The *Treasury* plays a co-ordinating role in the allocation of financial resources and as such has the ultimate responsibility, but is more concerned with the macro-economic consequences of investment strategy.

The *Department of Industry* is involved in transport to the extent that it has responsibility in manufacturing with such firms as Rolls Royce, British Leyland, Swan Hunter and British Aerospace. The fact that transport is a large consumer of energy and user of labour means also, of course, that the policies of the *Department of Energy* and *Employment* play an important role.

Examination questions

1 To what extent are government controls on competition between operators necessary for the sound development of the road passenger transport industry?
2 Discuss the advantages and disadvantages of moving responsibility for

the allocation of public expenditure on roads and public passenger transport from the central government to the local authorities.

3 Analyse local government responsibility for transport in your country. Explain how local government expenditure is funded, and consider what improvements, if any, should be made.

4 'It is impossible to reconcile the purposes of public ownership with the independence needed for vigorous and enterprising management.' Comment on this statement in relation to state transport corporations.

5 Outline the structure of central government in your country, identifying the departments with transport responsibilities. Assess its effectiveness and suggest those areas in which improvements might be made.

6 'Non-discriminatory (quality) licensing is desired by all; discriminatory (quantity) licensing only by governments and large operators.' Analyse this statement in relation to the control of road transport in your country.

7 Critically analyse the role and purpose of British structure plans, Public transport plans and transport policies and programmes.

8 Discuss critically the sources and priorities for major investment in the various transport modes in your country.

9 Outline the licensing policies and procedures designed to ensure the safe operation of two modes of transport in your country, identify any deficiencies in the system and recommend improvements accordingly.

10 'There is little merit in creating state transport corporations, or nationalizing existing transport assets, unless the provision of transport on a social service basis is a prime objective'. Discuss critically.

8

Transport Planning

8.1 Introduction

Travelling, particularly in built-up areas is seldom a pleasant experience. The situation seems to be deteriorating too as traffic levels increase. Yet we see many examples of things designed to make getting about easier and a little less frustrating; new motorways, synchronized traffic light systems, road-rail interchanges, one-way systems, and bus-lanes. These are all the easily identifiable results of the involved, expensive and lengthy process which is transport planning. We can divide transport planning into two parts. The first part (which we shall concentrate on) examines the factors which influence the level of travel demand and having analysed the relationship tries to predict future travel patterns. The second part (transport engineering) tries to deal in some way with the traffic flows expected.

First, we shall examine the way various factors influence the demand for transport in the national context. This is the area of traffic forecasting and we will pay particular attention to the techniques and problems of *car ownership forecasting*. We will then look at the relationship between land-use and transport demand which leads us into a description of the *transportation model*. This is the process which transport planners use for estimating demand in defined areas and testing and evaluating the solutions they have arrived at to deal with that demand. There then follows a brief outline of transport planning in practice in the U.K. including procedural, institutional and organizational matters.

8.2 Traffic forecasting

It is generally recognized that forecasting is an exercise full of uncertainty and inaccuracy. Table 8.1 compares the actual with forecast estimates of

Table 8.1 Comparison of predicted and observed flows on road schemes

Scheme	Flow predicted for 1974 (vehicles/16 h av day)	Date of forecast	Observed flow (vehicles/16 h av day in given month)
A64 York By-pass[1,4]	15,090	1970	20,000 (June 1977)
A63 Dualling Cowes By-pass[3,5]	22,000[11]	1963	12,100 (April 1977)
A108 Sunderland By-pass[1,4]	13,700	1964	20,900 (February 1977)
A55 Chester By-pass[1,6]	23,100	1966	11,500 (July 1977)
A38 Sutton Coldfield[1,6,7]	20,000	1964	{ 8,500 (August 1974) / 12,800 (August 1977)
M69 Coventry to Leicester[2,4,8]	29,500	1964	11,500 (July 1977)[12]
A12 Colchester By-pass[1,4]	6,090	1968	11,500 (August 1975)
A1–A111 Potters Bar[3,4]	26,000	1969	15,300 (April 1977)
A34 Abingdon By-pass[1,8]	14,000	—	12,300 (August 1976)
A2 Lyddon to Dover[1,4]	8,400	1968	11,800 (May 1977)
A30 Camborne By-pass[1,2,7]	14,600—18,300	1966	15,500 (August 1970)
M5 (junctions 28—31)[3,9]	40,000[11]	1965	{ 60,000 (typical Saturday August 1970) / 45,000 (annual average 1976)
A303 Wylye By-pass[1,7]	15,000	1968	8,000 (August 1970)
A1 Lemsford to Welwyn Diversion[3,6]	35,700	1968	31,600 (August 1976)

Notes

1 Predicted flow directly available as vehicles/16-hour average August day in 1974, no conversion required.
2 Range of predicted/observed flows covering the different sections of the scheme.
3 Predicted flow given as pcu/16-hour August day in 1974, converted to vehicle/16-hour August day using a pcu/veh ratio of 1:20.
4 Observed flow, originally quoted as axles/2, divided by 1.1 to give vehicles.
5 Observed flow originally quoted as vehicles per weekday, multiplied by 0.9 to give 7-day average flow.
6 Observed flow originally quoted as vehicles per 16-hour average day (i.e. averaged over 7 days).
7 Observed flow originally quoted as estimated vehicles/16-hour average August day.
8 Observed flow, originally quoted as per 24-hour day, multiplied by 0.95 to give per 16-hour day.
9 Because of the exceptional seasonal variation on this section of the M5 two figures have been quoted. The first gives a typical vehicular flow for an August Saturday, the second is an estimate of the annual average 16-hour day flow.
10 The predicted figures were originally quoted as urban pcu/peak hour in 1985. Adequate conversion factors cannot readily be derived from the information available.
11 Observed data collected within one month of the opening of the scheme and therefore unlikely to be a satisfactory measure of stable conditions on the scheme.

Source: Department of Transport. *Report of the Advisory Committee on Trunk Road Assessment* (HMSO: London, 1977)

traffic using various road schemes in the U.K.,[1] and we can see some significant differences.

Traffic forecasts for Concorde and the Humber Bridge appear very optimistic in retrospect, but the M4 needed to be widened not long after it was built and, in Hong Kong, there were even tentative plans to fit in an extra level for car traffic in the existing Cross-Harbour Tunnel! But traffic forecasting plays a fundamental role in transport planning. The size of a new airport runway or terminal and the design standards of new roads depend entirely on the traffic predicted. In addition, as we saw in Chapter 6, the 'worth' of a transport investment will increase with the amount of use it is expected to have. The planning procedures described in the previous chapter also rely heavily on forecasts of traffic levels as well as of economic growth, and perhaps the most critical area is that concerning energy where Government policy will depend crucially on traffic forecasts — transport accounts for about 25% of energy consumption.

8.2.1   Forecasting techniques

We will examine techniques, called models, for estimating car travel, goods traffic by road and air travel.

8.2.1.1   Car ownership forecasting

Car traffic depends on the number of cars owned per head of population, the total driving population, and the distance the vehicles travel. It is crucial then to be able to forecast car ownership levels accurately. Official estimates are based on two types of model — aggregate and disaggregate. The aggregate model was the one to be used first. It expressed growth in car ownership per person in terms of gross domestic product per capita and motoring costs. The future levels of these factors were estimated and applied to population projections. These were then related to assumptions about saturation levels of car ownership per head. The mathematical formula which 'pictures' this relationship is as follows:

$$y = \frac{s}{1+(a(t-T)+b \log i+c \log p)^{-n}}$$

where
   y is cars per person in Great Britain in year t,
   i is GDP per person in year t at fixed prices,
   p is cost of motoring in year t at fixed prices,
   s, a, b, c, T, n are parameters to be determined.

To the unmathematical this looks rather daunting but stripped of the mathematics it is quite simple. y is the thing we are looking for — future car ownership per head. s is the important assumed saturation level. The

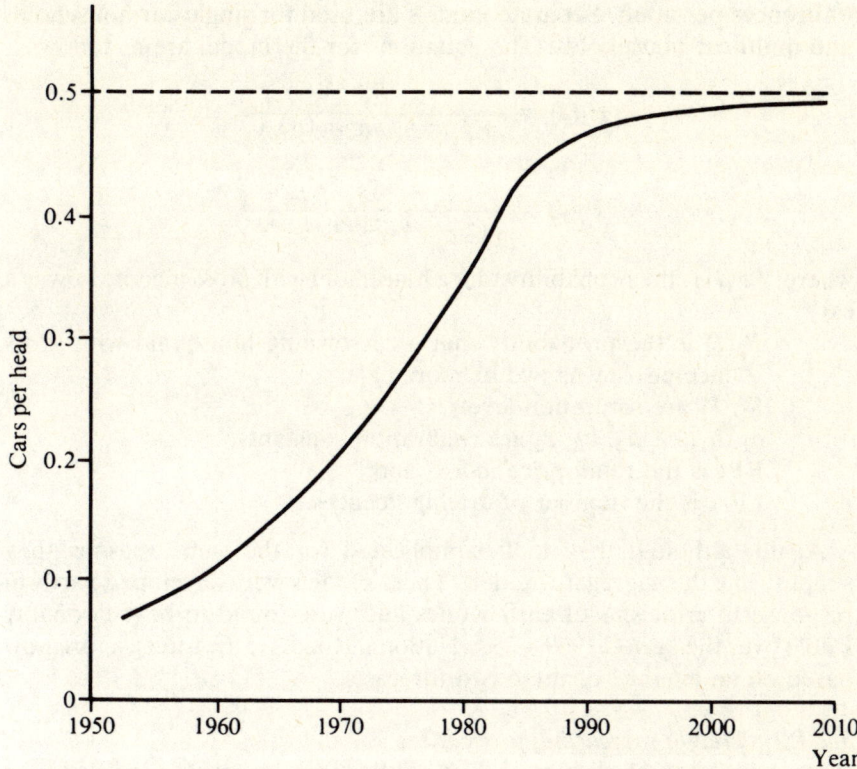

Figure 8.1 The s-shaped curve used in car ownership forecasting.

complicated part to the right of the 1+under the line relates to GDP, motoring costs and time. However, in time, or as GDP increases, they become small enough to ignore and the equation becomes

$$y = \frac{s}{1+0} \text{ or } s$$

If the equation was plotted on to a graph it would produce an S-shaped curve of the type shown in Figure 8.1. As you can see the top of the curve gets closer to the horizontal *s*-line without actually reaching it — we say it approaches it asymptotically. That saturation line is therefore critical. We will look at it again later.

The disaggregate model, instead of looking at car ownership over time compares it with a whole range of household incomes. This is called *cross-sectional analysis*. Forecasts are based on estimates of changes in real household income, changes in the distribution of income, and the number of licences per adult. Separate models are used for single-car households and multi-car households. The equations for the model are as follows:

$$P_1(I) = \frac{S_1}{(1+e^{a_1+b_1\,(I/\text{RPI})+c_1\text{LPA}})}$$

$$P_2(I) = \frac{S_2}{(1+e^{a_2+b_2\,(I/\text{RPI})+c_2\text{LPA}})}$$

where: $P_1(I)$ is the probability that a household with gross income I owns a car,

$P_2(I)$ is the probability that a car owning household with gross income I owns two or more cars,

S_1, S_2 are saturation levels,

a_1, b_1, c_1, a_2, b_2, c_2 are calibration constants,

RPI is the retail price index, and

LPA is the number of driving licences.

Again, although they look complicated for the same reasons they simplify like the aggregate models. These models were developed partly in response to criticisms of earlier ones and were found to be 'reasonably stable over the period 1969—75'[2]. National Road Traffic forecasts are now based on an average of these two forecasts.

8.2.1.2 Freight forecasting procedures

We are concerned here with the official forecasts for road freight in terms of the annual kilometres travelled by goods vehicles exceeding 30 cwt unladen weight. The procedure has two main parts. Firstly, forecasts of industrial and commercial requirements for freight movements in terms of tonne-kilometres by road are produced. This is the 'demand side'. Goods are divided into commodity groups found in official statistics, e.g., coal and coke, chemicals and food and drink. Forecasts are made using past trends, assumptions about GDP and population growth and any other relevant factors such as the economic outlook for particular industries. The 'supply side' is then calculated by matching fleet size and composition to the given demand.

8.2.1.3 The forecasting of air traffic

Only a small minority of the population travels regularly by air, but civil aviation is a large consumer of energy and the infrastructure required such as runways and terminals involve huge sums of investment. Consequently, great emphasis is placed on traffic forecasting. The 1978 White Paper on Airports Policy (Cmnd 7084) signalled the establishment of the Air Traffic Forecasting Working Party. Its role is to monitor air traffic forecasts in line

with the development of traffic and to keep assumptions and methodology under review. The model[3] which has been developed is very complicated and the explanatory variables numerous.
They are:

UKGDPP	UK gross domestic product per capita
WEGDPP	Western Europe gross domestic product per capita
RWGDPP	Rest of world gross domestic product per capita
UKGDP	UK gross domestic product
WEGDP	Western Europe gross domestic product
RWGDP	Rest of world gross domestic product
TLHBF	Total long haul business fare
UKSHLF	UK short haul leisure fare
FOSHLF	Foreign short haul leisure fare
UKLHLF	UK long haul leisure fare
FOLHLF	Foreign long haul leisure fare
RTP1A	UKSHL Relative tourist price
RTP2A	UKLHL Relative tourist price
RTP3A	FOSHL Relative tourist price
RTP4A	FOLHL Relative tourist price
UKPOP	UK population
WEPOP	Western Europe population
RWPOP	Rest of World population

Recent improvements have been made to the model in particular the introduction of tourist prices as a variable in leisure traffic equations and changes in the business traffic equations.

8.2.2 Some comments on the various forecasting models

There has been severe criticism of forecasting procedures. We have insufficient space to deal with them adequately and would refer you to the references below. However, we will outline some of the most important problems associated with these techniques.

8.2.2.1 Car ownership models

Both the aggregate and disaggregate models use readily available information and are therefore cheap and easy to produce and both are considered to be reasonably accurate in prediction. As with all the models they depend on the accuracy of predicted explanatory variables such as GDP but one of the fundamental drawbacks is that explanatory variables like income, cost of cars or motoring and time may really be replacements (or *proxies*) for much more complex factors. If the way these factors behave is not fully undertstood inaccuracies could occur. In addition, it is not possible to use these models to evaluate the effects of possible changes in transport, economic or social policy or of tastes or preferences. Recognizing these problems some recent work at the Transport and Road Research Laboratory of the DTp has centred on the role of social factors in forecasting car ownership[4].

We stressed the central role that the saturation figure played in these models. Forecasters have had great difficulty in agreeing a universal figure and it has varied between 0.4 and 0.6 even within one year. The difference is significant. It could mean the car ownership forecasts varying on one set of assumptions between 21.6 and 26.3 million vehicles for the year 2000. The S-shaped curve itself has its critics. At one public enquiry into a new motorway a Department of Transport representative defended the model by saying, 'If growth in car ownership behaves like other social and biological phenomena, it will lie on a logistic growth curve . . .' but one authority is not persuaded;[5] 'The car ownership growth process has not followed a logistic curve in the past and there is no reason why it should in the future either'. He points out that the Departmental spokesman was unable to produce an example of a social or biological phenomenon which followed the S-shaped curve sufficiently closely to make it useful for prediction! The Leitch Committee[1] examined traffic forecasting methods and it focused on the doubtful validity of the S-shaped curve;

> 'The logistic curve is only one of the many forms of curve it is possible to fit to the known data. Thus, there is nothing uniquely right about the S-shaped curve that determines the level of car ownership in future years.'

There are further criticisms of these models which we will have to omit for reasons of space but we would recommend reference[5] for an extremely thorough and illuminating treatment of this area.

8.2.2.2 *Goods traffic forecasting*

The Leitch Committee also examined the forecasting of goods traffic. It observed that the authors of the official predictions were not very confident themselves in the forecasts!

> 'the uncertainties in the various steps of this process are so great that the final results can be little better than guesses'.

The reason for this they suggest is that traffic levels and vehicle composition depend on many important factors such as the quality of the road system, the various legal and fiscal controls that may be applied, and the relation between the growth of freight and the growth of GDP.

8.2.2.3 *Air traffic forecasting*

The official air traffic forecasting model is obviously complicated including as it does so many explanatory variables. This signals the problems that are likely to arise. Predicting many of the factors themselves is a very inaccurate exercise. It also leads to the problem of multicollinearity; many of the variables react to each other in a way difficult to predict.

Dr. Adams also believes that the planners have overlooked the basic laws of economics;

'Britain's airport planning is based on forecasting methods that recognize no supply constraints whatever, either within the airport perimeter, in terms of airport runways or terminals, or beyond the perimeter in the areas for which the travellers are destined.'

The introduction of tourist prices as an explanatory variable goes some way to answering this criticism but the working party admits that their's is 'a hazardous undertaking'. It adds:

'it is quite impossible to forecast the course of the world economy to A.D. 2000 . . . In the specification of air traffic models only partial success has so far been achieved in distinguishing the role of general measures of economic progress such as GDP or consumers' expenditure from that of other factors to some degree correlated with them . . . Different forecasters will have different ideas about the factors which influence demand, and the relative weight given to each. They will also vary in the judgements they make and the assumptions they employ. As a result different forecasts may be produced even using identical assumptions.'

8.2.2.4 *Some general observations*

The individual models described in this section all have unique weaknesses but many of the problems lie in their dependence on external factors which themselves are difficult to predict. Figure 8.2 shows the various predictions made for U.K. population levels which would seem to be one of the easier forecasts.[1] Gross Domestic Product, an equally important variable is more difficult to predict. Our second observation is of a more general but ultimately more important nature. It concerns the role the forecaster/ planner plays in policy making. We saw above that car ownership models are unable to take account of changes in government policy. Therefore the forecasters have to make assumptions about future policy. In transport, as in other areas, there tends to exist a self-fulfilling prophecy. Growth is predicted and therefore facilities are provided to meet it. Then, because the facilities are there they are used, thereby justifying the original forecasts. Moreover, forecasters make predictions based on underlying trends in traffic growth which in turn depend on the assumption of

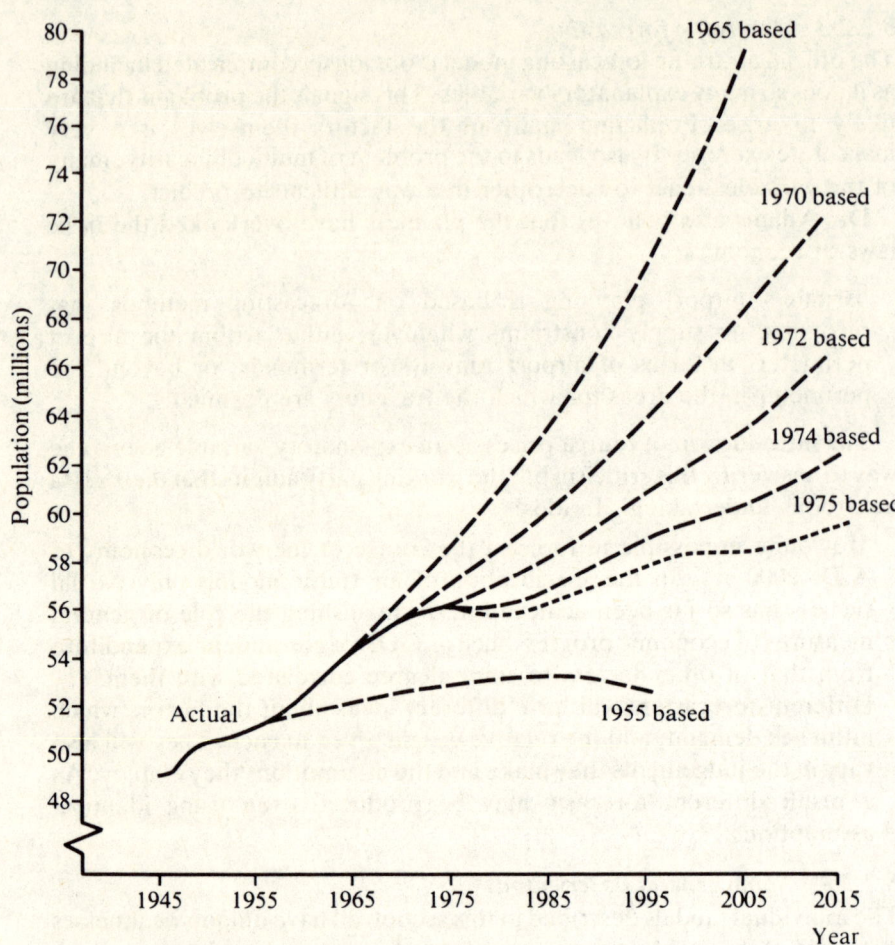

Figure 8.2 Past projections of population.
Source: Office of Population, Censuses and Surveys, p. 2, No. 7 (1977).

continued increasing road provision. But this is an area of policy i.e. the province of the politician not the planner.

There are therefore serious problems with traffic forecasting which cannot be taken lightly given the immense sums involved in transport provision and the consequences for scarce resources such as land or energy. But it is for these very reasons that forecasts have to be made. It would seem that planners consider erring on the side of overprovision, a lesser evil than underprovision, an attitude encouraged by the long lead times in transport investment and the relatively small marginal cost and impact of extra provision. This is understandable but to the economist there must be concern over the wastage of resources.

There is now amongst planners a general awareness of the growing public scepticism of forecasting procedures, particularly in the light of recent events at public inquiries into road schemes and the Third London Airport. The Leitch Committee commented:

'Uncertainty in forecasting is inevitable and it is important that such uncertainties should be exposed to public scrutiny and taken into account specifically in the decision-making process . . . The Department should never put itself in the position of appearing to defend a single figure as if it were uniquely correct.'

It is common practice in forecasting to use sensitivity analysis in order to determine whether assumptions made about such factors as income levels make a great deal of difference to the final result. One of the most encouraging developments is that now planners are more ready to explain to the public the assumptions and judgements they have made, to give a range of predictions based on different assumptions, and to illustrate, using sensitivity analysis, how important those assumptions are. This approach is to be applauded. Although the layman may not understand the technicalities of forecasting he should be given the range of forecasts and have explained the significance of the assumptions and judgements the planners have made in reaching those forecasts. It is also general policy now to develop 'high' and 'low' forecasts and, where practical, use the former for design purposes and the latter for economic evaluations. Environment impact assessments use both forecasts.

8.3 The traffic study

Planning for new transport facilities, particularly roads, used to be a case simply of extrapolation — looking at the way traffic flows had increased in the area over the past few years and continuing the trend into the future. However, no account was taken of changes in other activities in the area, say the building of a new office block, or the closure of a large factory. In other words, land use was not taken into consideration in predicting transport needs. But of course, land use plays a significant part. For example, the outward movement of residential areas in town and cities and the greater separation of home and workplace has increased the need for travel and the demand for road space whilst at the same time making public transport operation all the more difficult. On the other hand, transport facilities have an impact on land use patterns in, and therefore the shape and character of, towns and cities. We only have to compare Los Angeles with London, Paris or even New York. This is why local traffic studies have become more sophisticated since the mid-fifties and are now part of what is called *Land-use transportation planning*; the subject of this next section.

Land-use transportation planning is a very wide but detailed subject. It can be used in regions, such as the south-east of England, conurbations such as Greater Manchester or Calcutta, or free-standing towns like Brighton. The techniques can also be applied in the planning of by-passes, ring-roads, inter-urban motorways and public transport infrastructure such as modal interchanges. We do not have the space to examine the subject in as much detail as we would like and we must restrict ourselves to a broad outline of the techniques involved paying particular attention to the concepts upon which they are based.

Figure 8.3 outlines the main steps in a transport study. Notice box C encloses 4 elements. This represents the transport model itself which in essence is a series of mathematical equations usually used with a computer and which is used to 'picture' existing travel patterns in the area under study and then to forecast changes resulting from external factors of the type discussed above e.g. GDP and from the proposed alterations in transport facilities designed to solve the original problem. We will now examine the major steps involved.

8.3.1 The study area

Having defined the problem, be it general congestion in a conurbation or intolerable traffic levels passing through a village, identified possible solutions and decided the project worth pursuing in the face of various constraints the study area must be chosen. The main criterion in defining the study area is that all transport links affected by the scheme in question should be included. However, the bigger the area the greater the cost so ideally you should draw the boundary as close as possible to the problem consistent with the need for sufficient information, and with taking account of all the possible consequences of the scheme. In practice, planners would rather err on the big side just in case some affected areas are missed. The boundary should follow if possible natural and administrative boundaries, take account of possible development areas, and be compatible with adjacent transportation studies.

8.3.2 Zoning

You wish to obtain as much information as possible about the travel behaviour in the study area and to represent it on maps, diagrams and in the transportation model in the computer. You could go and ask every household to find out the addresses of all the places they visit, shops, cinemas, nightclubs, other houses and so on and record all the information on a data file. However, this would be prohibitively expensive and not worth all the trouble. So, we normally divide the study area into zones and take that zone as being representative of the people within it.

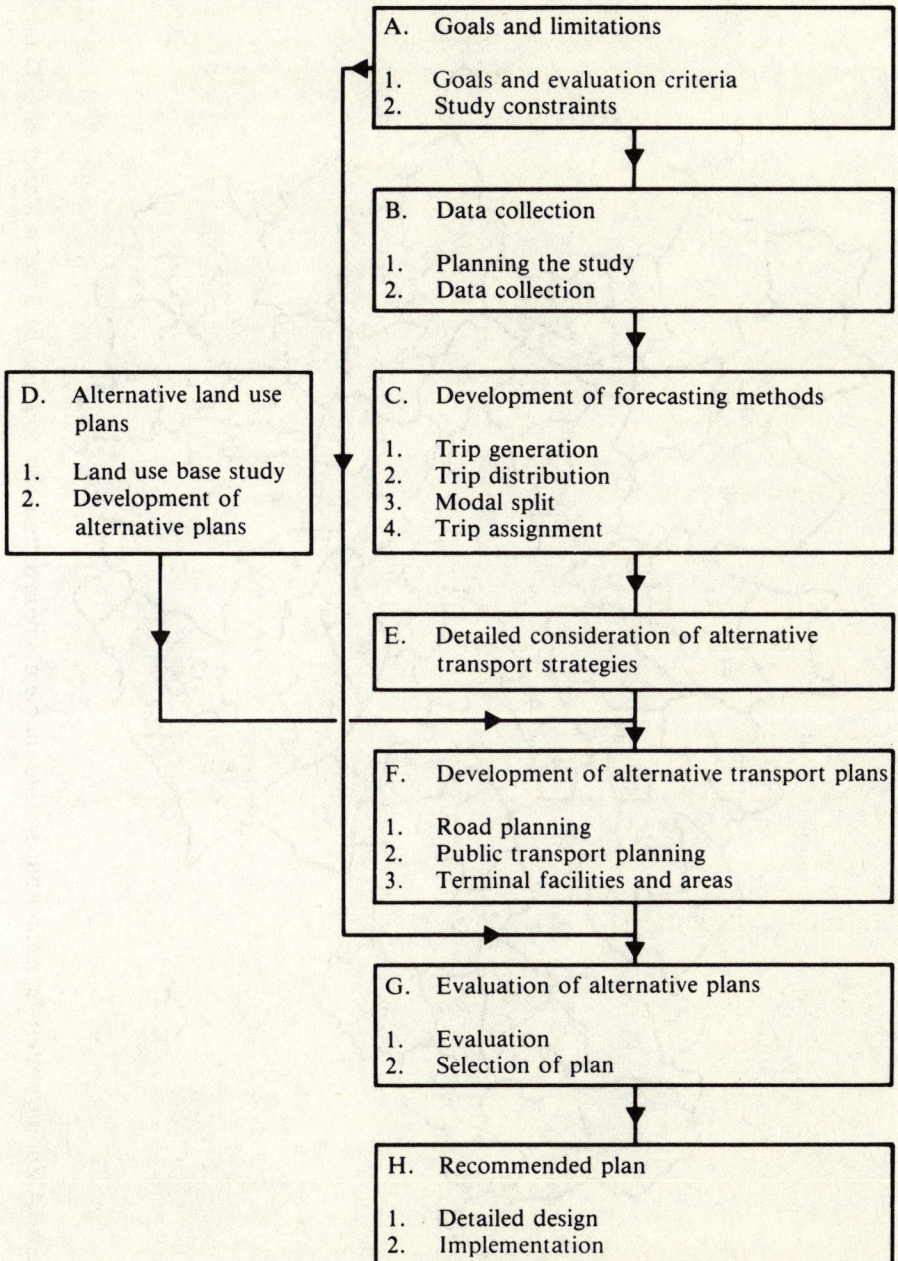

Figure 8.3 Simplified land use/transportation study programme.

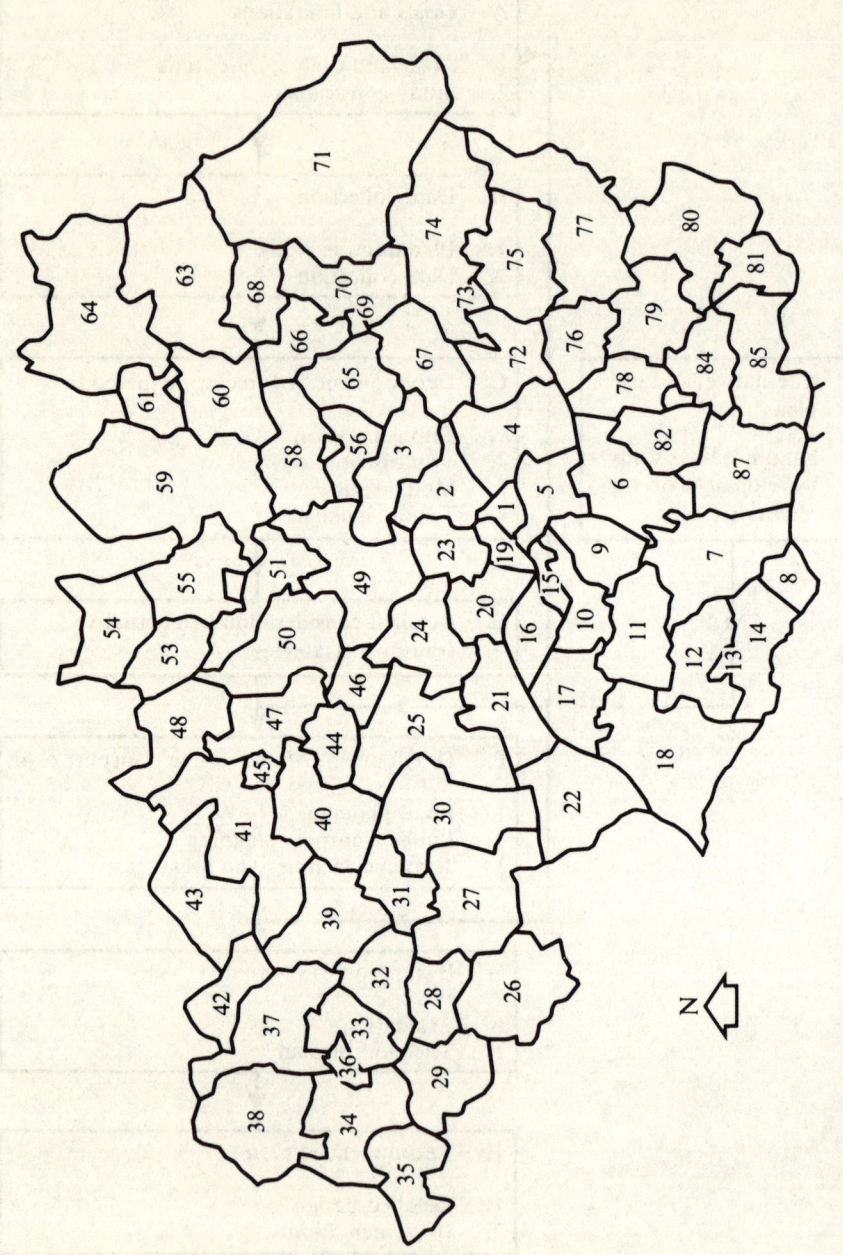

Figure 8.4 Zoning pattern for a conurbation, intermediate zoning pattern. By courtesy of Greater Manchester Council.

Figure 8.4 shows a zoning pattern for an urban area. Zones should be chosen so that they are:

1 As homogeneous as possible,
2 Small enough to ensure travel patterns are representative and big enough to be statistically significant,
3 Compatible with zones used by those with land-use data,
4 Compatible with natural and administrative boundaries,
5 Compatible with public transport catchment areas (where applicable).

Notice that in Figure 8.4 the zones get smaller the closer they are to the city centre. This is because travel patterns are more complex and if the zones were larger they would not be sufficiently representative and a lot of inter-zonal movement would be lost because it would be hidden within the zone. For the same reason the zones close to a particular scheme will be smaller because they will be the ones most affected.

8.3.3   The collection of information

After deciding on the size of the study area and dividing it into zones you will then want to set about collecting information on the activities within it and the travel behaviour resulting from those activities. The first thing to do is to decide what information you need and secondly to decide where you might obtain it.

8.3.3.1   Data requirements

The objective of the first part of the study is to enable a series of models to be constructed representing the present day travel patterns within the study area. These can then be used to predict future travel patterns. To build these models we will need information about trips made categorized by:

1 Purpose — whether for work, shopping, other personal business (like going to the dentist or the bank), education, or social/recreational.
2 Home-based or not — i.e. whether the trip started or ended at home,
3 Mode used — whether private or public transport and which form of public transport,
4 Time-period — this is usually divided into peak, off-peak or 16 or 24 hours,
5 Movement type — i.e. whether the trip is within a zone, between zones, or external (at least one end of the trip being outside the study area).

Information on commercial trips will also be required, and it is important to know whether or not those making trips have access to private transport as this will affect their modal choice.

We have already stressed the relationship between travel and land-use. Therefore as much information as possible is required on the location and intensity of land use for residential, commercial, industrial, leisure and other purposes.

8.3.3.2   Sources of information

There are two ways of collecting information for a particular transport study; asking the public about their travel behaviour or using existing data sources. The second approach is recommended by the DTp because it is less expensive and the public will not have to be involved. Firstly, then we will examine these sources.

Existing data sources

National based sources   Of course, the information required depends on the type of study but, assuming it is a large project, national-based data may be appropriate. The DTp has built up a data base available to planning authorities which contains the following:

1 1976 Survey data manual classified counts, roadside interviews and
    household interviews
Roadside interviews were carried out at 1,021 sites around the country and more than one million interviews were obtained from private and commercial vehicles. In the household survey 51,000 interviews were obtained in 21 areas. Information was collected on household size and trips made by all members of the family in the previous 24 hours.
2 National zoning and network system
The DTp has on file data representing a national zoning system comprising 3,613 areas in Great Britain. It also has route inventory files containing link characteristics for 13,000 lengths of road and drawings showing network layouts for each county available.
3 Planning data
Details of population, households, workforce and jobs are available for present and future years in the 3613 zones.
4 Automatic traffic counts
The data bank also includes the results of automatic traffic counts taken in 1977/78.

Local sources of information   Of course, national-based data will in many cases be insufficient and it will be necessary to supplement it with local information. In most areas, transport studies will have already been carried out so there will be existing information available and most local planning authorities will have already built up data banks on trip patterns and land-use characteristics. Land-use data can also be obtained from local authority staff in other disciplines.

Surveys

Data banks of course will become out of date and the information available may be insufficient. Planners therefore may have no alternative but to undertake surveys. The most common methods are as follows:

1 Traffic counts

Automatic traffic counts involve using pneumatic tube or inductance loop detection with recording equipment for short representative periods or continuously over a longer period. There will be a labour cost saving of course but installation costs are high and the equipment needs to be robust. Alternatively, more expensive manual counts may be used. It is estimated that one numerator can handle about 500—600 vehicles per hour. There is concern that manual counts are less accurate and the DTp has estimated that sixteen-hour counts of total traffic are probably within ±10% of the true flows with 95% confidence, but it has found no evidence of systematic bias.

2 Roadside interviews

These involve directing vehicles off the road so that interviewers can obtain information from the occupants by conversation. The success of these interviews depends on the co-operation of the police and the motorist. The interviewing site must therefore be efficiently laid out and organized and the interview as short as possible in relation to the information required.

3 Household interviews

These involve the interviewer obtaining information by conversation or by leaving a diary for the household to complete at a later stage. It is important that the respondents are motivated to help and understand what is required of them. It is therefore necessary to explain the purpose of the survey.

Of course it is not usual to interview all the relevant households so a sample is normally taken. This is often done by taking every nth household from the Electoral Register or Valuation List. Most major studies take a 1% household sample.

4 Public transport surveys

For the consideration of many transport problems the role of public transport is crucial. Information on public transport is normally collected under the following headings:

(a)   Routes and stopping places (to provide origins and destinations),
(b)   Frequency of service,
(c)   Fares,
(d)   Passengers carried, and
(e)   Waiting time.

5 Registration number surveys

Information is sometimes required on vehicles entering and leaving a small study area. To avoid using roadside interviews it is possible to observe registration numbers together with class of vehicle and the time to the nearest minute as vehicles pass the survey point. By subsequently comparing the records of all survey points it is possible to obtain points of entry and exit of all through journeys and the journey times. This method is unpopular as it is notoriously inaccurate and data analysis is time consuming.

6 Journey time measurement

In order to estimate the benefits of a proposed scheme it is necessary to determine existing travel times. This is particularly important where by-passes are proposed. The most common form of survey is the *Moving Observer Method* whereby information on journey times and its relation to traffic flows can be estimated by using observers in moving cars. The cars should each contain three observers in addition to the driver and be driven to and fro along the route of interest. One observer counts the cars in the opposite direction, one counts the cars overtaken and being overtaken and the third records times and the traffic flows counted by the other two.

7 Network information

The characteristics of the existing road network and public transport services need to be recorded for the transport model. Networks are normally divided into *links* which represent lengths of road of a uniform standard, separated by *nodes* representing junctions at the ends of those links. The model needs to know the characteristics of each link and node in terms of length, effective width, capacity, speeds, junction type and capacity, accident rates and aspects of the surrounding land-use. On the data file each link and node will have a number and the coded information relating to it. The public transport network is designed on similar principles but capacity will be determined by service levels and fare levels will be included. The nodes will represent boarding and alighting points rather than junctions.

8 Parking surveys

The availability and price of parking space plays an important role in travel behaviour so it is important to have an inventory of public and private, on- and off-street parking provision. In addition there must be information on the demand for spaces, the final destinations and trip purpose.

8.3.4   The transportation model

The transportation model represents in mathematical form travel patterns and is used to predict future patterns. It has four main stages:

1 Generation,
2 Distribution,
3 Modal split, and
4 Assignment.

Briefly, the generation stage estimates the number of trips originating and terminating in each zone; the distribution stage calculates between which zones those trips will be made; the modal split determines the proportions of trips by public and private transport and the assignment stage calculates route choice. We shall examine each in turn.

8.3.4.1   The generation or trip-end model

The objective of the generation or trip-end model is the estimation of the number of person trips originating and ending in each traffic zone. It uses information such as numbers of households, family structure, population, household income, employed persons, and car ownership, and comprises the trip production model and the trip attraction model.

The trip production model is concerned with trips originating from the home and uses a technique known as *category analysis*. The basic assumption with this technique is that households with the same characteristics exhibit the same level of trip making. Thus if you know the numbers of households with certain characteristics in a particular zone at a future date you can estimate how many trips will originate from that zone. The household characteristics used are income, the number of cars owned and the number of employed and non-employed members. Most models use six family-structure groups, three car-ownership groups and six income groups giving a total of 108 categories.

The trip attraction model is less complex than the production model and relates attractions to a zone to the intensities of the activities within that zone.

Defined land use types are used for describing activities and intensity of use is measured by the numbers of workers, households and educational establishments.

Two models are used to relate trip attractions to land use. One is a *multiple regression model* where the dependent variable is the total attractions and the explanatory variables are the various levels of activity by land use type. The other is a form of category analysis where each land-use type has a trip rate associated with it. Problems in achieving satisfactory co-efficients in the first model have tended to encourage the use of the category model.

8.3.4.2   The distribution model

The generation stage should result in estimates for trips produced in all the zones in the study area. If our area was made up of four zones then we may

Attraction zones / Generation zones	1	2	3	4	Total generations
1					60
2					40
3					80
4					120
Total attractions	100	60	80	60	300

Figure 8.5 The results of the generation stage.

arrive at generation figures for each zone as seen in Figure 8.5. The objective of the distribution model is to estimate the trips between all pairs of zones, i.e. to fill in the squares as shown in Figure 8.6. Two types of persons, car owning and non-car owning, are normally defined at this stage so that modal choice can be determined at a later stage.

A whole variety of distribution models have been developed. The early ones were *growth factor* models. The basic assumption behind these is that existing trip patterns can be projected into the future using zonal growth rates. The first and simplest model is the *uniform factor growth model* which merely uses a single growth factor. It can be expressed mathematically as follows:

$$T_{i-j} = t_{i-j}F$$

where $F = T/t$,
T_{i-j} = Future number of trips from zone i to zone j,

Attraction zones / Generation zones	1	2	3	4	Total generations
1		10	30	20	60
2	20		10	10	40
3	40	10		30	80
4	40	40	40		120
Total attractions	100	60	80	60	300

Figure 8.6 The results of the distribution stage.

t_{i-j} = Present number of trips from zone i to zone j,
T = Total future number of trips in study area, and
t = Total present number of trips in study area.
The obvious fault with this model is that it ignores the likely differential growth within the study area.

The *average factor* model partly overcomes this by using growth rates in each zone:

$$T_{i-j} = t_{i-j} (F_i + F_j)/2$$

where F_i and F_j are growth factors for zones i and j.

A further development was made by *T. J. Fratar*. He assumed that (a) the distribution of future trips from an origin zone is proportional to the present trip distribution from that zone, and (b) the distribution of these future trips is affected by the growth factor of the zone to which the trips are attracted. The model is also able to take account of the fact that trips to one zone may be influenced by the 'attraction' of nearby zones. The model is as follows:

$$T_{i-j} = \frac{T_{i(G)}\, t_{i-j} F_j}{t_{i-j}F_j + t_{i-k}F_k + \ldots t_{i-n}F_n}$$

where $T_{i(G)}$=expected future number of trips from zone i,

$t_{i-j} \ldots t_{i-n}$=present number of trips between zone i and all other zones $j \ldots n$,

$F_i \ldots F_n$=growth factors of individual zones $i \ldots n$.

The Fratar model requires an iteration process to balance the total number of trips predicted from the zone $T_{i(G)}$ and expected zone pairings T_{i-j}. To avoid this the *Detroit Model* was developed:

$$T_{i-j}=t_{i-j}\,(F_iF_j/F)$$

where F=growth factor for the study area.

The key assumption in this model is that the trips distributed to zone j will be in proportion to the appropriate growth factor F_j divided by the growth factor for the area as a whole.

Although these models are simple to use and do not require an understanding of the causes of distribution patterns they do have serious shortcomings. First of all they require very good origin—destination data and any irregularities will be compounded in prediction. They also assume that travel times and costs will not change in the future which is a fundamental weakness, as is the inability to cope with major land use changes.

Probably the most successful model used for this stage of the transportation model is the *gravity model*. Its underlying assumption is that trips to a given zone will be made (a) in direct proportion to its relative attractiveness, and (b) will depend on the separation of that zone from other zones. The structure of the model in its basic form is:

$$T_{i-j}=K\; G_iA_jF(C_{i-j})$$

where T_{i-j} = future trips between zones i and zones j,

G_i =total number of trips generated in zones i,

A_j =total number of trips attracted to zones j,

C_{i-j}=a measure of the separation between zones i and j. This is normally some form of Generalized Cost as described in Chapter 2. K and F are constants.

This model is used extensively for a variety of planning purposes, not only in large projects like the Third London Airport, and urban motorway development but also in smaller ones like traffic management schemes and the planning of shopping complexes. It is conceptually easy to follow and it can deal with changes in land use and travel costs. Although a great deal of work has been done on these models and they have become very sophisticated many planners are doubtful of their effectiveness and there is a trend back towards growth factor models particularly the Fratar method.

8.3.4.3 *The modal split model*
The objective of the modal split stage is the estimation of the numbers of person trips by public and private transport between all pairs of zones. It uses the estimated total trips by car owning and non-car owning persons from the distribution model and the estimated perceived costs between zone pairs for both public and private transport. It will also use forecasts from car ownership models which casts doubt on its reliability. The model used is normally the standard logit model and is of the form:

$$T_{i-j}k/T_{i-j} = \exp(-\lambda C_{i-j}k)/\exp(-\lambda C_{i-j}k')$$

where: $T_{i-j}k =$ the number of trips between zones i and j by mode k,
$\quad\quad T_{i-j} \;=$ the total number of trips between zones i and j,
$\quad\quad C_{i-j} \;=$ the cost of travel between zones i and j by models k and k',
$\quad\quad \lambda \quad=$ constant.

The concepts behind this model are quite simply that those with a car available will base their choice of mode on the relative generalized costs. Those without access to private transport are of course considered captive to public transport.

Some models include in addition to generalized costs a 'modal penalty' which reflects attributes of particular modes. In the case of private transport this would be convenience and comfort and in the case of public transport reduced stress, increased safety and being able to read or work while travelling.

The results of this model can be seen in a *diversion curve* of the type shown in Figure 8.7, which relates the proportion of trips made by private transport to the cost difference between public and private transport.

8.3.4.4 *Assignment stage*
Having estimated (1) how many trips are going to be made, (2) where they are going to and (3) which modes will be used, it is now necessary to determine which routes will be taken. This is the objective of the assignment stage. Two separate assignment models are used, one for private and one for public transport.

By this stage in the transport study, the characteristics of the network would have been established and placed on file in the computer. Thus, the least-cost routes (called *trees*) between zones will be known. It would then be a simple matter to 'load' all the trips on to those 'cheapest' routes. This

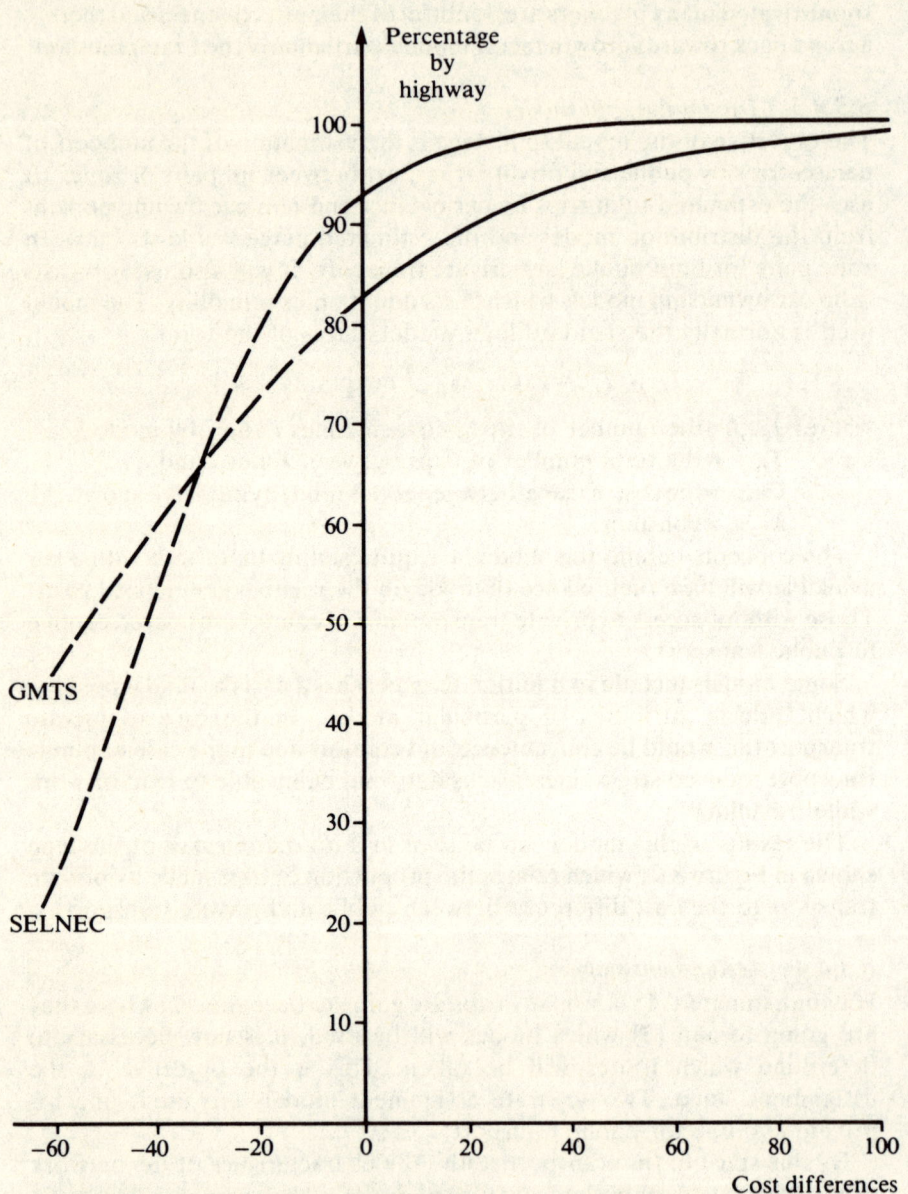

Figure 8.7 Examples of diversion curves used for modal split analysis.
By courtesy of Greater Manchester Council.

is sometimes done and is called 'all or nothing' assignment. However this ignores two important factors. Firstly, travellers may not know the true costs of the alternative routes and some through ignorance may take more expensive routes. A *multi-route* assignment may therefore be used. Secondly, account should be taken of the fact that roads become congested and consequently the route becomes more expensive. Therefore, a *capacity restraint model* is normally used. This is an iterative process which reduces the speed on a route if there are too many trips assigned to it. Consequently, in successive assignments some trips will be sent on alternative routes. To do this, the model makes use of *speed-flow curves* of the type illustrated in Figure 6.3.

In public transport assignment it is necessary to allocate trips to the different modes and this is done after a public transport network has been built and least-cost trees established. Generalized costs are used which include transit time, distance, fare levels and structure, and estimates of walking and waiting times. An interchange penalty is also included.

We have now examined briefly the four main elements of the transport model. The objective in using it is to represent as accurately as possible the travel behaviour within the study area. Once this has been achieved we can predict what will happen in the future if nothing is done to the transport network and/or if land use changes take place. We can also assess the impact of transport improvements. Before this can be done however it is very important to make sure that the model accurately reflects the existing travel patterns; in other words that it can predict closely what is happening now. This should be done at the *calibration stage* and is one of the longest, most expensive but most important steps in the transport planning process.

In general, many highway authorities around the country have transport models of their areas. To appraise a major scheme (say more than five or six miles in length in an urban area or say a motorway connecting to the motorway network) they may in practice use the last three stages but would probably not use the trip end model. For smaller schemes they would use only the last, the assignment model as the likely changes would be too small for the relatively insensitive trip end, distributional and modal split models. One outer ring road study for a major conurbation uses national trip-end model results, locally observed trip matrices growthed up to the forecast year and the local authority's assignment model. So neither a gravity nor a modal split model is used.

8.3.5 The development of solutions

Very often at the start of a project the planner has a good idea what the solution to the particular transport problem is. If a village is suffering from heavy through traffic the only solution might be the construction of a by-pass. However, there is always an alternative and that is to do nothing and most studies will compare proposals with the 'do nothing' (or more likely the 'do minimum') situation. For large urban transport studies though there may be a whole range of solutions ranging from highway-oriented schemes to proposals relying almost exclusively on the development of public transport. Emphasis on one side or the other is often a matter of political persuasion and the planner may need to be aware of this, developing a range of policies accordingly; but of course the greater the number of schemes tested the greater will be the cost and complexity. He has therefore a delicate balancing act to perform.

8.3.6 Evaluation and selection of proposal

Having put forward a number of proposals and perhaps carried out an initial screening process those that are left need to be evaluated. There are three parts to the evaluation stage; operational, economic and environmental. We have already outlined the economic analysis in Chapter 6 so we will concentrate on the operational and environmental evaluations and the way they should be presented.

8.3.6.1 *Operational appraisal*

This is a detailed form of traffic appraisal which is particularly needed in urban areas. It should be used at the earliest opportunity to test the model output for reasonableness and to identify the strengths and weaknesses of a scheme. We shall restrict ourselves to an outline of the areas an operational evaluation should be concerned with. They include:

1 *Safety*
Is the detailed layout the most suitable with respect to accidents? Can minor changes be made to reduce accidents? What are the accident costs as calculated by COBA?
2 *Network balance*
Are bottlenecks merely transferred elsewhere?
3 *Pedestrians*
Will new pedestrian facilities such as pelican crossings be required thereby reducing initial benefits?
4 *Interacting junctions*
Does the change in the pattern of flow affect junctions downstream?
5 *Access*
Are there any restrictions such as height, weight, or traffic management policies which might restrict access? Does the scheme encourage traffic on to unsuitable roads to gain access?
6 *Junctions*
Will there be any junctions which might become overloaded?

7 *Planning policies*
How consistent is the scheme with land use planning proposals?
8 *Enforcement*
What traffic orders will be required?
9 *Maintenance and policing*
What are the expected maintenance costs and how will traffic be affected during repairs?
10 *Staged openings*
Some part of the scheme may temporarily have demands imposed on it which are greater than intended when the scheme is complete. Will it be able to cope?

Some of these considerations will be fundamental to the working of the scheme. Others may be not so serious and may be dealt with easily at a later date, e.g. traffic signal settings.

8.3.6.2 *Environmental evaluation and the appraisal framework*
We have already seen in Chapter 6 that there are many environmental effects missing which are difficult to quantify. The DTp is studying the problem for a range of impacts including traffic noise, community severance, agricultural severance, air pollution, pedestrian amenity, visual impact, heritage and conservation, disruption from construction, and view from the road. However, it is generally accepted that in many areas we are far from being able to quantify effects satisfactorily. So rather than attach rather spurious monetary figures to these impacts it is felt far more realistic to show how many people, households or institutions are affected. This is normally done in an appraisal format as shown in Appendix 6.1. Notice that the framework identifies those groups affected by the scheme both those who benefit and those adversely affected. This approach reflects earlier criticism that many effects were 'hidden' inside single 'rate of return' figures. The framework does not produce an aggregate net benefit figure. Neither does it produce a ranking of options. The selection of projects is a matter of judgement by the planners and their political masters. The emphasis is, therefore, on giving the decision maker as much relevant information as possible presented in the clearest format.

8.3.7 Monitoring

It is considered good practice to monitor the actual effects of projects. It is recommended by the DTp for the following reasons:

(a) Satisfying the demands of good management and public accountability by providing information about the use of a new facility,
(b) Assisting in assessing compensation under Part 1 of the Land

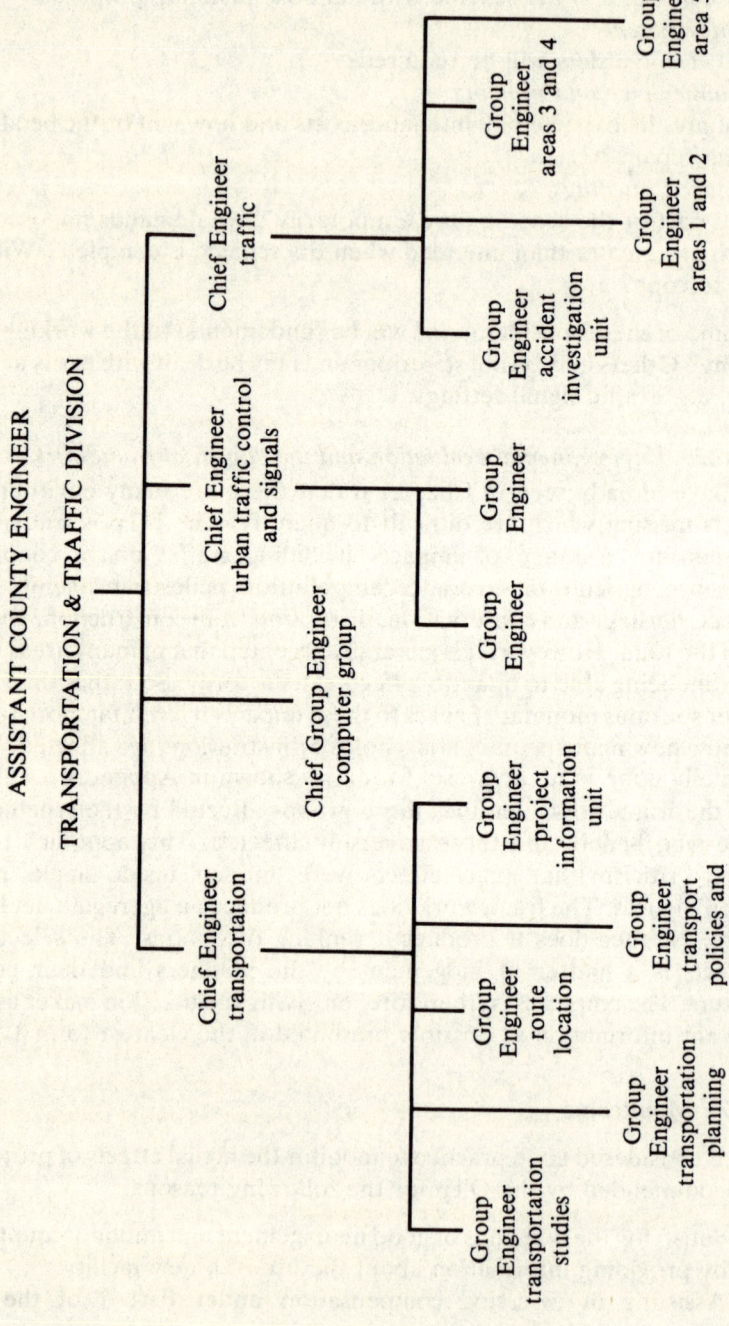

Figure 8.8 County Engineers Department: transportation and traffic division.

Compensation Act 1973 for depreciation due to the physical factors caused by the use of public works,

(c) Allowing the predictive ability of the models used to be monitored.

8.4 The organization for regional transportation planning

We have described the structure of the DTp at headquarters but there is also a need for a regional organization and we shall examine that for transport planning. In 1967, six Road Construction Units with sixteen sub-units were established to prepare and manage new trunk road schemes. The sub-units were based on counties and staffed mainly with local authority personnel. They were responsible for the detailed design and management of trunk road schemes. The units were closed in 1980 and the work was taken over by private consultants or local authorities acting as agents. The Departments of Transport and Environment also have regional offices and, from October 1981, regional directors took over the work of the units and the directors of the RCUs assumed the new title of Director (Transport) and reported to the regional directors on all regional transport work.

Local authorities therefore undertake work on trunk roads as well as local roads. The organization chart of a typical department responsible for transport in local authority is shown in Figure 8.8. The average trip length on major roads is quite short and many trunk roads form part of local networks. Therefore close co-operation between regional offices of the department and local authorities is an essential organizational feature.

8.5 Procedures in road planning

There has been a growing concern about the effects of road schemes on communities and their environment. One of the results of this pressure was a much more sensitive approach on the part of planners to the presentation of their project appraisals. There has also resulted an increasing criticism of the way that the road building programme in the U.K. is conducted; in particular the public inquiries into specific road proposals. In this section, we shall outline the procedures involved in the development of a scheme from inception to opening and then examine in more detail highway inquiry procedures.

8.5.1 Stages in trunk road development

A major road scheme may take anywhere between ten and fifteen years to complete and is therefore a complex and lengthy process. It will start at the

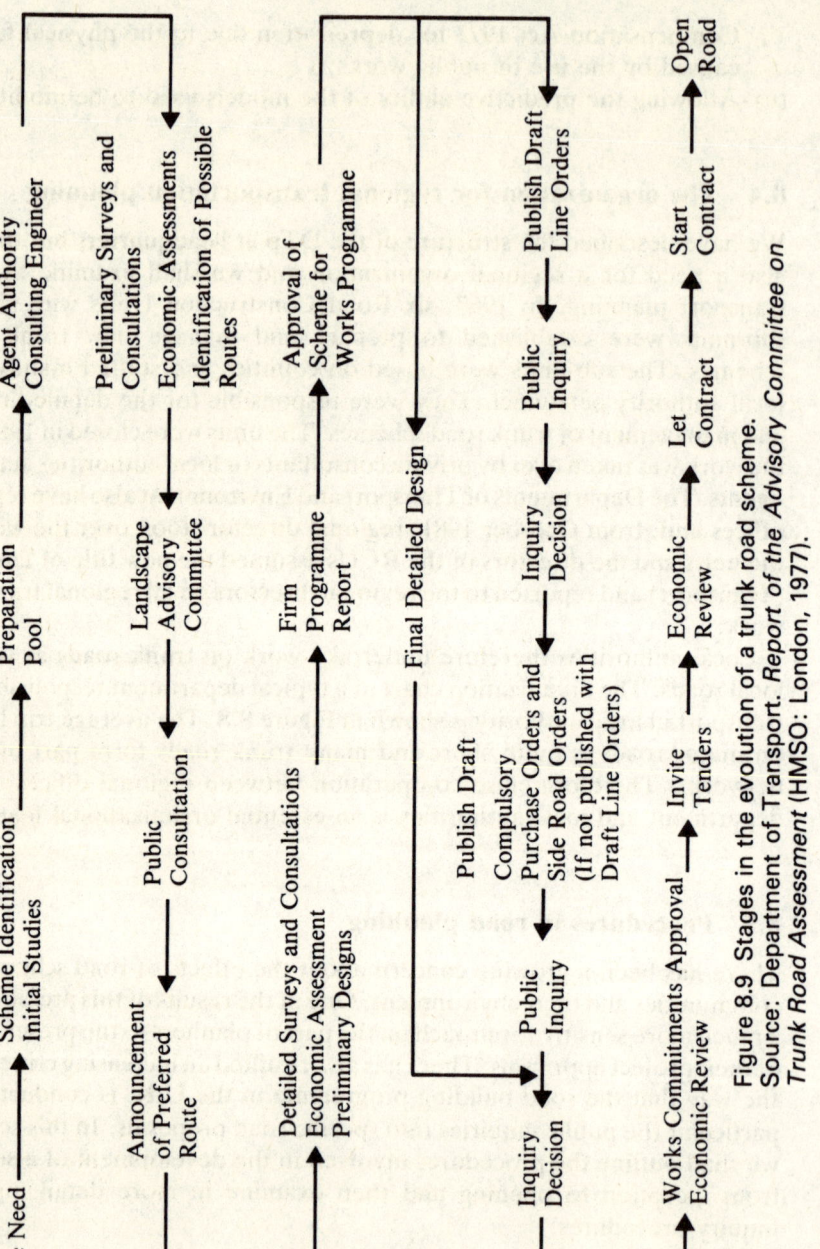

Figure 8.9 Stages in the evolution of a trunk road scheme.
Source: Department of Transport. *Report of the Advisory Committee on Trunk Road Assessment* (HMSO: London, 1977).

national level where central government develops a general roads policy, as part of a national transport policy. It decides how much expenditure should be allocated and in the annual White Paper seeks Parliamentary approval. Individual road schemes go through a series of stages which are illustrated in Figure 8.9. We shall now examine the most important ones.

Preparation pool
Schemes of a certain size and with an observed need are included in the pool and are then subject to detailed investigation. This normally takes about two years.

Public consultation
At the earliest opportunity local communities are asked for their views on the possible lines for the route.

Preliminary report
Once initial but adequate appraisal has been carried out a preliminary report is produced which includes a report on the consultations. It also recommends the route on which further analysis should be done.

Firm programme report
More detailed work is carried out on the preferred route when large scale drawings are made and costs, traffic forecasts and appraisals are refined enabling the preliminary report to be updated. At the same time detailed cost benefit analysis is carried out.

Draft orders and public inquiries
By law draft orders must be published for the preferred line of the road together with any side road compulsory purchase orders. Objections to the draft order may be received and public inquiries nearly always follow with major schemes. The inspectors at the inquiry submit a report to the Secretaries of State for Transport and the Environment who then decide whether to endorse the orders.

Works commitment and contract letting
A Works Commitment gives financial authority to complete the preparatory work on the basis of the firm programme report. Tenders can then be invited.

8.5.2 Highway inquiry procedures

'People rightly want to know why a new road is needed; how it fits into the national and regional planning context; what traffic demands it is intended to meet; and why it should be built to a certain standard . . . Perhaps above all, they seek an assurance that they are getting a fair deal; that what they have to say is given a fair and proper hearing; and that proper weight is given to their views by the Secretaries of State . . .'

In November 1975, local objectors to the proposed Airedale Trunk Road in Yorkshire prevented an inquiry from taking place because they did not think they were getting a fair deal. More particularly they felt that the terms of reference of the Inquiry excluded the most important issues; they doubted the independence of the inspector, they were not clear of their rights to participate; and they felt the results of the Inquiry were a foregone conclusion anyway. The quotation above from the *Report on the Review of Highway Inquiry Procedures*[1] indicates that the Government is aware of the problems associated with these procedures. However, it has always been concerned with the time and expense involved and the Highways Act 1971 was intended to reduce procedural delays by giving the Secretary of State wider powers. These were largely to the disadvantage of the objector. We shall examine the main objections and the Government's response to them and then see what problems remain.

There appear to be three main areas of objection. Firstly, is the road needed at all? Secondly, is the line of the road the most suitable? Thirdly, are the objectors fairly treated at the Inquiry?

8.5.2.1   Need for the road

As the report points out need can be argued at various levels — national, regional and local. National road planning must take place in the context of national transport policy which of course is part of wider economic policies. This is really the province of central government answerable to Parliament. The problem is, many observers suggest, that Parliament is unable or unwilling to devote sufficient time to analyse the policy thoroughly. In fact, one objector argued that particular Inquiries should not take place as there was no government transport policy and no effective parliamentary control over the road programme. Therefore the proposers of the scheme would be unable to show a need at the national level.

The fear is then that normal democratic procedures are replaced by a series of administrative decisions made by officials who develop individual road schemes on the basis of traffic forecasts and cost benefit analyses which are themselves of dubious accuracy.

The Government answers these criticisms by explaining the respective roles of the Ministers and the Inquiries:

'. . . Ministers personally make the major decisions about road policy and strategy . . . Ministers are themselves accountable to Parliament; . . . officials are subordinate to their Ministers; . . . and the purpose of highway inquiries is not to debate national issues nor to overrule the democratic decisions of Parliament, but to provide a means of communication on local issues between the people directly affected by the proposals and the Ministers . . .'

8.5.2.2   *The line of the road*

Objectors often feel that insufficient thought has been given to all the possible alternatives. This is partly because the inspector is concerned with the line taken for the draft Order. It is important then that planners give the local community adequate information on the alternative lines at an earlier stage in the development of the project so that objections can be made then.

8.5.2.3   *Fair treatment at the inquiry*

There has been criticism that in law only certain classes of objectors — local authorities, navigation and water authorities and property owners, occupiers and leaseholders directly affected — have a right to appear at the inquiry. In practice, inspectors hear anyone with relevant and non-repetitious contributions. The independence of Inspectors has also been questioned. They were drawn from a fee-paid panel which was managed by the Department of the Environment and the inspector was chosen by the Secretaries of State who of course eventually make the decision on whether the scheme should proceed. In response to this criticism they are now chosen by the Lord Chancellor.

Another problem facing the potential local objector is that he has insufficient information and knowledge to question the forecasts and analyses of the Departments' representatives armed with documents and computer print outs resulting from many years' preparation. Not only does he need sufficient information, it needs to be presented in a way that he can comprehend without too much difficulty. This was a particular criticism by the Leitch Committee[1]. It is the practice now that when a draft Order is published a public statement is made outlining the consultation already taken place, giving a summary of the views expressed, and giving the reasons for the line chosen. Incidentally, the normal procedure is to hold inquiries during the day thereby forcing objectors to take time off work.

There are two further difficulties which appear particularly important from the objector's point of view. When the Secretary of State is considering the Inspector's report he may seek advice from his officials. These are likely to be those who supported the proposal in the first place! Secondly, very often Inquiries take place for specific stretches of road when other sections of the same road have already been approved. The pressure to complete the final (and probably most contentious) part is therefore all the greater and in effect the decision is pre-empted.

It seems that many of the problems faced in Highway Inquiries are intractable although cosmetic improvements can be made. The fundamental question remains the relation between policy and objection. P. H. Levin in a study of these problems concludes that:

'the search for a generally applicable well-defined line between the realms of policy and of objections is in the last resort doomed to fail. National, regional and local policies and proposals shade into and have implications for one another.'[7]

The important thing is therefore to gain public respect where the line between the levels is blurred. Levin suggests that to achieve this, four conditions must be met. Firstly, the decision on a particular proposal must not be pre-empted in any way by previous decisions. Secondly, where there is a limit on the range of objections it should be made clear beforehand and should be generally acceptable. Thirdly, policy decisions and assumptions that are not open to objection should be acceptable and command respect. This means that policy should be adequately discussed and Parliament more involved. Fourthly, that objectors should participate on more equal terms.

Examination questions

1 Discuss the merits of the various models developed for the distribution stage of the transportation model.
2 If you had to present to local councillors the findings of a traffic study into the need for a by-pass round a small town what would you include in your report?
3 Assess the role of Highway Inquiries in transport planning.
4 Do you think the transportation planning modelling procedures are worth the time and expense?
5 What do you consider to be the major factors which might influence transport demand over the next 20 years? To what extent can the planning process in your country influence matters in this period?
6 Explain the methodologies available at present for traffic forecasting. Assess their strengths and weaknesses for decision-making on future road investment. What evidence is there available to support your assessment?
7 'Public participation is an expensive luxury designed to tell a small minority that what they want won't work'. Do you agree or disagree? How would you assess the effectiveness of such participation?
8 'Planning is the assembly of a series of events projected into the future which will be of guidance to an enterprise'. To what extent would you regard this statement to be an adequate description of the planning process as it affects transport provision and management?

9

International Transport

9.1 Introduction

The major theme running through several chapters in this book, is, having justified the market economy on efficiency grounds, to study the degree to which free market forces are restrained; to examine the reasons for restraint and to try to determine how inefficient are particular departures from the market economy.

In this chapter the theme will be continued in relation to three areas of international transport—shipping, civil aviation and the common transport policy of the European Economic Community. We shall see that market forces come under pressure to varying degrees and the reasons put forward for interfering in the economy are generally of a practical nature. In shipping we outline arguments that suggest the departures from market efficiency are slight but in the other two we really have to concentrate on the political realities of economic life. We shall also see that the question arising throughout the book — should the transport sector be regarded as a commercial one or as a social service? — is relevant in the international context too.

9.2 Maritime transport

9.2.1 Introduction

Shipping has traditionally been the most market-orientated of all the modes of transport with very little government control except for safety and, more recently, for environmental reasons. Most control over market forces has come from the industry itself and we shall consider how important these are. Since the Second World War, however, we have seen greater government intervention in shipping and we shall examine these methods and the implications.

9.2.2 The conference system

The conference system, which dominates the dry cargo liner (i.e. scheduled) services, has been discussed in great detail by economists because conferences are considered, as cartels, to act as a restraint on trade.

> '. . . they carry out policies which must be regarded as being against the best interests of shipping and trading. Indeed the wrath of the Restrictive Trade Practices Court would have fallen on them immediately it was established had they been operating within the United Kingdom . . .'[1].

Conferences take a variety of forms ranging from the relatively informal to the highly structured. One of the key problems facing the industry is the fact that it suffers from high overheads — on a voyage basis only 20% of total costs constitute variable costs. Rather like the road haulier looking for a back load if a ship is in port with spare capacity it would pay the company to accept any price above 20% of normal average costs to make some contribution to overheads. The industry lends itself readily to cut-throat competition in which firms cannot survive for long. The temptation then is to form a cartel to ensure rates are fixed to cover all costs. This is the minimum a conference might do; many also agree to restrict capacity, and shippers are encouraged to remain with the conference for long periods by use of a deferred rebate system. A further refinement is the pooling agreement whereby revenues are collected centrally and allocated on the basis of output.

9.2.3 Criticisms of conference pricing

In Chapter 4 it was suggested that a loss-making monopolist might adopt a policy of price discrimination. In this way it would roughly follow a marginal cost pricing policy at the same time as covering total costs. However, this may manifest itself in what Pigou called 'third degree price discrimination', i.e. a monopolist charges different prices for different commodities, according to their elasticity of demand. It might also be termed 'value of service' pricing or 'charging what the traffic will bear'. This may not be related very closely to costs and one of the major criticisms of conference pricing is that some 'high value' commodities are carried at prices above marginal cost to cross-subsidize those 'low value' goods carried at rates below marginal costs. This was the policy for which British Rail was severely criticized. It causes a waste of resources because, if commodities are carried at rates higher than the marginal cost, output will be less than the optimum and, if prices are below marginal cost, the marginal revenue product is lower in shipping than elsewhere.

This form of pricing adopted by conferences can also lead to excess capacity. It is unlikely that, when conferences are established, prices are fixed such that normal profits are achieved by having those commodities carried at greater than marginal cost exactly offset by those moved at below marginal cost. As conferences have some degree of monopoly power the average freight rate can be expected to be greater than marginal cost. Conference members cannot compete on price so service competition takes its place in the form of bigger, faster or more ships. Supernormal profits will be reduced to normal ones as excess capacity reduces load factors. In this way price discrimination, as described, together with fixed prices leads to excess capacity.[2]

Pricing in this way also causes wasteful competition as conference members call at ports they would have avoided to 'cream off' high-paying cargo. In addition, fixed rates mean that all the usual attributes of cost-based pricing such as peak/off peak pricing will not be used.

9.2.4 Alternative views on conference pricing

This, then, is the traditional criticism of 'value of service' pricing in this context. However, this view is not held by all economists. It is suggested that conferences really take costs as well as value into account. The two main criteria for charging what the traffic will bear appear to be (1) charge no rate so high as to stop traffic moving and (2) the rate must cover at least SRMC. Thus:

> 'By charging what the traffic can bear, conference lines can achieve discrimination of practically the first degree, which means that, in a monopolistic situation, output is increased to cater for almost total demand and little loss of utility, as indicated by total demand, occurs.'[3]

It is also suggested that to describe conferences as monopolists is misleading as the threat of competition (for example from non-conference lines and tramp shipping) and the need to leave outsiders little potential profit strongly influences conference pricing policies: 'to retain their position as apparent monopolies they have to act as if they were not.'[4]

Furthermore, it is argued that differential pricing is a natural result of competitive forces. Any ship in port, unless there are several others all scheduled to depart at the same time for the same destination, will have a temporary monopoly of supply in relation to shippers needing urgent dispatch of their goods. Rates will therefore be bid up on the basis of value of service or ability to pay. Once the high value goods have been assured of space, excess remaining space will cause prices to fall towards SRMC.

This kind of fluctuation is not in the interests of shippers who need some degree of uniformity in their costs and shippers of high value goods would accept higher prices to ensure consistency. It is suggested therefore that differential pricing has arisen not from monopolistic exploitation on the part of conferences but purely as a result of simple market forces. These competitive pressures are significant. Long-term elasticities are high as shippers, and therefore shipowners, face competition from goods delivered from other countries, from domestic suppliers and from substitutes.

Differential pricing may also arise for quite justifiable practical reasons. For example, some cargoes may be stowed safely in spaces unsuitable for other cargoes and others may be carried below cost in order to help stabilize the vessel.

Even those who defend the pricing policies of conferences would agree that they do not accord very closely with the economist's view on rationality or efficiency but they do relate closer to cost-based ones than perhaps a cursory examination would suggest. Practical considerations play a more important role: 'the liner conference system is necessary in order to secure stable rates and regular services.'[5] and external competition is considered sufficient to prevent the worse excesses of monopolistic exploitation. Tyson *et al.*, however, consider the growth of containerization to pose a threat to competitive forces because the massive investment required for terminal facilities has encouraged the establishment of consortia of shipping companies.[6]

9.2.5   Other restraints on trade

Although liner conferences receive most of the attention there are other features of maritime transport which might be considered to introduce imperfect competition. Flag discrimination is an obvious one whereby nations insist that a proportion of their trade be carried on their own vessels. The U.N. Liner code (popularly known as the 40:40:20 rule) is the result of this trend, amongst developing nations. This cargo sharing system ensures that of the trade between two countries 40 per cent should be carried by each of the participants leaving 20 per cent for third flags. This may not necessarily produce the benefits developing countries expect. If their ships carry mainly their own products then their cargoes will be of the high-bulk low-value nature leaving the developed nation to carry the more valuable traffic.[7]

Another threat is from heavily subsidized fleets, particularly of the Soviet Bloc nations. Soviet fleets have been estimated to under-cut conference carriers by as much as 40%. One report suggested the American warplane, the General Dynamics F-16 was carried across the Atlantic in Soviet and East German vessels as rates were one-third lower![8]

9.3 Civil aviation

9.3.1 Introduction — why air transport is different

In terms of regulatory control air transport is at the opposite end of the spectrum to shipping. There is no 'freedom of the skies' to compare with the liberal characteristics of maritime transport. The theme of this chapter is the degree to which free market forces are restricted in international transport, and the reasons for their large degree of absence in civil aviation are readily apparent in the political and economic realities of the operating environment. They include:

1 The ease with which aircraft can cross national boundaries creates problems of sovereignty, jurisdiction and defence.
2 Civil aviation has a major impact on international trade with consequences for balance of payments and employment.
3 In most nations, the national airlines are regarded as public utilities which requires them to offer adequate minimum networks and service levels and, of course, they are often a symbol of national virility.
4 Like all transport operations air transport's product is non-storeable but, unlike other modes, customers can switch their allegiance to operators in other countries.
5 Finally, the philosophies and actions of nations affect and are affected by those of other nations. There is bound to be conflict which must be resolved and there will inevitably be a need for compromise between national interests and international policy. There is an inbuilt advantage, then, in joint development and co-operation between governments.

9.3.2 Regulations

1944 saw the beginning of regulations when the International Air Transport Conference in Chicago formulated five privileges (or 'freedoms') which sovereign states would grant to each other for the operation of scheduled international air services:

1 The privilege of one State to fly across the territory of another State without landing;
2 The privilege of one State to land in another State for non-traffic purposes;
3 The privilege of one State to put down in the territory of another State passengers, mail and cargo taken on its own territory;
4 The privilege of one State to take on passengers, mail and cargo destined for its territory from the territory of another State;
5 The privilege of one State to take on passengers, mail and cargo in

another State destined for the territory of a third State and the privilege to put down passengers, mail and cargo coming from any such territory.

There are now more 'freedoms' the sixth being the most important. This enables an airline to participate in a route which does not start or finish in but passes through, connects at, or stops for a limited period at a point in its own country.

There are three main elements to regulation of international air transport. There is firstly, the work of the United Nations body, the International Civil Aviation Organization (ICAO) which is concerned with technical legal and operational matters. Secondly, governments have developed a system of bilateral agreements which cover specific routes and which agree capacity levels (i.e. number and size of aircraft) and the airlines to operate on them. These will incorporate the freedoms described above. Thirdly, there is governmental control over the passenger fares and cargo rates offered to the public. Since 1946, airlines themselves have developed their own fares policies, subject to governmental approval. However, there has not been anything like competitive pricing because fares and charges have been multilaterally agreed at regular conferences of the airlines' trade association the International Air Transport Association (IATA). Such tariff co-ordinating conferences take place at least every two years. The world is divided into three main areas and 50 sub-areas. Within those areas uniform rates are set.

It has always been agreed in the industry that this work is the province of the airlines because there is a need for a coherent fares and rates pattern and for the development of through and interlinable fares. There has always been a belief too in the advantages of the multilateral nature of the rate fixing arrangements.

In 1980 at the Special Air Transport Conference of ICAO in Montreal it was agreed by Government representatives that:

1 International tariffs should be established multilaterally;
2 The worldwide multilateral machinery of the IATA traffic conferences should be adopted as the first choice when establishing international fares and rates;
3 Unilateral action by governments on tariffs should be avoided;
4 Carriers should not be discouraged by governments from participation in the IATA system.

It is significant though that such reiteration of the belief should be made in 1980 when the system has been operating since 1946. It had obviously come under pressure.

9.3.3 Pressure to change tariff co-ordinating activities

The economist's criticism of a cartel like IATA has found strongest support in the United States which has had long standing anti-trust legislation. For a long time though, the multilateral price fixing of airlines received immunity from the anti-trust laws, but in 1977 and 1978 domestic airlines faced a 'deregulation' experiment on freight and passenger services. At the same time the U.S. Government began to arrange 'liberalized' bilateral agreements for international services. In return for being given long-sought-after 'gateways' to the U.S., smaller countries had to accept flexible fares and capacity levels which of course would be to the advantage of the larger U.S. airlines with excess capacity. Furthermore, in June 1978, the U.S. Civil Aeronautics Board required IATA and other interested parties to 'show cause' why the Board should not withdraw its approval of and, consequently, the anti-trust exemption for, the traffic conference machinery. In addition, there was the pressure from airlines (e.g. Laker Airways) with marketing policies which were directly opposed to any price-fixing agreements. Underlying all these pressures there was the general dissatisfaction from airline passengers with price levels on scheduled services.

IATA has always felt aggrieved that it receives so much criticism for such a small proportion (it estimates about 20%) of the work that it does but, in 1979, it bowed to the pressures and divided its activities into two distinct parts. There were the trade association activities and the tariff co-ordination side. Member airlines could choose whether to join the latter and the U.S. airlines, subject to the anti-trust legislation opted out. There resulted a fierce price war on the Atlantic route with ramifications elsewhere.

9.3.4 Arguments in favour

We do not need to repeat the economist's objections to a cartel. It is worth outlining though the arguments put in favour of the IATA price-fixing system. They are essentially of a more practical nature.

The first argument is that put forward for liner conferences. The variable costs of airline operation are such a small proportion of total costs that the industry is vulnerable to cut-throat competition. Since more flexible pricing arrangements have been introduced airline revenues have fallen and costs have risen. Many airlines are not only making insufficient profit to cover reinvestment, but are actually making losses, and several have ceased operation. IATA estimated 1981 losses at 1660 million dollars and 1982 at 1870 million dollars.

The second argument centres on the travelling and shipping public. Multilateral agreements prevent the confusion that would arise from a completely free competitive environment. The higher level of service that results for the passenger is seen in the way that any member airline will honour IATA tickets and help with any difficulties, e.g. baggage or rerouting problems, on an agreed basis.

Thirdly, there are advantages for governments. Instead of having to cope with a multitude of individual filings for rates and charges, a single fare or rate structure is provided for a geographical area. This is considered particularly relevant to developing countries. It is argued by IATA that deregulation can result in more rather than less government involvement as they become embroiled in bilateral pricing agreements. Moreover, where there are different regulatory philosophies, governments may clash over issues which airlines could solve multilaterally at the tariff co-ordination level.

The final argument put in favour of regulation is that capacity can be controlled, thereby saving on fuel consumption which comprises about 27% of total operating costs.

9.4 The European Economic Community and the Common Transport Policy

9.4.1 Introduction

The general belief in the advantages of free trade has resulted in the establishment of a number of free trade areas such as The Latin American and Caribbean Free Trade Associations, the Central American Common Market, and The East African Community. We will examine in some detail the European Economic Community (EEC), setting out the original aims with respect to transport and outlining progress towards a common transport policy.

9.4.2 The objectives

The goal of the Community's economic policy may be described as the promotion of economic growth by means of competition based on common rules. The Community transport policy has been regarded from the outset as an instrument of economic policy and it shares the same goal. The Treaty of Rome, 1957 which established the EEC required: 'the adoption of a common policy in the sphere of transport'. Article 3(e) (1)

The Treaty was concerned with three transport modes: rail, road and inland waterways. The general aims for transport were set out in Articles 74—84 (Title IV):

'The objectives of this Treaty shall, . . . be pursued by Member States within the framework of a common transport policy'. Article 74(1). The succeeding Articles in Title IV aimed to establish:

(a) Common rules applicable for international transport to, from, or passing across the territory of Member States. Art. 75(a) (1).
(b) Abolition of the charging of different rates and imposing different conditions for the carriage of the same goods over the same transport links. Art. 79(1).
(c) Prohibition of the imposition by a Member State of rates and conditions involving any element of support or protection in the interests of one or more particular undertakings or industries within the Community, unless authorized by the Commission. Art. 80(1).

In summary, the EEC stands for economic growth which is best achieved by the encouragement of competition. This means that any impediments to the workings of a free market economy should be reduced as far as possible. The transport sector will encourage economic growth within the Community only if it imposes no restriction on the free movement of commodities. In other words free market forces must be allowed to operate in the transport sector.

At this stage we should explain the respective roles of the Commission of the EEC and the Council of Ministers in relation to the transport sector. All member states appoint Commissioners who act independently of their own States and one of their functions is to put forward policy for the Council to consider for approval. The Council will comprise the Ministers of Transport of the member states. We see in the history of the EEC the Commission making proposals in the spirit of the Rome Treaty which the Council then considers against a background of national interest. This is one of the reasons why the proposals put forward by the Commission in the following paragraphs seem so much at variance with what actually becomes Community law.

In 1973 the lack of progress was evident:

'The efforts which have been made to eliminate impediments to trade and to create a common transport market have not fully succeeded, and the common transport policy is in an impasse.'[9]

The same thing could have been written in 1983.

In 1982 it was estimated that delays at frontiers increased transit costs in intra-Community road haulage alone by about £210 million excluding administrative costs, customs clearance and auditing agencies and so on. This was considered to be between 30% and 50% higher than necessary[10]. In 1981, it was found that almost half of international railway wagons were held up for more than 12 hours at frontiers, and two-thirds (65%) for more than six hours on transit routes.

Why are there still such problems and what progress has been made? We will try to answer these questions by tracing the history of transport policy through the sixties and seventies.

9.4.3   The progress towards a Common Transport Policy

Progress in the early sixties was slow. This is partly explained by the lengthy procedures that formulated policy is subjected to in the EEC but is also due to the vastly different philosophies that member states held on the role of transport. West Germany traditionally took a 'public utility' approach which resulted in state protection of the railways and very strict quantity control of road haulage. France had similar restrictions whereas the Netherlands favoured a more liberal approach, as did Italy.

A major step towards a more liberal transport policy was the publication in 1961 of the 'Schaus Memorandum', which set out an 'action programme', aimed at transforming national transport systems into an international one. It presented the main objectives of a common policy as:

1 The creation of healthy competition,
2 The removal of obstacles which transport might represent to the establishment of the common market for goods, and
3 The development of a transport system which would prove to be a powerful stimulant for the growth of trade and the widening of markets.

These objectives meant that discrimination by nationality, taxation, technical regulations and by state aid was to be discouraged. They also covered such factors as freedom of establishment, freedom of operation, technical harmonization and licensing policy. This overall policy on transport operations was prevented from progressing further by political problems in the mid-sixties.

Towards the end of the sixties there was a change of emphasis in transport policy on the part of the Commission, away from operational matters towards infrastructure provision. It was argued that, if the appropriate level and type of infrastructure were provided and the correct pricing principles applied, the right balance of transport provision would be achieved without much difficulty. Research in this area was carried out but, at the time, the chances of such a policy being accepted were slight. The inevitable conclusion is that little progress was made in the period up to 1972. Any progress that was made was confined to what Button describes as 'secondary areas'[11], rather than agreement on broad policy, as the following regulations show:

(a) Abolition of discrimination in transport rates and conditions (Reg. 11).
(b) Common rules for the international carriage of passengers by coach and bus (Reg. 117/66) and modal control documents for this (Reg. 1016/68).
(c) Harmonization of social legislation relating to road transport (manning driving time and rest period for paid drivers) (Reg. 543/69).

(d) Obligations inherent in the concept of a public service in transport (Reg. 1191/69).
(e) Common rules for the normalization of accounts of railway undertakings (Reg. 1192/69).
(f) Granting of aids for transport by rail, road and inland waterway (Reg. 1107/70).
(g) Introducing an accounting system for expenditure on infrastructure for the three modes (Reg. 1108/70).

In 1973, the Community was enlarged to include the United Kingdom, Denmark and Ireland. These new members were, of course, geographically on the edge of the Community. They also brought with them more liberal policies on road haulage and two of them are very much involved in shipping. In October 1973, there was a new 'communication' from the Commission to the Council[12] which pointed out that fundamental changes had occurred in the transport sector since the 1960s. Trade had increased considerably and raw materials no longer constituted the main traffic. Also there was a greater dependence on fuel from outside the Community. It was felt that fundamental questions on international trade were much more appropriate than the rather narrow views taken hitherto. 1973 was seen as the time for a 'new impetus' to develop a new transport policy.

By 1975, the Commission felt that, in general, there was no real need for capacity control except in specific circumstances. Its increasingly liberal outlook regarding operational matters can be seen in further suggestions:

1 That states should seek to provide a satisfactory balance between supply and demand without recourse to quotas or any quantitative restriction.
2 That existing restrictions should be lifted as international transport grows.
3 That non-resident hauliers should be allowed to operate within another member state whilst on international operation (i.e. cabotage).
4 That the trade itself should 'recommend' tariffs according to the type of goods and conditions of carriage.

In the early seventies the Commission was also proposing radical changes for the charging of infrastructure costs. It was felt that road operators should pay the full resource costs (infrastructure and environmental) associated with their operations and long-term marginal social cost pricing was put forward as a policy. (It seems that taxation would include provision for new construction as well as wear and tear.)

However, it is one thing for the Commission to make proposals and quite another for member states to approve them. These liberalizing policies were put forward at a time of economic recession and mounting financial difficulties for state railways. They were, as were those before them, doomed to failure.

More recently, the Council of Transport Ministers have approved several items on the Commission's list of priority measures which it wanted to see adopted by the end of 1983. In June 1982, the Council asked the Commission to select infrastructure projects to be included in an experimental 3—5 year programme. It also agreed to a draft directive establishing common rules for certain types of combined road/rail carriage of goods, including a system of tax reductions applicable to road vehicles engaged in combined transport. A Council decision was agreed on the fixing of rates for international carriage of goods by rail and the Commission was asked to submit proposals for an action programme to encourage railway co-operation. Legislation was agreed for the establishment of common technical requirements for inland waterway vessels. Finally, although the Ministers adopted a Directive on the beginning of summertime for 1983—1985 they were unable to agree on a date to end summertime but the Commission hopes that this may be achieved by 1986! Even discounting this last point we can see clearly by what was agreed how slow progress has been and how far things are from the ideal as outlined in the Treaty of Rome and subsequent Commission memoranda.

The reasons lie in the fundamental differences of philosophy towards transport within the Community and it is the same question that arises in many discussions on transport, i.e. whether transport should be regarded in some way as a 'social service' or whether it should be regarded in commercial terms. If member states take opposing views on something as fundamental as this then a common approach is going to be very difficult to achieve. We are left then with accepting the piecemeal approach rather than going for a global policy.

Examination questions

1 Discuss the economic factors that can be expected to exert a major influence on the future development of shipping.
2 Compare and contrast the economic policies of the International Air Transport Association with those of the various Shipping Conferences.
3 Are rigorous controls on operation and entry to the market necessary for the proper co-ordination of the transport sector? Discuss in relation to the development of a common transport policy for the European Economic Community.
4 As part of its common transport policy, the EEC proposes changes in the taxes levied on commercial vehicles. What are these changes and why are they being proposed?
5 Compare the role of the International Air Transport Association in scheduled air transport with that of the various conferences in international shipping. Why have these institutions often been described as 'cartels'?

6 The Regulations of the European Economic Community require the governments of member countries to compensate railways for 'public service obligations' imposed on them. What is meant by this requirement, and why was the measure agreed?

7 What are the major causes of 'excess capacity' in international air transport? Discuss the policies being pursued by scheduled airlines to cope with this problem.

8 In 1966, the original members of the European Economic Community agreed to institute a system of 'forked tariffs' (tarification à fourchettes) for the transport of freight by road and rail. What are the purposes of this system, and what are its defects?

9 The International Air Transport Association and the various Shipping Conferences are often described as 'cartels'. What is meant by this? How are these institutions being affected by current developments in the international airline and shipping industries?

10 Trace the development of a common transport policy (ctp) in the European Economic Community since the signing of the Treaty of Rome in 1960. Why has progress in the integration of freight transport been relatively slow?

Recommended Further Reading

GWILLIAM, K. M. and MACKIE, P. J. *Economics and Transport Policy* (George Allen and Unwin: London, 1975).

STUBBS, P. C., TYSON, W. J. and DALVI, M. Q., *Transport Economics* (George Allen and Unwin: London, 1980).

FOSTER, C. D., *The Transport Problem* (Croom Helm: London, 1975).

MILLWARD, R., *Public Expenditure Economics* (McGraw Hill: London, 1971).

NASH, C. A., *Economics of Public Transport* (Longman: London, 1982).

ADAMS, J., *Transport Planning-vision and practice* (Routledge and Kegan Paul: London, 1981).

MOSELEY, M. J., *Accessibility, the Rural Challenge* (Methuen: London, 1979).

WARDROPER, J., *Juggernaut* (Temple Smith: London, 1981).

BUCHANAN, C., *No Way to the Airport* (Longman: London, 1981).

HOYLE, B. S., (Ed.) *Transport and Development* (Macmillan: London, 1973).

Appendix A.1

The Multiplier

In Chapter 1 we referred to the importance of the 'multiplier effect' when governments invest in various parts of the economy. We pointed out that if a government's prime objective was to increase the country's national income (the measure of its wealth) then it would look to an investment which had the greatest multiplier effect. We will now explain how the multiplier effect works and to describe the factors which effect its magnitude.

Suppose the government of a developing country invests $1,000 million in a new road. Assuming private contractors plan and build the road they will receive the $1,000 million. They would use that money to purchase raw materials, pay wages to employees and dividends to shareholders. So the supplier of raw materials, the employees and shareholders would receive $1,000 million. But the cycle does not stop there. The suppliers of raw materials will pay wages and buy raw materials and machinery and the contractor's employees and shareholders will spend their wages and dividends on such items as food, clothing, domestic hardware and entertainment. People in those industries would benefit and so the process continues. That original $1,000 million is therefore spent over and over again.

National income can be measured by the income received by the various groups in the economy. Thus, we could add the original $1,000 million many times. How many times will determine the size of the multiplier effect.

The multiplier can be defined as the ratio of the change in national income to the initial change in expenditure that brings it about. That change in expenditure could come not only from government spending but also from an increase in private investment or from additional household consumption expenditure. If the initial $1,000 million investment resulted in a national income increase of $4,000 million then the multiplier would be 4, but why does it not increase indefinitely giving a multiplier of infinity?

The reason lies in the fact that not all income received is spent in the country's economy. Some will be claimed as tax by the government, some will be spent on imports and some will be saved. All these constitute withdrawals from the economy. The greater the *propensity to withdraw* money from the economy the lower will be the multiplier effect.

If we assume that every time people receive additional income they spend 60% of it and withdraw 40% for savings, taxation and expenditure on foreign goods and services then we say the marginal propensity to consume is 0.60 and the marginal propensity to withdraw is 0.40. The increase in national income resulting from the $1,000 million government investment in our example can be seen in the process below:

	$ Increase in Expenditure	Increase in Withdrawals
Initial government expenditure	1,000.00	
Increase in expenditure withdrawals		
round 1	600.00	400.00
round 2	360.00	240.00
round 3	216.00	144.00
round 4	129.60	86.40
round 5	77.760	51.84
Sum of 1st 5 rounds	2,383.36	922.24
all other rounds	116.64	77.76

Total increase in National Income $2,500.00 million. Total withdrawals $1,000.00 million.

Table A1.   The increase in national income resulting from an initial $1,000 million investment with a marginal propensity to withdraw of 0.40

The process will come to a halt when the increase in withdrawals equals the increase in the initial investment. Thus, in this example national income increases by $2,500 million when the initial investment was $1,000 million. The multiplier is therefore 2.5. So if the initial investment had been $2,000 million the increase in national income would have been $2,000 million×2.5=$5,000 million.

There is a quicker way of calculating the multiplier value. It is the reciprocal of the marginal propensity to withdraw. So in our example it is 1/0.4=2.5. What would be the multiplier and therefore the increase in national income following an investment of $1,000 million if the marginal propensity to withdraw is 0.30?

If we are concerned with the role that transport investment plays in economic development then we must try to determine what the multiplier effect would be relative to alternative sources for investment. This is a most difficult question to answer as the World Bank has pointed out (see Chapter 1). Probably the strongest arguments in favour of investment in, say, trunk roads or rail schemes are that, first, by their very nature they will reach a large number of communities and secondly, they are labour intensive and the marginal propensity to withdraw of the workers is likely to be low as they will be on relatively low incomes. The multiplier effect may therefore be quite significant.

Appendix B.1

Technological Change and the Future

Technological change is occuring in most modes of transport all the time. We have seen marked improvements in the transportation and handling of freight. As vehicles increase in size they are also becoming more sophisticated (but perhaps not as quickly as many environmentalists would wish!). The container revolution has continued and there have been tremendous strides in the automatic handling of parcels traffic at distribution centres. The use of pipelines increases and the scope for freight carrying 'trains' of air-balloons has been actively investigated. In terms of motive power we have seen developments in electric vehicles and nuclear-powered ships.
nuclear-powered ships.

On the passenger side there have been marginal changes in air transport but train technology has taken a leap forward with the French Railways' 'Train à Grand Vitesse' (TGV) and, more arguably, British Rail's 'Advanced Passenger Train' (APT). Major efforts are being made to help solve the urban transport problem by introducing new technology and it is this subject area that we concentrate on in this Appendix.

However, before we do we should also recognize that new technology can help the traveller not only enjoy a better level of transport service; it can also reduce the need for travel itself. Improvements in telecommunications together with computer technology may well, in the not too distant future, obviate the need for many present-day journeys. Examples would be those business trips requiring exchange of information in a form which at present cannot be done by telephone, some shopping trips and personal business journeys such as those to the bank, or even to the travel agent to arrange your next holiday.

From a very wide subject area we have chosen urban public transport for more detailed discussion because we feel that it is here that the largest problems remain and where significant developments are taking place.

B2   New Technology and Urban Public Transport

Developments in urban public transport can be divided into three groups. The first is the introduction of already established devices such as bus lanes, bus priority signals and other such systems intended to reduce operating costs and improve service reliability. The techniques for the economic appraisal for these schemes are already established although the actual introduction of schemes yielding an 'aimworthy' rate of return can still depend upon political will. The second group is the development of existing forms of transport and vehicle types by the application of new technology and comprises electric vehicles, dual-mode vehicles and light rapid transport (LRT). The third group involves the development of completely new modes. We are concentrating on the last two categories.

B3   The Development of Existing Forms of Transport

Such development has perhaps three objectives:

1 to provide a higher quality system with greater reliability and reduced journey times, with the criterion of altering modal split in favour of public transport;
2 to provide a system which is both more energy efficient and less dependent on oil-based fuels; and
3 to provide a system which is compatible with expectations for the urban environment.

The systems tested against these objectives are trolleybuses, and dual-mode vehicles and LRT.

B3.1   Trolleybuses

Trolleybuses were first operated in Britain in 1911 with the opening of systems in Bradford and Leeds. Bradford was the last British operator, closing its system in 1972. Trolleybuses were attractive to tramway operators because they retained the advantages of electric traction whilst avoiding the need for a fixed track (although still requiring an overhead electricity supply). Predictions that oil-based fuels will be both expensive and in reduced supply have renewed interest in electric traction. Indeed the successor to Bradford City Transport, the West Yorkshire Passenger Transport Executive (WYPTE) has proposed a demonstration project of modern trolleybus technology in Bradford.[1] Evaluation of three sample projects on a cross-city route yielded the following conclusion:

> 'None of the networks would save money in 1980 when the annual capital costs (discounted at 5%) are included in the calculations although substantial operating cost savings are predicted. For the other two specimen years (2000 and 2025) the operating cost savings outweigh the annual capital cost element leading to overall savings over the life of the systems. Although the fuel costs are important to these predicted annual operating cost savings the most significant savings arise from substantial reductions in vehicle maintenance costs.'[2]

The systems satisfied WYPTE's own target rate of return, of 5% in real terms, and perform well against the Department of Transport's rate of return. However, a study by Mercedes[3] showed that trolleybus costs were 128% of those for a diesel bus. The discrepancy between this and the WYPTE study arises partly from differing views on equipment life. Mercedes assumed a 12 year vehicle life and a 20 year life for the overhead wiring whilst WYPTE used 24 years and 40 years respectively. European operating experience would probably support WYPTE's view, certainly with respect to vehicle life. However, one must be aware of the sensitivity of the economic performance of a system to assumptions made about such matters as equipment life, vehicle utilization and operating costs over time.

B3.2   Dual Mode Vehicles

The Mercedes study also set out the relative total operating costs for a range of dual mode vehicles thus

	%
Diesel bus	100
Trolleybus	128
Battery-bus	145
Diesel-trolleybus	120
Diesel-batterybus	126
Trolley-batterybus	140

There are various combinations of power sources in dual-mode vehicles and differing views of patterns of operation. For example a trolley-battery vehicle could operate on batteries in the suburbs, to avoid the expense of wiring, but use the overhead for line-haul. An alternative view would see the duobus system as avoiding the need for 'unsightly' wiring in town centres. In general dual-mode vehicles perform badly in evaluations and the WYPTE study found that pure trolleybuses performed better in its appraisal than trolley-diesel duobuses. Battery-powered vehicles await the development of a cheap, lightweight replacement for the lead acid battery. The present poor performance of this battery results in battery vehicles that are relatively heavy and have restricted range. New battery technology, perhaps based on nickel-cadmium cells, would alter this, however.

B3.3   Light Rail Transit

Turning to LRT, these systems offer the possibility of providing a high quality and relatively high capacity urban public transport system. They have higher fixed costs but lower unit operating costs than diesel-bus based systems. As the recently opened Tyne and Wear Metro system shows LRT can also have very efficient manpower utilization. A study by the Transport and Road Research Laboratory (TRRL)[4] considered the applicability of LRT to Britain. It considered that a suitable area of LRT installation would need to have a population of between a half and several million and have six or more corridors with peak hour flows exceeding 3,000 passengers. However, in the future LRT may be seen as an alternative not to road-based systems but to 'heavy rail' suburban railways. There is some evidence that this is already happening in Germany and it is significant that London's Dockland development is likely to be served by a LRT system rather than an extension of the heavy rail Underground network.

B4   Advanced Urban Transport

The third category involves a departure from existing modes and uses advanced technology to produce new forms of transport. What then are the key features of these new urban transport systems? First of all they are automatic – the individual vehicle have no drivers. In this respect, of course, they are no different from passenger carrying machines like escalators or moving pavements but they can react to external demands in a more sophisticated way. The second feature plays an important part in this. They will be controlled largely by computers which will be able to react to changes in demand and deal with problems like vehicle breakdown. Thirdly, these systems will operate on reserved track. They may be at street level, underground or overhead. The last alternative is the most likely choice given the cost of building/services and physical difficulty in finding space in dense urban land-use. Finally, headways will be much closer than with conventional systems. They may be as low as 1 second but more normally up to 20 seconds. This compares with about 90 seconds for normally controlled urban railways.

B4.1   Types

From the multitude of designs produced we can distinguish two basic types of advanced urban transport and they can be described as *autotaxi* and *autotram*.

The autotaxi is the more sophisticated. It provides a service very close to that of a conventional taxi. The vehicle itself is quite small, carrying up to six people. At the station passengers can call up a vehicle by sending a message to the central computer, specifying the destination. Once they are aboard the vehicle will travel uninterrupted to that destination and no change of vehicle will be necessary. So the autotaxi provides the ultimate in personal transport by public means. Although the passenger has to walk to and from the system he is, once there, offered a fast, convenient, comfortable non-stop service in a vehicle provided for his exclusive use. Such a system, however, is unlikely to be seen in urban areas in the foreseeable future. The technical operating problems are immense as are the economic and environmental costs. For this reason we are paying more attention to the second major type – the autotram.

The autotram provides a service more akin to those conventional bus, tram or urban railway services, with vehicles following scheduled timetables along routes with fixed stopping places. The major differences are those outlined above, particularly the automatic operation with much closer headways. Vehicles could be coupled into trains and routes are normally two-way. Stations would be simple but probably manned. We shall now look a little more closely at the autotram to assess its viability as an alternative to conventional systems.

B4.2   The Autotram – an assessment

What we must try to do is to determine whether the autotram is intrinsically superior to conventional modes or whether many of its attractive features are merely the result of higher levels of investment. For example, it would be unfair to suggest higher levels of comfort because the seating was more luxurious.

B4.2.1   Compared with Urban Bus Operation

The autotram would appear to offer a higher level of service compared with conventional buses in respect of speed and reliability and of smoothness of ride with automatically controlled acceleration and deceleration and the absence of obstructions *en route*. However, there will be poorer accessibility to the system with stations less frequent than bus stops; walking distances will be greater and most likely the stations will be overhead presenting very difficult problems for the elderly and disabled. We should be aware, however, that autotram is not designed to replace many of the services offered by bus operation, for example, those routes away from main demand corridors. We should be equally clear about the respective roles of autotram and conventional rail systems.

B4.2.2   Compared with Urban Rail

Autotram is not capable of carrying the demand satisfied by full metros. Rather it is designed to carry maximum loadings of between 4,000 and 10,000 passengers an hour. It is perhaps viable where the larger rail-based systems would be too expensive to construct. Stations would be spaced more closely than other rail-based systems thus making the autotram more accessible particularly if conventional systems are underground.

B4.2.3 Other Considerations

Perhaps the biggest advantage for autotram lies with running costs. The major part, labour costs, with the attendant problems of staffing in unsocial hours will be avoided.

The biggest disadvantage would appear to be that the system, if it is going to work at all, must be (at least almost) completely built and it has got to be right first time! Experimentation is much easier with bus services although it must be said, the same problems would be faced in the construction of conventional rail operation. Capital costs, of course, will be high.

Many people have expressed fears on environmental grounds if the autotram is going to run overhead. This is quite justified, of course, but the advantage of the advanced systems is that they are more flexible than their conventional rail counterparts. The vehicles will be able to negotiate tighter bends which give greater scope in locating the tracks. They will be much quieter too. A study was carried out to test the viability of an autotram system based on Coventry[5]. Three routes totalling 27.7 km were chosen for detailed assessment. The vehicles were designed to hold 40 passengers in two cars powered by rotary electric motors and running on rubber tyres. The tracks would have side-walks for guidance. There would be 24 manned stations and the fixed block control system, guided by a central and vehicle based computers, would make a 24 second headway. The total capital cost (in 1973 prices) was estimated at £24.3 m and running costs at £6.4 m per annum. Costs and benefits were discounted over 25 years and the IRR was estimated to be nearly 13%. The authors compare this with rates of return for urban road investment which are in the region of 20%. They conclude that in strictly economic criteria the automated system does not represent a particularly attractive use of resources.

B4.3 Conclusions

The conclusions on these urban public transport developments must be that more scope lies in the improvement of existing operations and equipment. Tremendous advances have been made in urban traffic control systems and these will be more widely used. The advanced systems suffer from the need for area wide development with the resultant high capital costs and related environmental problems. Perhaps efforts should be concentrated on improving existing systems.

References

Chapter 1

1 *Annual Abstract of Statistics*, (HMSO: London, 1982).
2 THE MASEFIELD REPORT, Towards Better Transport – People and Qualifications, *Chartered Institute of Transport Journal*, 1977 May.
3 LORD LUGARD F. J. *The Dual Mandate in British Tropical Africa* (London, 1922).
4 FLINN, M. W., *Origins of the Industrial Revolution* (Longmans: London, 1966).
5 ROSTOW, W. W., *The Stages of Economic Growth* (Cambridge University Press: Cambridge, 1971).
6 YOUNGSON, A. J., *Overhead Capital: A Study in Development Economics* (Edinburgh University Press: Edinburgh, 1967).
7 SECTOR WORKING PAPER, *Transportation* (World Bank: Washington, 1972).
8 HARRISON-CHURCH, R. J. *The Evolution of Railways in French and British West Africa*, Congrès International de Géographie, Vol. 4, p. 113 (Lisbon, 1949).
see
MABOGUNJE, A. L. *The Development Process: A Spatial Perspective* (Hutchinson: London, 1980).
9 HOYLE, B. S. (ed.) *Transport and Development* (Macmillan Press: London, 1973).
10 LEITCH COMMITTEE REPORT, *Report of the Advisory Committee on Trunk Road Assessment* (HMSO: London, 1977).
11 DODGSON, J. S. 'Motorway Investment, Industrial Transport Costs and Sub-Regional Growth – A Case Study of the M62' Regional Studies, 1974.
12 WILSON, G. W., *Towards a Theory of Transport and Development* to be found in HOYLE, B. S.[9]
13 WORLD BANK ANNUAL REPORT 1982 (World Bank: Washington, 1982).

Chapter 2

1 TANNER, J. C., *Forecasts of Vehicles and Traffic in Great Britain*, TRRL Report LR 650 (Transport and Road Research Laboratory: Crowthorne, 1974).
2 NASH, C. A., *Economics of Public Transport* (Longman: London, 1982).
3 URQUHART, G. B. and BUCHANAN, C. M., *The Elasticity of Passenger Demand for Bus Services: A Case Study in Telford*, TRRL Supplementary Report 641 (Transport and Road Research Laboratory: Crowthorne, 1981).
4 LAYFIELD, R. E., *Demand for Bus Travel: the effects of service and fare changes in Gosport and Fareham*, TRRL Report 983 (Transport and Road Research Laboratory: Crowthorne, 1981).

5 OLDFIELD, R. H. and TYLER, E., *The Elasticity of Medium Distance Rail Travel*, TRRL Report LR 993 (Transport and Road Research Laboratory: Crowthorne, 1981).

6 FRERK, M. LINDSAY, I. and FAIRHURST, M. *Traffic Trends in the Seventies* (Economic Research Report R248: London Transport, December 1981).

7 OLDFIELD, R. H., *The Effect of Income on Bus Travel*, TRRL Supplementary Report 644 (Transport and Road Research Laboratory: Crowthorne, 1981).

8 HAYWOOD, P. J. and BLACKLEDGE, D. A. *The West Midlands Passenger Transport Executive Continuous On-Bus Survey: How the Data is Used* (PTRC Summer Annual Meeting: University of Warwick, 1980).

9 BARRETT, B. and BUCHANAN, M., *The NBC Market Analysis Project* (Traffic Engineering and Control: October, 1979), pp. 471–4.

10 HAYWOOD, P. J., *West Midlands Survey on Modes of Travel (Area Studies Programme)* (Seminar on Operations Research: University of Leeds, 1980).

11 ELLISON, P. B. and TEBB, R. G. P., *Costs and Benefits of a Bus Service Information Leaflet*, TRRL Report LR 825 (Transport and Road Research Laboratory: Crowthorne 1978).

12 ELLISON, P. B. and TEBB, R. G. P., *Benefits and Costs of Providing Additional Information about Urban Public Transport Services*, TRRL Report 991 (Transport and Road Research Laboratory: Crowthorne, 1981).

Chapter 3

1 COMMITTEE OF INQUIRY INTO CIVIL AIR TRANSPORT, *British Air Transport in the Seventies*, White Paper Cmnd 4018 (HMSO: London, 1969).

2 CHARTERED INSTITUTE OF PUBLIC FINANCE AND ACCOUNTANCY, *Passenger Transport Operations* (Chartered Institute of Public Finance and Accountancy: London, 1974).

3 CHARTERED INSTITUTE OF PUBLIC FINANCE AND ACCOUNTANCY, *Passenger Transport Operations Peak/Off-peak cost and revenue allocation* (Chartered Institute of Public Finance and Accountancy: London, 1979).

4 LIVESEY, F., *Economics* (Polytech Publishers: Stockport, 1972).

5 HUME, E. T., quoted in Livesey above.

6 LIPSEY, R. G., *An Introduction to Positive Economics* (Weidenfeld and Nicolson: London, 1979).

7 THOMSON, J. M., *Modern Transport Economics* (Penguin: London, 1974).

8 HARRISON, A. J., *Economies of Scale and the Structure of the Road Haulage Industry* (Oxford Economic Papers: Oxford, 1963).

9 BAYLISS, B. T., *The Small Firm in the Road Haulage Industry* (HMSO: London, 1971).

10 LEE N. and STEADMAN I., 'Economies of Scale in Bus Transport: Some British Results'. *Journal of Transport Economics and Policy Vol.* 4, 1970, pp. 15–28.

11 TRAVERS MORGAN, R. and PARTNERS., *Bradford Bus Study, Final Report*, (Travers Morgan R. and Partners: London, 1976).

Chapter 4

1 GWILLIAM, K. M. and MACKIE, P. J. *Economics and Transport Policy* (George Allen & Unwin: London, 1975).

2 *Nationalized Industries: a review of economic and financial objectives* White Paper Cmnd 3437, 1967.
3 *The Nationalized Industries* White Paper Cmnd 7131, 1978.
4 WALKER, B. *Welfare Economics and Urban Problems* (Hutchinson: London, 1981).
5 MILLWARD, R. *Public Expenditure Economics* (McGraw Hill: London, 1971).
6 FOSTER, C. D. *The Transport Problem* (Groom Helm: London, 1975).
7 MARGOLIS, J. and GUILTON, H. (Eds) *Public Economics* (Macmillan: London, 1969) Chapter 15.
8 *Flight International*, 6 June, 1981.
9 TYSON, W. J. 'The economic effects of bus season tickets'. *Tenth Annual Symposium on Public Transport Operational Research*, University of Leeds, 1978.
10 WHITE, P. R. *An Evaluation of the Long-term Effects of the West Midlands Travelcard* (West Midlands Passenger Transport Executive, Birmingham, 1981).
11 FAIRHURST, M. and MACK, T. *Consequences and Causes of Changes in Road Traffic Levels* (Economic Research Report R243 Planning Research Office, London Transport, January, 1981).
12 *The Role and Application of Traffic Restraint Document 107*, WYTCONSULT West Yorkshire Transportation Studies. July, 1976.
13 DEPARTMENT OF THE ENVIRONMENT, *Transport Policy*, Vol. 2. Consultant Document (HMSO: London, 1976) pp. 106–123.
14 *Report of the Inquiry into Lorries, People and the Environment*. The Armitage Report, (HMSO: London, 1980).
15 WALKER, B *Welfare Economics and Urban Problems* (Hutchinson: London, 1981).
16 HOLLAND, E. P. and WATSON, P. L. 'Traffic Restraint in Singapore' *Traffic Engineering & Control,* January 1978, pp. 14–22.

Chapter 5

1 TRAVERS MORGAN, R. AND PARTNERS, *Bradford Bus Study Final Report,* (Travers Morgan, R. and Partners, London, 1976).
2 BRITISH RAILWAYS BOARD, *The Reshaping of British Railways*, (HMSO: London, 1963).
3 Railway Invigoration Society, (*Can Bus replace Train*, London, 1977).
4 BUCHANAN, C., *No Way to the Airport* (Longman: London, 1981).
5 APPLEYARD, D. and LINTELL, M. 'Streets dead or alive', *New Society*, 3rd July 1975.
6 WARDROPER, J., *Juggernaut* (M. Temple Smith: London, 1981).
7 TYME, J., *Motorways versus Democracy* (Macmillan Press: London, 1978).
8 ADAMS, J., *Transport Planning — vision and practice*, (Routledge and Kegan Paul: London, 1981).
9 MOSELEY, M. J., *Accessibility: the Rural Challenge* (Methuen: London, 1979).
10 McLENTIN, J., *Kendal and Windermere Railway* (Dalesman: Clapham North Yorkshire, 1980).
11 OXLEY, P. R., *The Effects of the Withdrawal and Reduction of Bus Services* (SR 719) (Transport and Road Research Laboratory: Crowthorne, 1982).
12 MACKAY, G. A. and LAING, G., *Consumer Problems in Rural Areas*. (Scottish Consumer Council: Glasgow, 1982).

Chapter 6

1 BEESLEY, M. E., 'The value of time spent in travelling—some new evidence' *Economica*, Vol. 32, May 1965.
2 QUARMBY, D. A., 'Choice of travel mode for the journey to work' *Journal of Transport Economics and Policy*, Vol. 1, No. 3, 1967.
3 HARRISON, A. J. and QUARMBY, D. A., 'Theoretical and practical research on the estimation of the value of time savings' *Report of the Sixth Round Table on Transport Economics*, ECMT, Paris, November 1969.
4 *Commission on the Third London Airport* (The Roskill Commission) (HMSO: London, 1971).
5 MISHAN, E. J., 'What is wrong with Roskill?' *Journal of Transport Economics and Policy*, Vol. 4, No. 3, 1970.
6 *Report of the Advisory Committee on Trunk Road Assessment*, (The Leitch Committee) (HMSO: London, 1977).
7 FOSTER, C. D., *Social Cost/Benefit Study of Two Suburban Rail Passenger Services* (British Rail: London, 1974).
8 GENTLEMAN, H., MITCHELL, C. G. B., WALMSLEY, D. A. and WICKS, J., *The Glasgow Rail Impact Study* (TRRL Supplementary Report 650, Transport and Road Research Laboratory: Crowthorne: 1981).

Chapter 7

1 PONSONBY, G. J., *Transport Policy: Co-ordination through Competition.* Hobart Paper 49 (Institute of Economic Affairs: London, 1969).
2 HIBBS, J., *Transport without Politics . . . ?* (Institute of Economic Affairs: London, 1982).
3 FOSTER, C. D., *Politics, Finance and the Role of Economics* (George Allen & Unwin: London, 1971).
4 *'The McIntosh Report'* 'A Study of U.K. Nationalized Industries: their role in the economy and control in the future' National Economic Development Office: London, November 1976.
5 *The Nationalized Industries* White Paper Cmnd 7131 (HMSO: London 1978).
6 *Policy for Roads: England 1980* (HMSO: London, 1981).
7 *Department of the Environment, The Town and Country Planning Act 1971* (Part II as amended by the Town and Country Planning (Amendment) Act 1972, the Local Government Act 1972 and Inner Urban Areas Act 1978): *Memorandum on Structure and Local Plans* Circular 4/79, (HMSO: London, 1979).
8 FRIEND, J. K., LAFFIN, M. J. and NORRIS, M. E., 'Competition in Public Policy: The Structure Plan as Arena' *Journal of Public Administration*, Vol. 59, Winter 1981.
9 DEPARTMENT OF THE ENVIRONMENT, *Local Transport Grants* Circular 104/73, (HMSO: London, 1973).
10 MACKIE, P. J., 'The New Grant System for Local Transport—The First Five Years' *Journal of Public Administration*, Vol. 59, Summer 1980.
11 DEPARTMENT OF THE ENVIRONMENT, *Transport Supplementary Grant Submissions for 1975/76*, Circular 60/74 (HMSO: London, 1974).

Chapter 8

1 DEPARTMENT OF TRANSPORT, *Report of the Advisory Committee on Trunk Road Assessment* (The Leitch Committee) (HMSO: London, 1977).
2 TANNER, J. C., *Choice of model structure for car ownership forecasting* TRRL Supplementary Report 523 (Transport and Road Research Laboratory: Crowthorne, 1979).
3 DEPARTMENT OF TRADE, *United Kingdom Air Traffic Forecasting Research and Revised Forecasts* (HMSO: London, 1978), and
DEPARTMENT OF TRADE, *Report of the Air Traffic Forecasting Working Party 1981* (HMSO: London, September 1981).
4 HOPKIN, J. M., *The Role of an Understanding of Social Factors in Forecasting Car Ownership*, TRRL Supplementary Report 695 (Transport and Road Research Laboratory: Crowthorne, 1981).
5 ADAMS, J., *Transport Planning – Vision and Practice* (Routledge & Kegan Paul: London 1981).
6 DEPARTMENT OF TRANSPORT AND DEPARTMENT OF THE ENVIRONMENT, *Report on the Review of Highway Inquiry Procedures*, White Paper Cmnd 7133 (HMSO: London 1978).
7 LEVIN, P. H., 'Highway Inquiries: a study in governmental responsiveness', *Journal of Public Administration*, Vol. 57, Spring 1979.

Chapter 9

1 STURMEY, S. G., *Shipping Economics Collected Papers* (Macmillan Press: London, 1975).
2 SCHNEERSON, P., 'The rationality of conference pricing and output policies. A Commentary' *Maritime Studies and Management*, Vol. 3, No. 4, 1976. pp. 245–8.
3 EVANS, J. J., 'Liner freight rates, discrimination and cross-subsidization' *Maritime Policy and Management*, Vol. 4, No. 4, 1977. pp. 227–34.
4 LAING, E. T., *The Rationality of Conference Pricing and Output Policies*, Maritime Studies and Management, Vol. 3, No. 2 (1975) pp. 103–12 and Vol. 3, No. 3 (1976) pp. 141–52.
5 UNITED NATIONS CONFERENCE ON TRADE AND DEVELOPMENT (UNCTAD) *Common Measure of Understanding on Shipping Questions*, New York, 1964.
6 STUBBS, P. C., TYSON, W. J. and DALVI, M. Q., *Transport Economics* (George Allen & Unwin: London, 1980).
7 LAING as before.
8 *The Financial Times*, September 1978.
9 *Common Transport Policy: Objectives and Programme Communications of the Commission to the Council on the development of the Common Transport policy*. Submitted to the Council by the Commission on 25th October, 1973.
10 COMMISSION OF THE EUROPEAN COMMUNITY, *Expert Report on Difficulties encountered in International Road, Rail and Inland Waterway Transport*, April 1982.
11 BUTTON, K. J., 'Recent developments in EEC transport policy' *Three Banks Review*, Autumn, 1979.
12 BAYLISS, B. T., 'Transport in the European Communities' pp. 28–43. *Journal of Transport Economics and Policy*, January 1979.

Appendix B.1

1 *The Modern Trolleybus for West Yorkshire: Looking to the Future* (West Yorkshire PTE: Wakefield, 1981).
2 DAVIES, R. R., *The Modern Trolleybus for West Yorkshire (Summary)* (West Yorkshire PTE: Wakefield, 1981).
3 *Motor Transport* 23 September 1981.
4 KOMPFNER, P., *Notes on Light Rail Transit in Great Britain* (Transport and Road Research Laboratory: Crowthorne, 1980).
5 BLACK, I., GILLIE, R., HENDERSON, R. and THOMAS, T., *Advanced Urban Transport* (Saxon House Studies: Farnborough 1975).
We recommend this book as a particularly thorough analysis of the scope for advanced urban transport.

Index